24118

P9-ECR-921

1.

ISBN 9971–941–12–0 English edition, softcover
ISBN 285–700–088–X French edition, hardcover
ISBN 9971–941–31–7 German edition, softcover

Library of Congress Catalog Card Number: 80-117745

Typesetting:
Asco Trade Typesetting, Hong Kong
Printed in Singapore
by Koon Wah Printing Pte. Ltd.

malaysia

Created and Designed by
Hans Johannes Hoefer

Written by
Harold Stephens
Star Black
Marcus Brooke

Revised and Updated by
Annabelle Morgan

Published by Apa Productions (HK) Ltd
and Times Publishing Berhad

Sixth Edition 1980

The *Insight Guide to Malaysia* was conceived in the early 70s, shortly after the first book in the Apa series, *Bali*, which won warm acclaim, awards, and eager anticipation of more.

Inspired by the reaction to *Bali* and its sister publication *Java*, the original Apa team — photographer/designer Hans Hoefer and writer Star Black — conferred on the possibility of producing an equally insightful book on Malaysia, then relatively undiscovered by international travel.

Hoefer and Black had previously collaborated on the multiple-award-winning *Bali Guide* and the *Guide to Java*, both of which

icum of anthropological/historical data. Armed with every possible piece of information they could garner, Hoefer set off on a systematic two-year exploration covering the length and breadth of the country, with Black and writer Harold Stephens.

By landrover, plane, riverboat and shank's mare, the intrepid threesome followed trail after trail on what at times appeared to be a wild-goose chase through remote jungles, lonely islands, forgotten villages and isolated hill stations.

By 1972, they had turned up some amazing discoveries about Malaysia, which they shared with the world when the book was published

Hoefer   Stephens   Black   Brooke   Morgan

were declared the Official Guides to their respective regions by the Tourist Authorities of Indonesia upon publication.

Faced with the task of producing a book on Malaysia that would require a minimum of two years' research, writing, editing, photography and production, Hoefer and Black flew to Bali, for a brief respite before setting off on their self-inspired mission of discovery.

The beneficent spirit that had watched over Apa's previous efforts now took the first step in making the new book a reality: while ideating on the calm beaches of Bali, Hoefer and Black met up with veteran traveler/explorer/ photojournalist Harold Stephens.

As chance would have it, Stephens was himself considering a similar project, and the chance to work with two other professionals of high standing was not one to be missed.

Initial discussions led to countless hours of research in museum and library archives, looking up every rumour, legend, and mod-

in cooperation with the Straits Times Group, one of the region's biggest publishers, later that year.

One of these was the mysterious Kelly's Castle, a crumbling old remnant of colonial glory now half-buried in the jungles of northern Malaysia.

Many hours were also spent exploring less-known trails and byways, and special thanks go to Encik Muhammad Khan, who guided the intrepid explorers through the depths of Malaysia's National Park.

The book has since seen several comprehensive revisions to keep pace with the rapid and sweeping changes taking place in Malaysia, and now appears in its sixth and most up-to-date edition. The revision was undertaken by writer Annabelle Morgan.

Hans Hoefer started his career in the "black arts" as a printer's and typographer's apprentice in 1960 in a down-to-earth German printing and publishing firm. After 4 years' study in one of Germany's leading art academies in the city of Krefeld, he graduated with a degree in graphic design and photography. Equipped with a background based on the traditional Bauhaus concepts of design and the practical integration of all art forms, Hoefer traveled extensively, combining photojournalism with his love for exploration and adventure.

In search of the medium to communicate his new concepts in travel literature, he created Apa Productions, producing and publishing a series of award-winning photographic guide books on Asian and Pacific destinations under the Apa banner. To date, the countries covered include Thailand, Bali, Java, Singapore, Malaysia, Philippines, and, in the first step toward new horizons, Hawaii.

Apa's guides to Asian and Pacific destinations have been warmly received in Europe and the West, and as a result have seen translation into French, German and Dutch and Japanese greatly increasing their invaluability to non-English-speaking travelers.

California-born author Star Black, who evolved the style of the book and also made major contributions to the Bali and Singapore Guides, has since returned to New York, where she is an editor and photographer with UPI (United Press International). Ms. Black holds degrees in literature and art, has lived in Washington, Paris and Hawaii, and has covered much of Asia in her travels. She is currently working on a photographic book for Penguin-Viking.

Co-author Harold Stephens served with the Marines in China, then returned to the US to take degrees in Foreign Service and International Law at Georgetown U, Washington. After a brief jaunt in Paris, he gave up his job and family life in exchange for travel and adventure. He has spent the last 19 years in various parts of the South Pacific and Southeast Asia, including 7 years in Tahiti, and is currently traveling through the Pacific on a 60-foot schooner built with the help of friends. He has authored six books and over 500 magazine articles.

Scots-born writer Marcus Brooke, who has also contributed text and photographs to the recently-published Philippine Guide and authored/edited Apa's *Insider's Guide to Thailand*, has served on the faculty of both Harvard U and the Massachusetts Institute of Technology. At various times an agriculturist, bacteriologist, biochemist and immunologist, Brooke left academia fifteen years ago to travel. He has written and photographed extensively for various magazines/newspapers around the world, including the *New York Times* and *National Geographic*, while pursuing his interest in anthropology and archaeology.

Writer Annabelle Morgan, also a contributor to the *Guide to Singapore,* was born and educated in London, where she worked as an advertising copywriter for some time. Since she moved to Singapore fifteen years ago, she has been a frequent contributor to magazines and papers in S.E. Asia, and continues to call this region home.

Thanks go to the people of Malaysia who aided in bringing about this book with their inimitable hospitality, generous nature and warm smiles. Especially, we would like to thank Encik Muhammad Khan, who helped us discover the National Park, and Tan Sri Mubin Sheppard, whose willingness to share his knowledge of the Malaysian culture was invaluable. Thanks also go to the Tourist Development Authorities of Malaysia for their constant and invaluable aid.

Apa Productions

TABLE OF CONTENTS

Part One:

Malaysia, A Step Closer

Introduction to the Unexpected   13

Keynotes from the Past   22

The Jungle, Ever Beginning   27
Leaping Lizards!   29
Trees Topple in Clouds of Sawdust   30
Shifting Horizons   33
Sabah and Sarawak   35
Sunken Cities and Giant Men?   36

Tides Upon the Sea   40
The Lucrative Spice Trade   42
Greatest Seaport in the Old World   42
Too Precious not to be Shared   45

The Countryside Evergreen   51
Honoring the Rice Spirit   52
A Fortune in a Tin Pan   54
Rubber Seeds, a Reckless Gamble   56

City and Town — Wild West to Big Time   62
Pioneers in Wild West Malaysia   64
A Spontaneous Tack-up Job   64
Our Town Today   66
Dreaming of the Big Time   69
Tomorrow's City   70

Cultural Expressions   74
The Malays: "Son of the Soil"   74
The Chinese: From the Bottom Up   75
The Indians   75
Islam: The Binding Spirit   76
Silat   78
Top Spinning   80
Sepak Raga   80
Wayang Kulit and Dancing Shadows   83
The Kris: Quintessence of Power   84
Thaipusam: Fulfilling the Holy Vow   87
Chinese New Year   90
Sarawak Art   93

Part Two:

Exploring Malaysia

Finding Your Way   98

Kuala Lumpur and Surroundings   103-124

From Shacks to Booming Capital   105
Praises to Allah   107
Memories of a Chinese Pioneer   109
Drumbeats at Dusk   109
Parks and Gardens   110
Mirror of Malaysia's Imagination   112
Something for Everybody   113
Shopping Tour   114
Saturday Night's Sunday Market   115
A Punter's Paradise   116
Loke Mansion   117
Le Coq d'Or   117
Dining by Starlight   118
Highlights After Dark   119

Side Trips from the Capital   120
Tackling Tigers   120
Pilgrimage   121
Fun for All   123
Wooing Lady Luck   123
Paradise on a Mule Track   124

North of Kuala Lumpur   127-164

Beaches and Mountain Retreats   129
Golf Clubs and Blowpipes   131
Riches Underground   133
Kellie's Castle   136
Why Fight Tropical Traffic?   136
Gold Dome in a Royal Town   138
Side Trip via Grik   139
Graceful, Tree-Lined Town   140
Privacy in a Rose Garden   141

Penang: Island of Many Dimensions   144
Traces of Old Penang   145
Streets of George Town   148
Dragons on the Rooftops   150
Joss Sticks for Goddess of Mercy   151
Penang Buddhism   153
Inspired by a Vision   155
Botanical Gardens   155
Penang Hill   156

Round-the-Island Trip	158
Aquarium and Snake Temple	159
Malay Fishing Villages	160

Penang's Beaches and to Langkawi **163**
| The Sound of Drums | 163 |
| The Sea, a Secretive Labyrinth | 164 |

South of Kuala Lumpur **169-185**

Travelling South Through History **170**
| Seremban: True to the Past | 170 |
| By the Blue Lagoon | 171 |

Malacca: History's Sleepy Hollow **174**
Walking Through History	176
Architecture from Holland	179
The River: Ever Constant	180
Santiago: Gate without a Wall	181
Churches	181
Portuguese-Eurasian Settlement	183
Sumatra Comes to Malaysia	184
A Princess and a Magic Well	185

Jungle Interlude **187-193**

The Green Heart **189**

Johore and the South **195-205**

Steadfast and Prospering **197**
Sulphur Springs and Sultans' Tombs	199
Pots and Chili Crabs	199
Like a Stage Curtain	200
Spectacle for the Dinner Guest	201
Suntans on the South China Sea	202
In Search of Mythical Islands	203
The Endau River	205

East Coast of the Peninsula **207-227**

Far From the Madding Crowd **209**
Islam, Royalty and Polo	211
Bustling, Yet in a Trance	211
Side Trips from Kuantan	212
The Road North	214
Turtle Watching	216
Setting its own Pace	218
Impromptu Festivals	219
Weavers and Silversmiths	222
Remote and Unspoiled	224

South of the Thai Border	225
Beach of Passionate Love	227

Sabah **229-247**

In An Island of Legends **231**
"Where the Eye Lingers"	232
Southeast Asia's Highest Mountain	235
Ranau and Hot Springs	240
Kota Belud	242
Round Trip to Tenom	244
The Other Side of the Mountain	247

Sarawak **249-262**

Tales from the Longhouse **251**
Sampans in Midtown	252
Images Charged with Intensity	257
Temples and Side trips	259
Journey up the Rajang River	260
Secrets from the Stone Age	262

Brunei **267-269**

Southeast Asia's Oil Sultanate **268**

Part Three:

Guide in Brief **263-297**

Index-Glossary **298-304**

Maps and Plans

Peninsular Malaysia	96
The Region (insert)	96
Sabah and Sarawak	97
Kuala Lumpur Street Plan	104
Kuala Lumpur Surroundings	120
North of Kuala Lumpur	128
Penang Island	144
Georgetown Street Plan	145
South of Kuala Lumpur	171
Malacca Street Plan	174
National Park (insert)	190
Johore and the South	196
East Coast of the Peninsula	208
Sabah	230
Sarawak	250
Brunei (insert)	268

introduction to the unexpected

A graceful, mosque-like structure with taxis screeching and blaring under its arched eaves stands near the busiest intersection in Malaysia. It seems at first bizarre that traffic assaults the building, but the mosque-like edifice is the capital's main railway station. Malaysia is full of such surprises.

Take the name, for example. "Malay" is clear enough: the ethnic term for the Muslim, tradition-abiding people with handsome features and a regal past who make up about half the population. But the "-sia" covers an additional six million Chinese, Indians, tribesmen, aborigines, Eurasians and others who settled there generations, if not centuries, ago.

Malaysia, the nation, is a federation of thirteen states which were fused into a political entity in 1963. Formerly, it comprised a collection of British colonies, and before that the realm of various Malay sultans whose powers reached their zenith in the 15th century.

Peninsular Malaysia was originally Malaya, the lower 132,000 square kilometers of the long finger of land shared in the north with Thailand and Burma, and reaching down to the Indonesian islands in the south. Sabah and Sarawak, two colorful and distinctive Malaysian states on the giant eastern island of Borneo, are separated from Peninsular Malaysia by nearly 1,000 kilometers of the South China Sea.

The federal capital, Kuala Lumpur, is a throbbing but relaxed city of nearly one million that grew from tin miners' shacks to its present size in less than a century. "KL" rocks to electric guitars and sways to ancient flutes. Neon signs in English advertise Japanese television sets while hand-lettered placards announce a Punjabi newspaper. It is a safe bet that no linguist in the East can understand all of KL's street-corner conversation or read all the writing on its walls.

As any city sidewalk immediately reveals, it is the Malaysian, all thirteen million of them,

At a top-spinning contest (left) children crowd the scene, while an elderly master awaits his turn to hurl the hardwood cone

who are the key to the country's vitality, diversity, and character. Few other nationalities have such a knack for eluding the stereotype. The man on the street in Malaysia may be a Malay teenager shouting "Hello John" from behind the handle bars of a motorbike. He also can be a wizened Chinese chef boiling noodles below a row of plucked chickens hung on hooks. Or an Indian at a newsstand selling paperback palmistry books wrapped in cellophane.

Truthfully, one cannot even speak about the man on the street in Malaysia, because there are nomadic aborigines roaming the deep jungle who have never seen asphalt, much less roads.

Each of Malaysia's many ethnic groups adds a distinct heritage to the pluralistic society. Malays, early settlers of the land, retain a continuity with their past. Many pursue a rural, traditional life as farmers and fishermen. Their carved, wooden dwellings standing on stilts overlook fruit trees and flower gardens. Malay *kampungs* (villages) merge with fields of golden rice. Yet, just when the indelible image of the rice farmer seems sealed, along comes a young Malay executive in a chic shirt. In cities, Malay technicians and economists find jobs at airport counters or on the top floors of the Parliament building.

Malays contribute largely to the country's identity: Islam is the national religion, Malay the national language. Sultans, descendants of the original Malay royal families, remain ceremonial rulers in most states. Every five years they elect one of their number King of Malaysia, to reign under yellow umbrellas amid court etiquette that survives from the earliest days.

Malaysia's Chinese community adds a hard-driving workaday spirit recalling the early 1800s when thousands of migrant laborers arrived from China's southern provinces to hack down the jungle and to pan for tin. In every town of any size, splashy red characters are to be seen on two-story "shop houses" — stores on the ground floor, bedrooms on the upper.

Today, the Chinese control fortunes in rubber, import and export companies, and in industries — dominating the country's economy to a far greater extent than the 35 percent

A Malay girl eyes a visitor with friendly curiosity, in a country accustomed to greeting newcomers since early times. Malays constitute 45 percent of the population, shaping most strongly the country's identity.

that they constitute in numbers. Even their Chineseness has modern aspects.

Indians, a bright minority of 10 percent whose ancestors came as rural laborers under British management, sprinkle flavors from the subcontinent in a myriad of trades. In corners of Malaysia's towns that resemble Old Delhi, some Indians sell sugared peanuts and candied limes. Others trade in rupees, francs, and dollars. Tamils from South India, Sikhs, Bengalis have all settled in Malaysia, attaining distinguished positions in the civil service, manning rubber estates and the railways.

Travelers wishing to meet other Malaysians can journey by steel-plated motorboat up Sarawak's log-ridden rivers and chat with an Iban patriarch about the times when "white Rajahs" ruled and war dances were common. Human skulls bound in raffia still hang from eaves in some longhouses, but head hunting is the pride of bygone generations. Most of Sabah's and Sarawak's nearly one million tribesmen have long since settled down to rustic lives, farming hill rice or pepper. Still, some old customs remain to embellish the present with vivid contrasts. One Kenyah chief in Sarawak startles visitors by wearing a shiny, black business suit with brown shoes, no socks, and boar's tusks through his pierced ears.

Malaysia's varied people now get along with remarkable harmony, although some communal tensions do exist. The waves of immigrants that flooded the country during British rule in the last century changed the social structure so rapidly that the indigenous population soon found that it was no longer an assured majority. Economic imbalances between the races remain a sensitive issue. Young Malaysians grow up aspiring to common national goals, yet their elders continue to practice their widely divergent cultures and customs.

Amid the colorful confusion, travelers eventually discover that the basic unity about Malaysia — the one solid invariable — is the ground on which they stand. It is Malaysia the country that links all the pieces together in a comfortable continuity. In Sabah the land drops from Southeast Asia's tallest mountain down to its most strategic waterways. On the mainland it moves from ageless,

A Hindu holy man tells fortunes beside a gnarled roadside tree. Constituting 10 percent of the population, Indians also distinguish themselves in the civil service, and man rubber estates and the railways.

untamed wilderness to fast-growing urban centers with suburban sprawl, and in between it catches the vitality of a nation in transition.

The jungles are Malaysia's ever-present greenhouse of untapped potential. Two-thirds of the country lies under a dangling profusion of incredibly dense rain forest and mangrove swamp. Timber camps trim the jungle's edge, toppling giant trees in a cloud of sawdust. But they hardly touch the vast hinterland that has covered Malaysia for a hundred million years.

Economic development has been, and still is, carving up virgin jungle into the geometry of well-ordered countrysides, where roads sweep past innumerable lines of rubber trees and sticky-looking oil palms. Tin dredges sputter and creak, gouging out rich tin ore from the red earth. Ribbons of asphalt increasingly pierce the jungle floor, as bulldozers crush forested terrain into modern highways. And huge tankers stand by offshore oil rigs like sea-going mammoths loading precious cargoes of black gold in the new-found oil fields off the coasts of Trengganu, Sabah and Sarawak.

Traffic includes shiny imported sedans and Mercedes taxis, whose drivers spend half their time dodging cumbersome lorries that carry logs to the sawmills. Rubber, petroleum, tin, timber, and palm oil all bring to Malaysia a steady wealth in export earnings, and constitute the mainstay of a solid economy that supports one of Asia's highest standards of living. The further the jungle recedes, the faster change accelerates; and the jungle hardly seems visible behind the glistening bank buildings and luxury hotels that spring up in the big towns. Urban Malaysia is a mixture of East and West, where an American denim jacket is as much a teenage status symbol as is knowledge of the Chinese martial arts.

But the overlay of Western imports and new-fangled fashions extends far beyond the busy downtown districts. Cities send out their vibrations to all corners of Malaysia, extending cosmopolitan greetings on television which reaches more and more remote villages. A Borneo tribesman may find it difficult to follow the plot of an English drama set in the 1930s, but the TV novelty is too exciting to miss, and it leaves a lasting impression.

A Chinese opera star admires his grease-paint portrait of a character from the ancient imperial court. Constituting 35 percent of the population, the Chinese have contributed beyond their numbers to the culture and economy of Malaysia.

keynotes from
the past

35000 B.C. Possibly the first *Homo sapiens* in the East settled in gigantic limestone caves in the Malay peninsula and Borneo. While the Ice Age continued to carve out most of the world's terrain, early man in Malaysia carried on a primitive existence using crude choppers chiseled from stone.

8000–2000 B.C. The jungle marathons began. Ancestors of today's aborigines wandered down the peninsula from Yunnan in southwest China, moving from cave to cave as generations passed. Before long, they were driven back into the wilderness by the more sophisticated Proto-Malays who forged metal tools and settled in fishing villages along the coasts.

A.D. 160. Claudius Ptolemy, the celebrated Roman geographer, drew the Malay peninsula on his map under ancient letters spelling "Golden Chersonese."

A.D. 200. The first Oriental gold rush was in full swing, luring adventurous seafarers from India, Rome, and China. The Indians were the most ambitious, arriving in 60-meter-long vessels with 1,000 tonnes of cargo, live goats and chickens, and even a vegetable garden on board. Some merchants stayed to keep an eye on Malaya's early gold mines. They married local women and introduced Hinduism to the native aristocracy.

A.D. 500. Hindu "river states" sprang up on estuaries along the coasts, each ruled by a Malay king and his court. Kings lived in walled palaces and hardly saw the peasantry, except from under a white howdah on an elephant's back when they journeyed outside their gates. Hindu belief sanctioned absolute despotism. Kings, it was believed, were "made of the essences of the gods."

1292. Marco Polo sailed through the Malacca Straits to do some sightseeing for the Great Khan of Mongolia.

1403. A Sumatran prince, called Parameswara, founded the city of Malacca, and his settlement soon blossomed into the most opulent spice bazaar in the East. Malaya never smelled so good. Sales pavilions were permeated with exotic aromas — cloves from the Moluccas; sandalwood from Timor;

Red paint encrusts the bolted doors of the Stadhuys *(previous pages) built by the Dutch in 17th-century Malacca.*

camphor from Borneo; drugs, dyes and perfumes from Persia, Arabia, Siam and the Philippines.

1405. Admiral Cheng Ho sailed into Malacca, liked what he saw, and later returned with a fabulous fleet bearing gifts from the "Son of Heaven." Parameswara returned the favor by journeying to China, whereupon the emperor proclaimed him King of Malacca and the mountains beyond. Before the Sumatran died, he converted to Islam. His successors extended their "mountains" to include the entire south of the peninsula.

1511. Ten Portuguese soldiers perished from poisoned arrows during a bloody siege of Malacca. The sultan fought with war elephants and 20,000 fighting men, but he was outdone by gunpowder and forced to flee south, leaving his harbor to the invaders. A Portuguese soldier gloated: "Men cannot estimate the worth of Malacca on account of its greatness and profit." He spoke too soon. Within little more than a century, Portuguese Malacca fell to the Dutch, who later traded it with the British.

1786. Captain Francis Light loaded his ship's cannon with silver dollars and fired it into the jungles of Penang Island, thus inducing Indian laborers to clear the land, which he then claimed for Britain. The East India Company was slow to respond, but in 1826 Penang joined Singapore and Malacca as part of the newly established Straits Settlements. With these colonies, Britain became the dominant Western power on the peninsula.

1807. Pirates crept aboard a British sloop-of-war and left eighty sailors "in a most mangled state" on deck. Piracy was a popular and ancient pursuit to the seacoast dweller. To the European merchant, it was "a great and blighting curse" that threatened every vessel in the straits into the 19th century.

1839. The dashing, young British adventurer, James Brooke, chatted with the ladies on the Singapore cocktail circuit, promising them he would keep in touch after his voyage to Borneo. Within three years he had come up with a worthy conversation piece. For helping Borneo rulers subdue a rebellion of native chiefs, Brooke was proclaimed "white Rajah" of Sarawak, a position he and his family held for a hundred years.

1864. A prospecting party of Chinese tin miners poled their boats to the swampy confluence of the Klang and Gombak Rivers. Here a couple of merchants set up shop selling supplies. They called their outpost Kuala Lumpur, or "Muddy Estuary." It was a remote, wooded, and diseased town. Within the first month, seventy of the original eighty-seven settlers died of fever.

1870s. Chinese secret societies warred over tin-mining rights to the point where a mere gambling dispute between two men could explode into a vicious feud lasting a decade. In Larut, a mining settlement in Perak, 1,000 Chinese were killed by rival gangs in a single day. The Governor of the Straits Settlements, Andrew Clarke, de-scribed Larut as "one huge cockpit where nothing but fighting and murder and piracy" went on. Clarke finally stepped in to procure peace. The Treaty of Pangkor in 1874 marked the end of the Larut disputes and the begin-ning of direct British intervention in the Malay states.

1878. As an experiment that no one took seriously, nine Brazilian rubber trees were sent from London's Kew Gardens and planted in Kuala Kangsar. Few estate owners paid much attention to the new crop, until John Dunlop invented the pneumatic tire.

1900. In northern Borneo, the formidable rebel chief, Mat Salleh, made his last stand from an underground fortress in the jungle. With the rebel's death, the British North Borneo Company gained full control over the land now called Sabah.

1901. Sir Malcolm Watson, a govern-ment district surgeon in Klang, took Malaya's mosquito threat seriously. Despite objections from the Home Office that he was spending too much time with his "bugs," Watson ordered the marshlands around the towns cleared and succeeded in curbing malaria epidemics.

1910s. The Sanitary Board had done much to shape Kuala Lumpur's shambles into paved roads and brick buildings. The town settled comfortably into its genteel role as British capital of the Protected Malay States. Daily newspapers chatted about the comings and goings of countless officials and planters. KL now had lightbulbs hanging in the rail-way station and the first train had steamed into town. A news report marveled about "the run of about twenty miles having been done in ninety minutes!"

1941. On 8 December the Nippon Im-perial Army landed north of Kota Bharu and rumbled down the Malay peninsula in tanks and on bicycles, while their torpedo-bombers demolished British battleships offshore. "In all the war I have never received a more direct shock," wrote Winston Churchill. For three and a half years British, Malay, and Chinese guerrillas fought the Japanese from hideouts in the deep jungle.

1948. Some guerrillas had refused to come out of hiding when the war was over, casting their lot with the Malayan Communist Party and its struggle against colonialism. Terrorist attacks became so menacing that the British administration declared a state of em-ergency and called in troops. The Communist guerrillas were eventually defeated, but it was a war of nerves that lasted twelve long years.

1957. On 31 August a new flag rose over the country with an eleven-point star sym-bolizing each Malay State. Britain fulfilled its promise of self-government and Malaya pro-claimed independence. Two days later, the Yang di-Pertuan Agong, "King and Ruler of the Federation of Malaya," unsheathed his gold Kris of State and kissed its blade as a gesture of the acceptance of office. He em-bodied a future era.

1963. On 16 September the national flag was once again hoisted to the masthead, but its star now had fourteen points instead of eleven. Malaya became Malaysia, a new federation that included the former British colonies of Sabah, Sarawak, and Singapore. In one case, it was a brief experiment. Two years later, Singapore split from the federa-tion and became a separate nation.

1970. In September Tunku Abdul Rahman, the "Father of Malaysia," retired. After bringing the country to independence and leading it through the first years, the easygoing and widely revered Prime Minister of the royal Malay family handed over his job to his deputy, Tun Abdul Razak.

1976. Tun Abdul Razak died. Datuk Hussein Onn became Prime Minister.

1979. More than 122,000 desperate "boat people" from Vietnam landed on Malaysian shores. They came packed tightly in motor launches, dilapidated fishing smacks, rowing boats and rafts. Camps were set up and by the end of the year, 85,000 refugges had been repatriated, mostly to the U.S.A.

the jungle
ever beginning

Naked, save for a breech cloth, a man, dark as stained mahogany, stands with feet apart upon a crude bamboo raft which floats silently downstream. Sitting cross-legged in front of him is a girl, perhaps fifteen, maybe sixteen. Her bare arms give warmth and protection to an infant child.

The man, his woman, and their child are Negritos. Their only possessions are freshly picked jungle fruit, a blowpipe, a bamboo container packed with poison darts and a *parang* ("long knife"). Their needs are few. They inhabit the Malaysian jungle.

The raft moves among the strange wreckage of the jungle in the slow motion of the stream. It hugs the bank to take advantage of the swifter current there. From the darkened forest, startled monkeys watch it pass, until a sudden shrill cry scatters them. In order to ward off rocks and giant trees floating downstream like themselves, the young Negrito uses a long pole. He steers the raft at a careful angle as the current quickens into rapids. In a moment the gushing and gurgling ends, and again there is silence.

Man, woman, and child are surrounded by an ageless jungle, living free from the realization that they and their world are growing older, for to them life is not a timetable, divided and subdivided into units of time. Time is but a vague concept and not a pattern. They live in the 20th century, but it could be the year 1000. Like his father, and his father's father, and his before him, the young Negrito on the raft lives in a timeless environment. His history is his memory; his present is what he can see and hear around him; his future is what is beyond the next bend in the river.

The Negritos, like other aboriginal people of Malaysia, inhabit the oldest jungles on this planet, so old they make the tropical rain forests of Africa and South America seem adolescent by comparison. While creeping ice fronts were swelling and shrinking across the Northern Hemisphere, the Malaysian jungles slept through an estimated 100 million years of uninterrupted slumber. And

A blue-green canopy of forest (previous pages) has covered Malaysia's hinterland since the dawn of time. These rain forests make those of Africa or South America seem young in comparison.

while the far-reaching climatic changes were affecting the rest of the globe, and the animal species there were forced into new evolutionary channels, Malaysia's wildlife was left undisturbed.

Leaping Lizards!

The process of evolution is slow and mysterious. Given enough time, under the right conditions, anything can happen. In the upper foliage of the jungle trees, where branches are dense and interlaced, there live bizarre species. Frogs and lizards, which have grown leathery membranes that pass for wings, fly from tree to tree. Then there is the flying lemur, a furry animal that has existed on earth for about seventy million years, dwelling only in the Malaysian region and in the southern Philippines. There are also tree snakes living in the same matted vegetation 10 meters above ground. These reptiles have developed over centuries of existence without ever coming down to earth, while their nearest relatives elsewhere in the world burrow in the ground.

Malaysia's profusion of rare wildlife stimulated a trade in luxuries which has thrived for more than a millennium. Before the days of Kublai Khan, Chinese merchants journeyed to Borneo in quest of exotic medicines like bezoar stones, extracted from the stomach of a monkey, and rhinoceros horn, used to make cups which could detect poison. Powdered rhinoceros horn is still an expensive ingredient for the Chinese apothecary, just as birds' nests, fetched from gigantic caves in Sarawak, are for the Chinese chef. Recently a young Indian girl, riding a bicycle on a deserted *kampung* road, sighted a tiger lying motionless by the roadside and went to pluck out its whiskers. Tiger whiskers, some believe, have extraordinary medicinal powers. But in this case, the cat was only taking a nap and the girl was lucky to escape injury.

Leopards, tapirs, elephants, deer, wild pigs, and porcupines still roam the isolated hinterland. But big game is elusive. Due to the denseness of the undergrowth, animals other than monkeys and gibbons are frequently heard but seldom seen. Years of callous butchery at the hands of profiteering hunters have depleted the ranks of some beasts. The

Only thin shafts of light pierce the dense foliage of the triple-canopy forest, which is home to a profusion of unusual wildlife, including flying lizards, flying lemurs, and tree snakes.

One-horned Rhino, which Marco Polo mistook for the mythical unicorn, has vanished from Malaysia's jungles and is on the verge of extinction. The Orang Utans, famous "wild men" of Borneo, have been rounded up and placed in a special sanctuary in Sabah.

The Malaysian government has set aside vast tracts of land as game reserves, and strict hunting laws are enforced. The Chief Game Warden has proposed that instead of shooting wild elephants that tear up garden patches in remote *kampungs*, the elephants should be captured and relocated in protected park areas. The Taman Negara, "National Park," is one game reserve where visitors are invited to perch on elevated lookouts above salt licks that attract big game. A snapshot of a wild tiger may take a long wait, however. For many travelers exploring the jungle, the most vivid encounter with Malaysia's wildlife is nothing more hair-raising than an occasional leech bite.

Trees Topple in Clouds of Sawdust

More than two-thirds of Malaysia is jungle. The green cover begins at the edge of the sea and climbs to the highest point of land. Along the coastline there are extensive areas of mud swamps and mangrove forests. Behind the mangroves are the "lowland" dipterocarp forests which extend up to an altitude of 600 meters. Trees grow to majestic heights of 60 meters or more, with the first branches perhaps 30 meters above ground. They call it "the triple-canopy" forest. Commercially, this region is the most important: from here comes timber for the sawmills.

It is difficult to imagine Malaysian traffic without the picture of a huge, sputtering lorry rumbling down a narrow country road with 15 tonnes of giant logs chained to its back. Hundreds of logs float downriver from inland camps in Sabah and Sarawak, and sawdust is a common denominator in Peninsular Malaysia's industrial towns. After rubber and tin, sawn timber is Malaysia's largest export. Timber exploitation is carefully controlled, and the immense fecundity of the Malaysian jungle assures the industry a green future.

The next level of forest is mostly oak and chestnut, and above 1,500 meters it becomes a

At home in the jungle, Negrito aborigines gather near their encampment in northern Peninsular Malaysia. Until recently leading a Stone-Age existence, the orang asli *("original people") now are moving into government-sponsored settlements.*

kind of never-never land with elfin forests consisting of small, gnarled trees 3 to 5 meters high, covered with folds of hanging mosses and lichens. The highland forests, for the most part, are left untouched as catchment areas which ensure the fertility of the soil. Some, like the silvery "Cloud Forest" that twists 4,000 meters up Mount Kinabalu, are scenic jewels.

Shifting Horizons for the Jungle Dweller

The aboriginal tribesmen who have inhabited the Malaysian hinterland for 7,000 years call themselves Orang Asli, meaning "Original Man," a name in which they take pride. They are the residue of various early migrations down the peninsula from southern China. They are physically and racially mixed, some resembling South Sea islanders, others the Khmer people of Cambodia. Their forefathers were hunters and food gatherers who lived in caves and rock shelters. They knew the use of fire and cooked their own food with the aid of crude instruments hewn from stone. Their migrations were hardly a conscious effort. Children were born into a family, grew up, mated, needed more space for their family, and shifted to the next cave. In twenty generations they had moved only 200 kilometers.

Sixty percent of the Orang Asli are deep jungle dwellers, living in closely knit groups under the leadership of a headman. They are animists, acutely aware of the benevolence of nature and of its wrath. The *pawang,* or tribal medicine man, mediates with the spirit world to cure sickness through incantations and a knowledgeable use of herbs. The Orang Asli's beliefs, their diverse and difficult languages, are little known outside their tribes. The isolation of the jungle has set them eons apart from city life nearer the coasts. What material goods they do exchange for jungle products are basic necessities, such as iron objects and salt.

However, although the Orang Asli remain an economically depressed group, the pattern is fast changing. With government support, the Department of Orang Asli Affairs is providing land settlements, schools, hospitals, and medical training in an effort to provide channels of integration with Malaysian society should the Orang Asli want them.

In Sarawak, tattooed patterns like twisting vines decorate the torso of an Iban tribesman, whose village occupies a single close-knit longhouse. Ibans have just recently abandoned headhunting for more peaceful ways.

Many tribesmen now live in clearings on the jungle's fringe where they cultivate crops of hill rice, maize, and tapioca. But the bonds which have sustained a self-contained inland community are not easily broken, and the identity of the "Original Man" remains strong.

Sabah and Sarawak

The people of Sabah and Sarawak, 1,000 kilometers to the east across the South China Sea, have an entirely different heritage from that of the Orang Asli of the peninsula. Their links stretch back 40,000 years to the earliest known *Homo sapiens* to inhabit Borneo. Provocative cave paintings of burial ships survive from a civilization that frequented Sarawak's Niah Caves forty millennia ago.

Many inland jungle dwellers — the Ibans and Land Dyaks in Sarawak, the Muruts in Sabah — live in longhouses close to the innumerable rivers that serve as the highways and byways of Borneo. Most of them have given up the hunt and have cleared surrounding jungle to grow hill rice and pepper. The Punans, who dwell in the far recesses of Sarawak's jungles, carry on the nomadic life that once characterized all the Borneo tribes, but instead of hunting with blowpipes they hunt with guns. Sabah's Kadazan people gave up the impermanence of shifting cultivation generations ago and have settled in rural villages nestling in rice fields.

There are 900,000 indigenous jungle dwellers in Sabah and Sarawak. Their folklore, languages and spiritual beliefs are as diverse as the striking designs they tattoo on their bodies. Their heroes are great warring chiefs who either rebelled against the encroachments of British rule or aligned themselves with foreign rulers to establish unprecedented peace treaties. Now, movie magazines, toothbrushes, tennis shoes and other Western imports have found a prominent niche in longhouse life. Barter trade has bowed to a money economy which holds more promises in the towns than in the jungle. More and more young tribesmen who leave the longhouse for the school in the city will never return.

While Punans and Negritos use the jungle as a living room, urban Malaysians

An orangutan makes a rare appearance through the tangled treetops in a wildlife reserve of East Malaysia. Some members of this endangered species must attend clinics to help them return to their natural habitat.

fight a constant battle to make sure the jungle stays beyond their backyard. Less than a half-hour's drive from the national capital is wilderness without any trace of civilization. Stretches of Malaysia's roads are nothing more than ribbons of asphalt that skirt beneath the triple-canopy forest. Pragmatic gardeners, who know they could spend a lifetime ceaselessly trimming the foliage, clear weeds by burning them.

Sunken Cities and Giant Men?

What other ruins and rarities the jungles conceal will always remain a Malaysian mystery. Rumors tell of a lost, sunken city beneath Lake Chini in the Pahang wilds. Aerial photographs suggest that an ancient city might have existed, but all that is known of it are Orang Asli stories about a walled palace, surrounded by lily ponds, on an island. Jungle dwellers further insist that the lost city is guarded by a sea monster that occasionally rises above the lake's surface. About fifteen years ago, a British engineer working in the area swore he saw a strange water beast "with a red eye the size of a tennis ball."

More recently, two Americans on a fishing trip up the Endau River came upon what appeared to be human footprints that measured 45 centimeters long. Their Orang Asli guides casually explained that they were left by "big foot," a subhuman giant covered with hair who roams the deepest part of the jungle. Whether there is any more to "big foot" than an enigmatical footprint is an open question. Large parts of the Malaysian jungles are only minimally recorded on maps. Many trails have been left totally deserted since the state of emergency more than a decade ago, and there are many more dark corners of the jungle that remain totally unexplored.

Malaysia's green carpet is its foundation. The jungle's importance to Malaysia's economic future is inestimable. The jungle controls the flow of water feeding the rice fields and valuable agriculture lands; and it prevents the erosion of hills and the flooding of rivers. Yet the jungle is forbidding and harsh, its soil difficult to till, its terrain dangerous to live in. The jungle dwellers who developed their separate societies within were left isolated by the uninviting triple-canopy forest. Their existence was self-contained. They had no visitors until the last century, and even then foreigners in the hinterland were few and far between.

tides upon the sea

The sky, a misty gray umbrella, releases streaks of rain that splash down on a white-capped sea. Along the coast fishermen have built barriers of thatched palm leaves to meet the winds sweeping inland from an unsettled surf. Their wooden huts are bleached silver from the intense sun and heavy downpour. The willowy casuarina trees that line the shore bend low in windblown curves. Fishing *prahu*s, deprived of their buoyancy on turbulent seas, wait empty-handed on the beach. Tires squeak on the film of water covering the coastal roads. The rivers run quick and high: it is the monsoon season in Malaysia.

Three months in a year, Malay fishing folk who live in small villages along the East Coast of the Malay peninsula store away their fishing nets, dock and repair their boats, and settle down in the shelter of their clapboard houses to wait for the winds to change. They cannot sail their *prahu*s against the force of the monsoon. The food they have gathered during fair weather must last them through this period.

This pattern of life has characterized Malaysia's shores for ages. Seas were the thoroughfares of antiquity. Long before the Christian era, bold sailors sailed over unknown seas in low, square-rigged sailing craft. They came from India with the southwest monsoon in search of gold nuggets, camphor, clove, pepper, and sandalwood. They came from China in primitive junks loaded with silks and porcelain, blown across the China Sea by the northeast monsoon. Almost surrounded by water, Malaysia was where the monsoons met, where the tides of the Indian Ocean and the South China Sea flowed together in the Straits of Malacca. Seafaring merchants traveling in either direction stopped along these coasts to wait for the winds to change. Malaysia was the halfway point in the ancient interchange, linking China to India, and India to the Spice Isles.

Along the eastern coast of Peninsular Malaysia (previous pages), a swift tide sweeps out upon the South China Sea, leaving behind a shell-strewn littoral and a stranded rock islet. Through the Straits of Malacca, which links the South China Sea and the Indian Ocean, plies a weathered Chinese junk (right) trading as its forebears did in ancient times.

The Lucrative Spice Trade

It was the Spice Isles, a small cluster of islands in the Indonesian archipelago, that set Asian maritime kingdoms against each other and in Europe sparked off the Age of Discovery in the 16th century, impelling Columbus to cross the Atlantic and Magellan to circumnavigate the globe. The Moluccas produced the spices which European aristocrats craved. In time the exports to Europe became so lucrative that a vessel loaded with spices from the Far East could make enough profit from one trip to pay ten times over the cost of the voyage, including the value of the ship.

Trade, however, was a hazardous business. Traders sailed on merchant ships carrying up to 200 men who endured violent storms and a constant fear of pirates. A Buddhist pilgrim named Fa-Hsien, sailing from Sumatra to China in A.D. 414, wrote: "In the darkness of the night, only great waves were to be seen breaking on one another and emitting a brightness like that of fire. Large turtles and other monsters of the deep were all about." Ships cautiously hugged the coasts and called at various river-mouth settlements for supplies and water. Where these settlements prospered as commercial centers, merchants remained behind to look after the business of the port. One such port grew into an empire.

Greatest Seaport in the Old World

Malacca today is like an eccentric old lady adept at hiding her age. The little sea town spreads out under low red-tiled roofs in a maze of narrow alleys and well-trodden roads. Streets come alive with the jingle of trishaw bells, the buzz of rickety sewing machines at the tailor's shop on the corner, and the steady thumping by the local cobbler who still does most of his business on the sidewalk. The tallest building has nine stories. It seems a bit odd, then, that in about 1460, merchants who bartered for luxuries in the local bazaar conversed in no less than eighty-four different languages. "Malacca is the richest seaport with the greatest number of merchants and abundance of shipping that can be found in the whole world," wrote a Portuguese sailor in the 16th century. Yet

In the early morning market at Trengganu, a young fishmonger sells the previous night's catch of cuttlefish, a Malay delicacy when fried with chilies. Fish along with rice are Malay staples.

even by then the illustrious harbor-kingdom had passed its prime.

Early Malacca epitomized the Malay bazaar that dealt in everything from Persian perfumes to Javanese daggers. A Sumatran prince named Parameswara, who claimed to be descended from Alexander the Great, founded the city in 1403 and swiftly established an opulent emporium that lured all ships passing through the straits. Five years later, the Emperor of China sent his Imperial Envoy Cheng Ho to Malacca laden with gifts. The Chinese admiral arrived with 62 ships and 37,000 men. Parameswara returned the magnanimous gesture by visiting China in 1411; he returned to Malacca on a ship half-submerged under the weight of precious stones, horses with saddles, gold, silver, and copper.

Prosperous merchants from India and the Middle East married into the local aristocracy, and before Parameswara died, Islam had become the religion of the Malay elite. The sultans who succeeded him guided the Malacca court to the heights of ceremonial pageantry. Whenever the ruler left his walled palace, he was carried on a litter by his ministers and surrounded by retainers beating drums and gongs.

The heritage of the international trade bazaars had a lasting effect on Malaysian life. While the Cambodians of Angkor and the Javanese of Borobudur built astounding monuments of stone to immortalize their more isolated inland kingdoms, Malaysia's ancient monarchs ruled over realms that touched upon dozens of distant civilizations via the diplomacy of the sea. Entrepôt trade instilled a cultural give-and-take that probably explains why the greatest monument the ancient Malays built is the Malay language, replete with words adopted from Arabic, Sanskrit, Persian, Portuguese, and, lately, English. The inhabitants of the harbor towns were as cosmopolitan as the trade was diverse. What remained uniquely Malaysian was the selectivity of the native rulers, who retained Hindu customs while adopting Islamic laws.

Too Precious Not To Be Shared

It took Western explorers little time to realize that whoever controlled the sea controlled the wealth of the land behind it. Marco

Stevedores in Penang Island unload cargo from a flotilla of merchant ships anchored in this emporium's strategic harbor, which is nestled between the island and the railhead of Butterworth on the mainland coast.

Polo sailed through the Straits of Malacca in 1292, but it was not until the 16th century that the first European traders decided to step ashore. They landed with a bang. On St. James' Day, 25 July 1511, Portuguese soldiers knelt on the decks of their ships to receive the blessing of the Holy Church before beginning a bloody siege on Malacca that lasted for ten days. Malacca's sultan fled, leaving the prosperous harbor in the hands of the conquerors who opened the first direct trade links with the West.

Trade with the Spice Isles was too precious not to be coveted, and within two centuries Portuguese Malacca had fallen to the Dutch who eventually traded it with the British in 1795. Britain's Honorable East India Company hastily established itself with an additional settlement on the island of Penang. Handsome *Indiamen* competed for harbor space with ancient junks from China and Siam. Treaties with Malay sultans secured for the British the use of several ports, and these prospered so quickly that some local rulers soon discovered that their signatures had granted more concessions than they had intended. The spheres of influence emanating from London and encompassing the British Empire had reached Malaysia and were to remain there for 150 years.

In the early 19th century there was still a spirit of adventure on the high seas that fired the fantasies of armchair travelers back in England. No one embodied the heroic image of the dashing young adventurer who left home to seek his fortune in the Orient more than James Brooke, ex-officer in the Bengal army. Brooke bought a 140-tonne schooner and set sail for Borneo on a commercial venture that was never to materialize. By chance, the young captain helped quell a rebellion of native chiefs in Sarawak. He was so successful in procuring a peace treaty that the local governor offered him land in return. In February 1841, James Brooke became the first "white Rajah" of Sarawak. It took him the next two decades to convince the world that it really happened.

Brooke, along with a hardy band of British captains, was a pirate hunter who set out in a warship to extinguish probably the

Schoolboys from Kelantan play a sandy game of barefoot soccer, on one of the many beaches along the eastern coast of Peninsular Malaysia that attract oceangoing turtles, skin divers, and sun bathers.

most lucrative profession on the South China Sea. Piracy was a widespread and an honorable calling in Brooke's day, one which attracted merchants, noblemen, and fishermen alike. A native aristocrat who replenished his treasury through a fleet manned by highly skilled seamen hardly considered himself an outlaw. He was more likely to define Brooke as a pirate for stealing land from fellow chieftains. Nonetheless, for centuries sailors trembled at the thought of passing unarmed through Malaysian waters at night. The most formidable pirate bands were the Lanuns from Mindanao. They would pounce on innocent ships with the terror of an approaching torpedo, in crude but frighteningly swift boats. Sometimes they recruited head-hunting warriors from the Borneo interior, and while the captains pillaged the cargoes, the crew collected war trophies.

Malaysian seas today hold untold riches from ships wrecked by storms or plundered by pirates. Rumors still circulate of hidden treasures buried in caves on islands off the east coast of the peninsula. D'Albuquerque, the Portuguese captain who demolished ancient Malacca, set sail three months later with a fleet laden with the spoils of war, only to see all his ships lost in a storm. His loss was never recovered.

Now, a steady stream of 200,000-tonne oil tankers and cargo vessels, replacing silks and porcelain with black gold, rubber, and tin, sail through the Malacca Straits, which still has the same strategic importance that spurred ancient kingdoms to war. Control of the Straits of Malacca remains an international controversy because both Malaysia and Indonesia claim rights to supervise all traffic sailing within their territorial waters. The recent increase in offshore oil exploration has greatly enhanced the value of sea territory, and the trading ports established by the British are now the leading commercial centers of the region. Even the wide, white beaches that spread over much of Malaysia's 5,500-kilometer shoreline have taken on profitable possibilities as tourists, eager for sunshine and palm fringed coral strands, flock to newly developed holiday resorts on the East Coast.

Living on water in houseboats or homes on stilts, fishing folk grow up with the sea in Kota Kinabalu, Sabah, East Malaysia. The Malaysian coasts are dotted with such villages, from where the menfolk set out in traditional wooden prahus *to catch cuttlefish, squid, carp, crab, cockleshells and tiny* ikan bilis.

the countryside evergreen

Eighty years ago the Malayan press reported an unprecedented mishap. While thundering over newly laid track in dense jungle near Telok Anson, a passenger train met head-on with a wild bull elephant. Defending his herd and territorial right, the elephant charged and derailed the train.

Malaysia today makes the gallant beast seem like a hero of a tall tale. Order and propriety now pervade much of the countryside. A smooth, well-maintained highway unrolls through green hills. Rubber trees flash by in never-ending, even rows. Monstrous tipples of tin mines, with pole scaffoldings spread out over white sludge, appear where plantations leave off. Freshly planted oil palms stitch the horizon in a patchwork of deep green against cleared and cultivated red earth. In the northern and coastal areas, fields are rich with stalks of golden rice.

As far as the eye can see, the lush, green vegetation of the tropics smothers the landscape. Yet, contrary to its looks, Malaysia is not ideally suited for agriculture. Unlike the Nile River Basin or the Ganges Valley, where seasonal rains flooding the land bring new fertile soil, the torrential downpours in Malaysia wash away the valuable top soil. In many places, only harsh red mud remains.

Erosion is one of Malaysia's oldest problems. For millenia, the land and its fertility have been washing out to sea. The many limestone outcrops that protrude from the lowlands like huge bubbles are evidence of this. Geologists believe the Malay peninsula and Borneo beyond were once a lofty, rugged land mass running the entire length of the Indonesian archipelago. It was the meticulous work of nature, the slow process of wearing down of the earth by the sun, rain, wind, and more rain that over the ages reduced mountains to hillocks and outcrops. Such changes continue to take place today. Stand on the ramparts of St. John's Fort in Malacca and you may wonder how the old cannons could shoot so far out to sea. Maps of that early period show that the area, including the

Monsoon showers splash the wet rice fields of Negri Sembilan, Peninsular Malaysia. Rice was probably introduced from India more than a millennium ago, and the planting cycle from seeding to harvesting sets the pace of rural life.

present parade ground, was then all covered by sea. Alluvial soil washing down from the hills has reclaimed it in less than 400 years.

Despite the shifting landscape, Malaysia's early settlers were basically food growers as well as fishermen. As far back as A.D. 500 Malays were growing crops for export: sugarcane, bananas, pepper, coconuts.

In centuries past, control of the land rested entirely in the hands of the aristocracy. The sultans were the source of all authority. They alone, in theory at least, held the powers of life and death. Their realms were administered by district chiefs, who could call for compulsory labor for any length of time, should they wish. Slavery was a regal institution. The deputy of the last Sultan of Malacca had so many slaves that if one of them arrived to work smartly dressed he might be mistaken for a stranger and invited into the royal *kampung* — until his identity was discovered.

The *raayat-raayat*, or common people, lived only to serve and obey their ruler. Yet often the ruler was as far away from a village as a one-month river trip. Communications were slow; travel was arduous. Little of the power struggles among the ruling class penetrated the rural *kampung*. Farmlands passed from generation to generation with scarcely a ripple of change.

Honoring the Rice Spirit

The continuity persists. Nothing typifies the Malaysian countryside more than the small, wooden homes shaded by a green awning of coconut palms and papaya trees. *Kampung* houses, as always, are propped up on stilts above a neatly swept courtyard to keep the living rooms dust-free and breezy. The sound of chicken feathers rustling under the house mingles with the smell of cooking curry. A portrait of the Yang di-Pertuan Agong, King of Malaysia, formally clothed in the rich, traditional garb of the sultanate, hangs prominently from a clapboard wall decorated with glossy calendars and magazine clippings. Narrow paths weave from house to house to the flooded rice fields behind the *kampung*, where farmers trudge through soft mud behind a water buffalo and a single-blade plow.

The planting cycle of rice, a crop introduced from India 1,000 years ago, continues

A Malay farmer in Kedah, Peninsular Malaysia, can reap two harvests annually with hybrid rice which has a shorter growing season. This helps Malaysia decrease its dependence on imported rice.

to dominate rural Malay life. Women hide their faces under wide, conical hats and hitch their sarongs up to the knee when they plant seedlings in the hot sun. Men tend the fields until harvest time when the women return to help reap the riches. Rice, the staple food and a prime source of income for the rural Malay, is a recognized and respected necessity. The ancestors of today's farmers believed all living things were imbibed with a spirit, called *semangat*. A bountiful harvest was followed by a thanksgiving feast in honor of the rice spirit during which villagers reveled in gay rounds of flirtatious folk dances and shadow plays that lasted for days.

The tempo of *kampung* life has quickened with double cropping, using new rice hybrids which permit farmers to reap a second crop during the time that was once off-season. Malaysia produces 85 percent of the rice it consumes, filling the gap with imports from Thailand and China. However, a rice revolution is high on the list of objectives in the government's development plans, and more and more fields are yielding two crops a year.

A Fortune in a Tin Pan

Remnants of the dynamic expansion inland linger alongside country roads in the shape of huge mounds of dirt gouged out of the earth to tap the tin deposits below. Malaysia is not exceedingly rich in mineral deposits, with the exception of tin, and there the country knows no rivals. When the mining boom was in full swing during the 19th century, it seemed that half the tin cans in Europe originated in Malaya. Tin mining led to new settlements that sprang from a few prospectors' shacks and became cities as big as Kuala Lumpur. It gave the British administration the revenue to build roads and railways through jagged jungle terrain, and it introduced the Chinese pioneer to the heartland of Malaya.

Envoys from the Dragon Throne were nothing new. Chinese navigators had charted Malayan waters when the Roman Empire was at its peak. But it was not until the last century, when the British established the Straits Settlements, that Chinese immigrants came en masse as merchants, artisans, and traders.

Mesmerizing rows of rubber trees will earn Malaysia millions in export earnings. Plantations of rubber and oil palm cover most of the peninsula's cultivated land.

In the late 1820s, when rich deposits of tin ore were discovered in the state of Perak, Malay chiefs encouraged Chinese immigrants to journey inland to work their mines and to prospect for new fields. When news reached China of the profitable opportunities awaiting the pioneer, thousands of workers arrived from the southern provinces, many bringing nothing but a spare change of clothes.

All-male mining settlements were rough and risky. Malaria and cholera, at that time diseases which medicine was unable to cure, wiped out hundreds of prospectors who sweated in the intense heat. Those who survived did so under a constant threat of tiger attacks, recorded at one stage as a daily occurrence. Law and order was a vicious balancing act between rival Chinese secret societies clashing over mining rights. Societies imported professional fighters from China and would commonly signal the success of a fight by dyeing their shirts with the blood of the vanquished. Thousands perished in gang wars. Others made a fortune.

To maintain a semblance of government in the early mining communities, the Malay chiefs appointed a sort of civil governor called "Kapitan China," who was often a Chinese prospector who had gained power and respect among his compatriots. This practice of self-rule through the Kapitans continued after British intervention in the Malay States in 1874. For the most part the Chinese were not interested in politics. They were contented working the mines and engaging in commerce. For decades, they held a virtual monopoly on the tin mining industry and their settlements slowly grew into towns, as women from China made their way inland. Their descendants continue to operate huge tin-dredges that pour metal into Malaysia's second largest industry. For more than seventy years, Malaysia has been producing over one-third of the world's tin.

Rubber Seeds, a Reckless Gamble

But what stands out on the green scene countless times more frequently than the cumbersome tin tipple is a plant first grown in the soil of Brazil—the rubber tree. Its modest debut in Malaysia hardly heralded a crop that was later to take up three-fourths of all the developed land in the nation. Coffee planters, who had been fighting a losing battle against plant diseases, pests, and plum-

Called the Asian tractor, the versatile water buffalo is also a source of milk, meat, hide, manure, and dried dung fuel.

meting prices, greeted the idea of rubber trees with wry pessimism. Many simply packed up and returned home to England. Those who stayed on and ventured to plant a few rubber seedlings in the soil of their estates considered their effort a reckless gamble.

The man who did not agree was Henry Ridley, Director of Gardens for the Straits Settlements at the end of the 19th century. "Rubber Ridley," as the planters called him, was convinced that his crop had great possibilities and was known to journey around the countryside with seeds in his pocket for anyone he could convince to plant them. Ridley's was a far-sighted and lonely crusade, until John Dunlop invented the bicycle tire and Henry Ford put the automobile on the assembly line. By that time, humbled planters had to wait their turn to get the seeds that Ridley once could not give away. The man who could claim "I told you so" has been remembered fondly ever since.

The rubber boom brought new waves of immigrants from South India and Ceylon. Planters with long experience on the Indian subcontinent imported the laborers they knew best, and before long Tamil and Singhalese became the new languages of the rubber estates. Though Indian merchants had been trading along the peninsula for 2,000 years, the freshly recruited rubber tapper found himself estranged from a familiar society, and the separation from the motherland was keenly felt. Workers bound to one estate for a number of years under a harsh, indentured labor system, clung to the village life they knew in India. Soon lighted prayer lamps in small Hindu temples and the electrifying beat of Indian drums merged with Malaya's increasingly varied ways of life.

The rubber tapper continues to set out before dawn to collect the cups of latex that make up 42 percent of the world's natural rubber supply, but now he often stops short of the old boundaries of his estate to view a field planted with oil palm trees. The government encourages farmers to diversify their crops by growing coconut, coffee, tea, fruits, nuts, and spices. Palm oil increased in dollars earned in the late 1970s by 20 percent a year, bringing Malaysia's share up to nearly half of the world's palm oil production. Then again, so did the number of television antennas, Japanese-made motorcycles, and Western synthetic clothes seen in the country.

On his way from an evening bath, a boy in Perak, Peninsular Malaysia, walks on the clearing for a new road slicing through the red-clay jungle hills.

58

city and town—
from 'wild west' to
the big time

Half of Malaysia's population is engaged in agriculture, but the once isolated and self-sufficient village is now linked by paved road and out-station taxi to the nearest town, where a farmer can stock up on Guinness stout and rubber boots as well as the age-old dried fish and batek sarongs. Villagers, who toil day after day on the same small plot of rice, can return home and tune in their portable radio for news from anywhere between London and Peking. The lure of big city life enters the daydreams of more and more teenagers in rural Malaysia. Many young men leave the family and the farm in pursuit of other worlds.

Encik Mansor bin Zainal Abidin, agricultural officer in the town of Pasir Mas, let his pencil drop on his desk. Glass doors that swish open at the weight of a footstep, push-button elevators with piped-in music, and a prim secretary in high heels flashed through his mind. He picked up his pencil and filled in an application requesting a transfer to the booming capital of Kuala Lumpur.

If most Malaysians do not live in the big city, enough hear about it to make life under neon signboards and revolving restaurants the topic of long conversations. Country youths let their imaginations glide up escalators and down jet runways in the place where TV Malaysia began. The only hitch attached to their vision of boundless possibilities is the "before generation" — *kampung* grandparents who may listen in wonder, but relate to far different times.

One hundred and twenty years ago Kuala Lumpur did not exist. Apart from a dense jumble of jungle trees with their simian occupants, all that was there were the swampy banks of the Gombak and Klang Rivers. The scene stood out from the rest of Malaysia's interior as much as one swell on the high seas. It was only by chance that a couple of Chinese merchants poling their boats upriver decided that they had had enough exercise for the day and set up shop selling supplies to tin miners in nearby Ampang. Being down-to-earth

Monsoon rains do not deter village women from going to market (previous pages), a colorful collection of stalls and shops that links town and country. On sunnier days bamboo shades unfurl (right) advertising what is sold inside.

pioneers, they named the place exactly as they saw it: Kuala Lumpur, "Muddy Estuary."

Pioneers in Wild West Malaysia

Dirty feet hardly got scarcer as the years went by. After the first shop gained some haphazard neighbors, Kuala Lumpur developed into a shockingly filthy, diseased, and violent village, plagued by fires, floods, and feuds. Chinese secret societies warred over tin holdings; nightfall became a dangerous time. The toughest men around wielded power like a hatchet on the downswing. Kapitan China Yap Ah Loy, the town's boss, was a racketeer with interests in gambling, brothels, dormitories, and tin. He was also the most astute administrator that squalid Kuala Lumpur could hope to find in the 1860s. His formula for law and order was clear-cut: He paid M$100 for the heads of his enemies; and he once remarked, "It has been as much as I could do to count out the money fast enough."

The days of Wild West Malaysia have almost vanished beyond memory in the innumerable small towns that sprang up as the tin miners dug in. However, there are still traces of the cluttered trading posts that provided pioneers and farmers with their basic supplies. Main street of an average Malaysian town today has become a trunk road slicing through the center of town, on which traffic consists of a peddler gliding by on a bicycle, or a huge timber lorry trundling past at highway speed. Enough through-traffic pulls up at the curb to give streetside stalls a steady clientele. The Chinese frying pan sizzles and steams as a burly cook in an undershirt and drawers tosses noodles, sprinkles spices, and takes orders at the same time.

In the sundry-shops located side by side on main street, Malay housewives browse over counters overhung with mops, dusters, school bags, pots and pans. A gruff mechanic, whose work clothes would shame a chimney sweep, revs engines and adjusts spark plugs amid a debris of disemboweled motorbikes spilling onto the street.

A Spontaneous Tack-Up Job

Typical Malaysian small towns have no sidewalks. The business of the day goes on

Chinese festive mobiles are on sale in the arcades beneath two-story shop houses, where Chinese merchants work and live.

under the shade of "five-foot ways," arcades under double-storied shop houses whose tenants only have to descend the staircase to work. Many shop houses plastered together in town blocks have festoons and flower pots carved on their pastel facades bearing a date in the 1920s; but these old-fashioned adornments now face keen competition from plastic petrol signs and garish movie posters.

The Pepsi Cola cult, at most, is a veneer. Much about a small town falls into an easy pattern established at the turn of the century. Main street branches off at right angles into smaller lanes that crisscross into alleys fanned by flapping clothes lines. A bird's-eye view in most cases would reveal that town planning amounted to little more than a spontaneous tack-up job, as more merchants moved in to compete with the man next door.

Our Town Today

Over the decades, hometown Malaysia grew in size and character. Beyond the cramped commercial center today still rise the stately trimmings of the colonial past, under which Order, Health and Cleanliness were the reigning deities. Though the whitewash may look drip-dried and the Doric pillars slightly out of date, government buildings still exude the stolid, if somewhat faded, dignity of the British Raj. Invariably, there is the *Padang*, a wide rectangle of green that gallantly bears up beneath football boots and Sunday picnics. The Lake Gardens, the most attractive of the innovations introduced by British residents, mirror nature with a manicure.

Not all towns popped up in the wake of the tin mining boom. Many grew around the fringes of the sultan's royal residence, or in Sarawak across the river from the majestic estate inhabited by the "white Rajahs." Roads terminate at riverbanks in the timber centers of Sabah and Sarawak, where waterborne laborers reinforce the bindings of giant logs floating downstream. On Sundays in Sabah's rural towns, the central square transforms into a Borneo bazaar, down to which barefoot tribeswomen trudge from the hills carrying baskets of bananas and betel nut. The marketplace, where fishermen dump their catch and farmers' wives collect the dollars, remains the prime link binding countryside to town.

Whether it is the local movie house, coffee shop, or billiard hall, Port Dickson offers a welcome change in entertainment for its rural neighbors. Towns lure thousands of newcomers each year in search of work and excitement.

Dreaming of the Big Time

Yet, instant kitchens on the main street of town and betel nut bazaars are but peepholes to the flashy city centers that lie at the intersection of rail tracks and trunk roads. Ambition links the towns to the new cities. Kuala Lumpur, now basking in its role as the national capital and nexus of new happenings, is heavily endowed with number one status.

Top-level students, leaving longhouses and *kampung*s to enter Standard Six at a high school in the nearest town, can aspire to serious studies (and more traveling) by joining the young elite behind the musty library shelves in the national university. Kuala Lumpur's two dozen technical training institutes offer courses ranging from dental surgery to radio operating.

Prestige as well as opportunity lures out-of-towners dreaming of the big time. A village athlete who kicks his way to the state soccer championships can set his goals on the ultimate match in the National Stadium. Even the venerable court musician, who once played music for his sultan's pleasure, may be re-called to his gongs in the banquet room of a luxury hotel to entertain visiting VIPs.

The capital is also the destination of religious pilgrimages. Indian rubber tappers, who seldom see horizons beyond the trees, count away days on the Hindu calendar until Thaipusam, the great celebration when past sins are purged and divine blessings bestowed. For three days, Kuala Lumpur's Indian curry cafeterias are monopolized by more than 300,000 pilgrims who arrive in busloads at the lofty shrine in Batu Caves.

On Prophet Muhammad's birthday, the traffic police turn out in full force to keep cars away from the ceremonies. Malay drums pound over avenues in the midst of a jubilant parade of Muslims representing hundreds of *kampung*s throughout the country. Banners fly atop the marble steps of the National Mosque, center of Islam, symbol of the national faith. Behind its tapered minaret soars the new Parliament Building, commanding a skyline that creeps a little higher every other week.

Kuala Lumpur, like most Malaysian state capitals, is half complete. The future hangs in the air as heavily as the humidity. All that remains of the rickety water-wheels that

Conviviality a keynote of Malaysian life, friends in Kuala Lumpur get together to enjoy evening satay and fried noodles at an instant kitchen on wheels.

scooped tin ore from the ground are warped, sepia-toned photographs salvaged from scrapbooks. Clapboard rooftops that tumbled down the hillsides in the back of the town are slowly disappearing. Behind the nostalgic serenity of colonial bungalows, forests receive a clean shave by the bulldozer. Geometric neighborhoods, offering a house and a garden in the same style for all, have become as Malaysian as satay.

Tomorrow's City

Urban Malaysians live in places no one would have dreamed of before World War II. Twenty eight years ago, city planners in Kuala Lumpur struck upon the idea of building a low-cost squatter resettlement 6 kilometers away. It is now Petaling Jaya, boasting 160 factories and a population of 222,000, a satellite city and industrial showpiece where government ministers and blue-collar workers share the same post office.

Tomorrow's city offers a scintillating range of services. "PJ" residents can shop for caviar and cream cheese at the local supermarket, dine on root beer and Texas hot dogs at the A&W Drive-in, or munch on Chinese spring rolls in sparkling new hawkers' stalls. They can pray at a Thai wat, Hindu temple, Malay mosque or Cantonese clan house. They need not journey to KL for recreation, since PJ provides everything from lectures on child care to judo.

Despite sporadic signs of the stereotype metropolis, there are Asiatic overtones in Malaysia's towns totally undiminished by the concrete cosmetics favored by urban planners. The Chinese assert the culture of their ancestors by combining pioneer stamina with the romantic memories of ancient Cathay. Signboards spring out from shop houses, painted with elegant calligraphy that spells "Everlasting Harmony Shoemakers," or "Virtuous Accomplishment Goldsmiths," or "Mercers of the Thousand Prosperities." There is not a town in Malaysia without Chinese opera singers wailing over the radio.

Yet cities have neighborhoods completely Malay where the urban squeeze and the *kampung* sprawl compromise with neat rows of bungalows on stilts, so that the Malay bureaucrat can still spend days at his office and cultivate fruit trees outside his living-room window.

Once a ramshackle collection of squatters' huts, Petaling Jaya today brimming with modern skyscrapers is the capital's satellite city of tomorrow.

cultural expressions

A Malaysian cultural expression is about as predictable as a Miss Universe contest. It can appear before you as a Malay farm lad in a rice field demanding recognition from passengers in a passing train by communicating via "the peace sign." Or a light-hearted, bare-breasted Iban grandmother unpacking her betel-nut kit, while her grandchildren pass around a snapshot of their brother studying in England. It can be a Chinese fishmonger cracking up with laughter when a foreign photographer asks him to pose with a 7-kilogram carp as if he had won it in a fishing contest. Or an Orang Asli guide explaining to hikers deep in the jungle about the time a tiger followed him to his village, when one false move would have been fatal — for the tiger, of course. It is a thousand other revelations characterized more by where they happen than by a common source.

"Malaysia" as a word is as new as the postwar baby boom. Before it entered the language of nationalism during the '50s, Malaysia was eleven states on the Malay peninsula, North Borneo, and Sarawak. The people in these regions spoke one of a dozen languages, followed one of several religions, and adhered to traditional beliefs that varied from the exorcism of evil spirits to portents bought from a 25¢ fortune-telling machine. The roots of family trees reach over the globe — to Sumatra, India, Sri Lanka, England, Portugal, Fukien, Canton, Thailand, Java, and the Philippines. Malaysians unify the land and the land unifies them, but within the recesses of private homes, customs are as varied as the ingredients of curry.

The Malays: "Sons of the Soil"

The Malays, long linked to the land as *Bumiputras*, "Sons of the Soil," generally prefer the sound of a cock crowing in the morning and crickets at night to noisy traffic horns and congested sidewalks. As farmers and fishermen living in close-knit neighborhoods, rural Malays cherish the simplicity of

Like a Confucian Disneyland (previous pages), lucky dragons and signs decorate the enameled rooftop gardens of a Chinese clan house in Penang. Chinese immigrants have contributed distinctive elements to Malaysia's cultural expressions.

an uncluttered outdoor life. In between harvests and fishing seasons, men pass their free afternoons lounging in a communal open-air pavilion or knotting fishing nets on a wooden platform by the shore. Women dust off the front shelves behind the sunlit facade of a traditional *kampung* house, or spend hours tending the small flower garden clustered around their doorsteps. Everyday routine gives way to an exuberant show of flying kites, spinning tops and bouncing *sepak raga* balls when villagers celebrate during a festive season. Come nightfall, the pattern returns. Children gather at the religious teacher's house to recite verses from the Koran under the glow of a gas lamp. *Kampung* life nurtures a provincial conformity laid down centuries ago. The ultimate of travel is a prestigious journey to Mecca, but other than the great pilgrimage, few *kampung* dwellers wander far.

The inherent talents of the Malays, however, find outlets far from the countryside. Well-groomed professionals, educated at Oxford and speaking impeccable English, make up the cream of the government service. Though a village elder may look askance at the freewheeling city life which permits strip-tease and the brandy glass, a city Malay edges his Alfa Romeo into the parking lot of a high-class restaurant with the ease that comes with practice. Urban youths pick up the latest mod styles in clothing only weeks after they first appear in fashion magazines imported from London or Tokyo. Some young men arrive at religious ceremonies with long tufts of hair under their traditional *songkok* caps, in a style that resembles a rock musician — and many are. A suburban clapboard house may have electrical wiring running through the premises like cobweb, in order to hook up an amplifier for the lead singer in the local band practicing his Mick Jagger accent.

Though the rift between the farm and the city widens as years go by, it does not threaten the strong unity Malays derive from a common faith. The laws of Islam immediately set a Malay apart from fellow Malaysians. Pork, a food relished by the Chinese, is forbidden to Malays. Intermarriage between races is uncommon, though Malays will accept a foreigner into the family if he or she is Muslim.

Yet Islam in Malaysia has little of the rigid dogma it has in the Middle East. Malays are an easy-going, shy people with an abhorrence of open conflicts and clashes of words. Their way of life, and their faith, is marked by a tolerance and self-control that have largely contributed to the peace Malaysia now enjoys.

The Chinese: From the Bottom Up

The Chinese, forming about 35 percent of the population, have a heritage so different from the Malays that for generations neither group knew much about the other. Malaysian Chinese worked their way up the hard route —from scratch. In the turmoil of 19th-century China, leisure was a luxury no one could afford. The Manchu dynasty took its toll on those who refused to bow to its tyranny. Class structure was disintegrating; officialdom was corrupt; the land was riven by floods, famine, and rebellions. Yet not even the rugged, seafaring Chinese of the southern ports of Amoy and Canton were anxious to part from a motherland with 4,000 years of written literature. It was half escapism and half necessity that drove pioneers to Nan-yang, "the Southern Seas," and to save up meager wages earned from backbreaking labor. They arrived willing to endure hardships other men shunned. They tolerated constant outbreaks of jungle fever to build railroads, mine tin, and establish new settlements. It was a transient existence with a definite goal: to return to China a rich man. The pastimes of the migrant laborers were not the carefree sports which Malay farmers enjoyed, but the more sedate preoccupations of gambling and opium — the quickest means to ease the tensions of a laborious day.

Nanyang as a whole was a gamble, taken at great risks but with tantalizing promises of wealth to those who succeeded. Rags-to-riches stories kept migrant laborers awake far into the night, and it was universally understood that any man who worked hard enough could become a millionaire.

Many did. The stately row of mansions along Jalan Ampang in Kuala Lumpur was built largely by Chinese *towkay*s who made fortunes from tin. Spinning roulette wheels in the gaming rooms at Genting Highlands casino are surrounded by intense Chinese businessmen who calmly place a fistful of chips on a dozen numbers before each throw. There are places among the cluttered alleys in Malaysia's Chinatowns that resemble the seedy Shanghai of five decades ago The Chinese opera continues to ignore all realities other than the powdered, pampered, glorious days of the Chinese imperial court.

The parents who pack up bundles of clothing for relatives back in China have children more intent on buying a new car to show the neighbors, or a new evening dress for a Saturday night party. Uniformed students march off to the local high school loaded with bundles of science, engineering, and economic textbooks. If a scruffy, old shopkeeper has trouble deciphering the foreign accent of his customer, he calls for his twelve-year-old son who is proficient in Malay, Mandarin, Cantonese, Hokkien, and English. Malaysian Chinese, descended from a hardy class of merchants, continue to work their way up in the professional world. China provides the tradition — a festive calendar, a focal point for family ancestry, a language and a religion — but Malaysia provides the future.

The Indians: Stargazing and Rain Prevention

Indians came to Malaysia much as the Chinese did, following rumors of fortune in a land their ancestors knew as the "golden peninsula." They came from South India in the early years of this century to tap rubber. The dream of instant wealth attracted many credulous villagers who later found themselves yoked to an alien rubber estate as indentured laborers. Thousands returned to India at the earliest opportunity and the Indians who remained, now forming 10 percent of the population, kept a close watch on the old country.

The rural culture of South India left a bright stamp on Malaysian life as vivid as a saffron silk sari. There are still hundreds of solitary men who live in humble barracks upstairs in an Indian shop house where they accumulate savings for a trip to the village back home. Indian weekly magazines, vegetable curries on banana leaves, the astrologer's calling card and the indomitable prevalence of the Hindu faith that continues to absorb change like an ink blotter have all become part of Malaysia. So has the Indian newspaper editor who plays golf in the morning, commands the news desk in the afternoon, and drinks beer with fellow journalists and diplomats at his favorite pub in the evening.

With the awakening of a national consciousness and with the ever-increasing stimulus of modernization, Malaysian leaders seek an overriding unity to their plural society. National Culture Congresses convene to redefine the country's history and art with a pragmatic inclusiveness that draws upon the new and the old. Often the result is an eclectic collection of elements that span several centuries. Malaysian stage shows now combine Borneo war drums with ultraviolet floodlights. Even at the most prestigious diplomatic reception, when government dignitaries stand at crisp attention above a lavish parade ground, there will also be present a *bomoh* — Malay village magician — hired by the protocol committee to make sure that it does not rain that day.

Islam: The Binding Spirit

If Malaysia has a single sound, it is the deep, melodious chanting of the muezzin — the man who turns the country's spiritual hourglass by calling Muslims to prayer five times each day. Though Indians, Sumatrans, Chinese, Thais, and Europeans each played their role in the history of Malaya, it was the Arab merchants who introduced Islam and it was Islam that revolutionized Malay life.

The two are synonymous: all Malays are Muslim, identified by Arabic names, married by Islamic law, guided by the moral precepts revealed in the Koran. Kuala Lumpur, the national capital, resembles a tropical dream of the Moors. Mecca is the supreme destination for any Malay villager wealthy enough to leave the country. Sultans, traditional rulers of the land, have combined spiritual prestige and political power for centuries. Today, Islam is the religion of the state, Friday *the* day of worship, and Islamic bonds the basis of diplomacy with the Muslim world.

Islam permeates everything Malay, from a soft-spoken greeting to the daily meal. The local *surau,* or village mosque, is the heart of every Malay neighborhood. There is not a wardrobe in the entire village that does not contain the *songkok* cap men wear to mosque and the long, white garment women drape over their bodies when praying. Cleanliness

If you could single out a particular sound heard throughout the country, it is the chanting of the muezzin, calling together the faithful five times a day. Although all Malays are Muslim, freedom of worship is extended to all religions.

is a prime virtue. Villagers say the brighter the house, the more blessings God will bestow. A devout housewife keeps her dominion spotless. The typical Malay home, propped up on stilts to assure dust-free floors, is a picture of bright flower pots arranged on a freshly-swept courtyard. Each house has large, open windows to catch the sunlight, and a water basin at the foot of the stairs for bathing the feet before ascending. Unclean things — pig's meat and the saliva of a dog — are never touched. Food is prepared in accordance with religious law; wisdom is acquired through the words of God as spoken through His Prophet.

Kampung children, under the keen eye of the *Ustaz*, or religious teacher, can read and recite Koranic verses in Arabic long before they are able to cope with multiplication tables. Koran-reading contests merit prime time on national television and attract almost as many viewers as Muhammad Ali did during the heavyweight championship fight. Traffic is hopelessly snarled in Kuala Lumpur on Prophet Muhammad's birthday when thousands of Muslims parade through the streets singing praises to the chosen one whose word has united much of mankind in faith.

Silat: Slithering Serpent, Glaring Owl

In some countries it may be lucrative to corner an unarmed man in a dark alley. In Asia it is fatal. Enough young men study the martial arts to form a weaponless army, and one expert can take on ten amateurs single-handed. In *silat,* the ancient Malay art of self-defence, unarmed fighters mimic a kris duel unto death—a reality in ancient times when a Malay who did not master the *silat* art dared not leave his *kampung.* During the lawless years of World War II, Malay leaders revived the martial art by creating a uniform system of teaching *silat* as a means of promoting godliness, loyalty, self-defence and self-discipline. Now, black-clad youths practice studied forms of potential violence behind the seclusion of high walls. Modesty and secrecy are among the basic precepts of a *silat* fighter. Like Japanese *karate,* Korean *tae kwon-do* and Chinese *koon tuo*—the legendary feats of which appear in popular Asian thriller films—expertise in *silat* in-

Malaysia has its own traditional martial art of self defense called silat. *Enjoying a revival since World War II,* silat *like most Asian martial arts calls for gracefully disciplined movement and inner power—cloaked by modesty and secrecy.*

volves meditation and spiritual powers, believed to help ward off evil blows. Fortunately, today evil blows are so few and far between that *silat* fighters are much more likely to highlight a national youth rally than to bruise an opponent. The most popular form of *silat* is merely a refined dance that epitomizes masculine grace.

One sideshow at almost every *kampung* wedding is a spontaneous round of exhibition *silat* to the dramatic tunes of long drums, gongs and melodious *serunai* trumpets. As the music speeds up, all eyes focus on the two fighters who crouch like wary panthers, lunge like arrogant cocks, slither like serpents and glare like owls. With limbs taut for instant reflex, they encircle each other in slow but perfected motion. Toes grip the earth for instinctive balance. Eyes meet in conniving attacks of psychological warfare.

Exhibition *silat* has great impact. Its latent violence sets the audience on edge. Its refined control conjures up all the virtuosities of the unvanquished Malay warrior. It was not so long ago when a *silat* fighter had to possess all these qualities. Fifty years ago, a Jelui chieftain humbled Mat Aris of Kelantan, who was the most famous *silat* fighter of his time. Said the proud Jelui man: "I slewed around and beheld him leaping upon me. A swift movement to one side served to avoid his blow, and as he passed by me my hand smote him full in the face. He was caught completely off his balance, and with a crash came headlong to the ground, but not so quick that I, with the bony edge of my left foot, had cut his face open from chin to eyebrow."

Top Spinning: Hottest Item in the Village

Throughout most of the countryside top spinning is a teenage pastime, but among the Malay communities on the northeast coast, a champion spinner is the village folk hero. Tops there have mythical origins. No one knows when they first started spinning in Malaysia, but Semang aborigines who live in the jungles insist that lightning is the flashing of top-cords in heaven, where dead medicine men compete in a game; and thunder is the murmuring of the tops as they spin.

On the northeast coast, husky villagers hurl their platters of polished hardwood like Olympian discus throwers and send them twirling for a record time of one hour and forty-seven minutes. Top spinning requires such strength that boys under sixteen are barred from village contests for fear they may tear the ligaments in their shoulders. Tops

vary from a simple wooden cylinder that a farmer whittled in his spare time to fantastically streamlined discs with spindles trimmed with inlaid gold. A master top-maker, who does not even begin work until he first inspects the tree, is admired throughout the region.

With the harvest completed and all the rice stored, farmers settle down to betting on the local top team. Contests feature either the long-time spinners or the war-like strikers who spin down 7-kilogram fighting tops faster than a speeding bullet. Attackers need as much skill as muscle, since the defensive team contrives sinister spinning formations designed to eliminate an attacker's top from the tiny playing circle. In addition to enemy strategy, top spinners have to contend with the roars from the peanut gallery. Every other farmer looking on is an amateur spinner, and no rope cracks without a loud comment.

Top spinning in the rice fields is like British wrestling on TV: totally absorbing — the answer to how to forget the monotony of a workday without even trying. Farmers follow their champions to neighboring villages or receive an outside challenger and his band of supporters by holding a feast. The long-time spinners are most revered in village lore since in their flawless form, they can send a top purring for over an hour. In contests, the two village champions meet like rustic gladiators. Teammates scoop up each top in a flash and place it under a bamboo-canopied stand. Long-time spinning tops are said to be "sleeping" and perhaps in the shade they will sleep longer.

Sepak Raga: Bobbing in Space for Hours

In the backyard of a clapboard *kampung* house, on a stretch of beach in south Sabah, in the parking lot of a shopping center or on a ship's deck, Malaysian youths shed working clothes for T-shirt and shorts, and start kicking and heading a ball about. *Sepak raga* is the most adaptable popular sport in Malaysia. All that is necessary is a small ball made of rattan and an open space, thus permitting a contest that demands the agility of a tap dancer, high jumper and sharpshooter combined.

Sepak raga traces its origins to a regal show-off in the 15th century, when four Malay

Top spinning has been raised to a major sport in Malaysia, where masters can keep the hardwood cones turning for hours. Played during the period of ripening of the padi main gasing, as it is called, is reputed to bring in a good harvest.

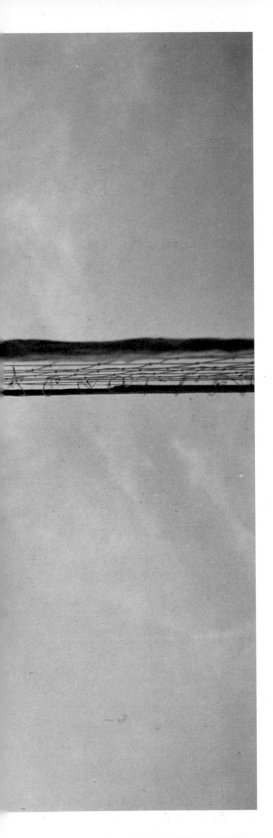

rulers strolled out of the Malacca throne room to a space within the palace walls and proceeded to engage in some fancy footwork that sent the rattan ball bobbing in space for hours on end. The star of the show was the Raja of the Moluccas Isles, who held his audience spellbound by sending the ball skyward with foot, heel, sole, instep, calf, thigh, knee, shoulder, head (everything but the hands), without letting it touch the ground until it had risen and fallen more than 200 times.

Kampung folks have been following his illustrious example ever since. A village festival crowd breaks into circles as soon as the ceremonies permit, each circle of men giving the rattan ball a full aerial workout until someone's legs tire of the expertly aimed kicks, jabs and jumps. Comical dramatics and a show of muscle embellish the big games. A *sepak raga* superstar delights not only his ebullient sports fans. The ladies of the village are watching, too.

Other Southeast Asian countries play variations of *sepak raga*. Arising from a desire to standardize the game and gain international recognition for the sport, Laos, Thailand, Singapore and Malaysia met in 1965 and devised a game with a set of rules acceptable to all. *Sepak takraw* made its appearance at the first Southeast Asian Peninsular Games in 1965 and Malaysia walked off with the gold medal. They have dominated the game ever since. Who knows, but if interest in *sepak takraw* continues to grow the rattan ball may soon be bobbing in the midst of the Olympic Games.

Wayang Kulit and the Dancing Shadows

No one knows who the first man was who tapped the heavens and invited the mythical personalities dwelling there to appear on earth as shadows. A thousand years ago, puppeteers of the shadow theater were entertaining imperial hosts in the courts of China. Otherworld figurines punched out of buffalo hide have bickered and flickered in the lamp light for centuries, in Turkey, India, Burma, Cambodia, Java, Thailand and Malaysia. Malaysia's shadows allude to immortal tales spun through the great *Ramayana* Hindu epic — tales revealing the heavenly virtues of filial

Action-packed volleying and balletic movements may someday carry sepak takraw *beyond Southeast Asia to worldwide arenas of sport. Malaysians excel in this game, in which every part of the body except the hands may be used.*

piety, marital devotion, valor in war, loyalty to one's brethren. The *Wayang Kulit*, or "Shadow Play," is unabashedly moralistic. The characters, after all, are either immortalized heroes or infinitely doomed villains. They clash in shadow battles time and time again, yet everyone knows that Prince Rama, personification of godly grace, will eventually prevail over the hideous, ten-headed demon king called Rawana. The question, and the entertainment, is simply: how? This is left to the skill of "the Master of the Mysteries," known to Malays as *To'Dalang*.

The *To'Dalang*, puppeteer and almighty guiding hand behind the shadows, has a nearly superhuman task. It is a tremendous job to memorize, conduct and sing all the parts of as many as fifty different puppets, lead the Malay orchestra providing the background music, and direct the action on screen all at the same time. Yet the *To'Dalang* carries on a single-handed performance for up to six hours without stopping. His repertoire of personalities includes strange animals in warrior's clothing, princes, priests, sages, giants, ghouls and the inevitable monkeys. But his favorite characters, as every shadow fan knows, are two sassy slapstick clowns named Pa'Dogah and Wak Long. Their wit and acrobatic contortions can keep a village audience howling until their eyes water.

The Kris: Quintessence of Power

In the 15th century a wavy-bladed double-edged dagger entered the courtly intrigues of the Malacca Sultanate. Some scholars insisted it originated from a stingray's bone, others pointed to Javanese ironsmiths who forged the vicious dagger, or kris, as a royal weapon.

Small, poisoned-tipped krisses could easily be concealed in a sarong. The pistol-like grip, designed for thrusting with greatest reach, made the kris most lethal. It was not long before every man carried at least one kris into combat. By 1586, Europeans sent out warnings about "daggers as sharp as a razor." The kris soon took on regal overtones as the symbol of kingship and authority. To the Malay bridegroom, the kris sealed his position as *Raja Sahari*, "King for a Day." To a royal

For more than a thousand years the puppet master has entranced audiences of the shadow play. Episodes from the Indian epic, the Ramayana *provide the basic plot for* Wayang Kulit *performances, but the puppeteer is free to improvise, mixing in anecdotes and local news.*

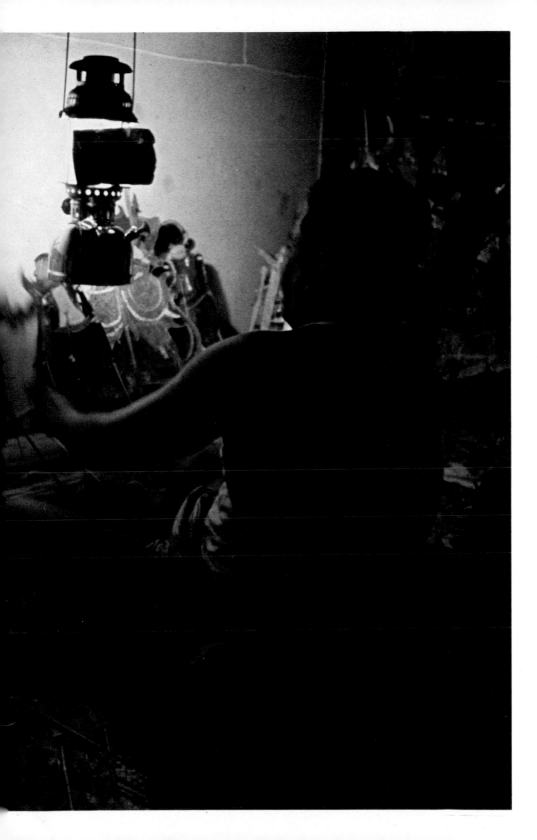

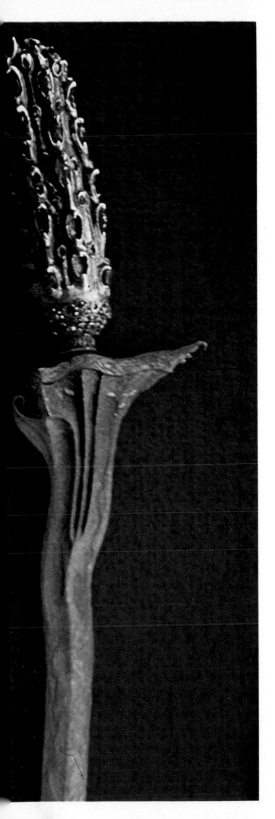

attendant, a golden kris was the ultimate status symbol.

In olden days, when psychic powers were on the prowl, the kris attracted cosmic vibrations like a magnet. Each kris was thought to be possessed by a spirit. The exquisite carvings on the hilt — a kingfisher's head or a stylized figure of a Rajah hugging himself to keep warm — were thought to please the spirit. But though the spirit could be appeased, the kris still had a will of its own. Its mystical qualities generated a slew of popular legends. It was said that a man might be killed if his footprints were stabbed by a kris. To so much as point a kris at anyone was to place him in danger. Some "magic" krisses could suck fire away from an object, cure snake bites or break evil spells. One old farmer insisted that his kris could bring relief to people with a hair stuck in their throat.

The wavy blade was the key to its powers. Malays call the blade *mata keris*, "eye of the kris," and treasure it above all else. The kris of Hang Tuah, a heroic Malay warrior, contained twenty varieties of iron. As late as 1952 an item appeared in the press about a kris named *Berok Bergayun*, "The Singing Ape," which had taken ninety-nine lives. Its blade, it was claimed, was made from ape bones and steel. Its original owner was a wicked monkey who lurked in the trees where he dangled his kris from a string and dropped it on unwary travelers.

Now most kris fables have been rationalized out of existence and emerge only in occasional headlines such as "Poison Kris Stolen from Flat." But if the magic is gone, the glory remains. To Malay rulers, the kris is still the quintessence of power, present at every investiture, served by a warrior on a silver tray, unsheathed and kissed by the king.

Thaipusam: Fulfilling the Holy Vow

At four o'clock in the morning mesmerizing Hindu drums ricochet off the limestone domes of Batu Caves like the heartbeat of a long-distance runner. Dark streams of pilgrims flood the roadside, arriving by the hundreds in lorries and buses. Breakfast foodstalls along the parking lots whip up hot cups of Ceylon tea and *murthaba*. Young,

In the annals of Malayan history, the kris became a legendary weapon to which magic powers and heroic exploits were attributed. Though the aura has waned, it remains a symbol of power, displayed at royal ceremonies.

lanky girls dressed in Day-Glo colors, on their first big trip from a rubber plantation in a year, shyly giggle at an ambitious Western journalist laden with camera equipment. By 4:30 the 3-kilometer-long parking lot is jammed. The massive limestone outcrop turns from an opaque glob to a gray specter as the sky pales. Under a gateway inscribed "Divine Life Society, Malaysia Branch" hang strings of Christmas tree bulbs illuminating the path up the gigantic staircase that disappears into the sacred cave.

The day is Thaipusam, a day of reckoning among Hindu devotees, who vow to repent for past sins and who ask future favors by making an extraordinary pilgrimage up the steep steps to Batu Caves. It is a day of thanksgiving and prayer.

Before ascending, repenters drench their bodies in the purifying stream, yield their minds to the frenetic drumbeats and prepare for absolution. The riverbank is a scene of yellow-clothed devotees passing from consciousness into religious abandon. Relatives and supporters gather around the entranced to dab their foreheads with sacred ashes, and pierce their cheeks with long skewers and spikes. Mortification of the flesh is an act of repentance, and the *kavadi*, a simple wooden frame strewn with peacock feathers, is the symbolic burden one carries in sublimated pain. As electric chanting pours out of loudspeakers and crowds thicken, *kavadi*-carriers slowly rise with the heavy weight fastened into their skin through metal hooks. Some zealous helpers use whips to spur on the devotees, others walk away quietly beside them, offering a gentle hand and constant prayers.

Within the hallowed destination is a dim sea of light bulbs, scattered fires and innumerable pilgrims. Shafts of sunlight shoot down hundreds of meters from cracks in the limestone ceiling. In a deep grotto framed with stalactites rests the jewel-encrusted image of Lord Subramaniam, The Spotless One, Son of Siva. A dozen white-clad priests tend to thousands of worshipers and bestow blessings and sacred ash upon the spent *kavadi*-carriers. The burden is lifted, the trance subsides. A coconut is dashed to the ground and camphor burned. The holy vow made unto God has been fulfilled.

Pain is transcended, then joyousness overcomes this Hindu fulfilling his vow to Subramaniam, son of Siva. In February each year worshippers flock to Penang and the Batu Caves near Kuala Lumpur for the Thaipusam ritual of purification.

Chinese New Year: Mystical, Musical Cats

Silence has never been at a premium on a Chinese street. Operatic love songs blare from portable transistors in every other balcony. Sputtering lorries draw up outside the local hardware store where workers heave heavy machinery. Gears growl on command at the motorcycle repair shop two doors down, not to mention the carpenters' hammers or the hefty cooks shouting orders at the corner coffee shop where the best meals are enjoyed in the loudest company.

But that is just normal. On Chinese New Year the bustle is amplified across the nation as shopkeepers on holiday splash their doorways with vermilion "lucky" scrolls and dragon-studded signboards shouting happiness and prosperity greetings to everyone in sight. Traffic creeps around a pedestrian parade of fashionable shoppers selecting *Nien Koay* — "cakes of the year" — for the dinner table or bright-colored greeting cards inscribed with joyous tidings. Tickets for the latest Hong Kong swordfighting film have been sold out weeks in advance, and those who are not in the cinema bring their foldout chairs to the neighborhood parking lot and resign themselves to the tears and laughter of Chinese opera stars.

All things positive, powerful and brilliant spark off the new year. Fantastic "lions" appear on the streets and start dancing — in and out of cluttered shop houses, around the corner coffee shop and under the window of a typical tiny hotel room with plastic curtains. As if the everyday radio racket was not enough, on New Year's day music-loving Chinese are blessed with a live cymbal orchestra. Mystical lions always bring their band along, even if the oldest musician has not yet reached his teens.

Every 3 meters or so, the clever and comical king of the beasts strikes up a mischievous song and dance routine, wiggling his hindquarters below a glistening coat of mirror sequins, drinking a soda pop and spraying it out, flapping his jaw and generally captivating his sympathetic onlookers with a wild display of high-stepping joy. Dancing lions are called down from the fantasy world on every momentous occasion. As guardians of the legendary empire and protectors of the

Cymbals crash and horns screech while a mythical lion dances in the Chinese New Year. Things positive, powerful, and brilliant are invoked by the Chinese to chase away the bad and welcome the bearers of good fortune.

faith, lions of stone snarl from the balustrades of Taoist temples. But on Chinese New Year, the mystical cats just dance around from shop to shop collecting *ang pows* — the cash gift packets of the season — and this is more than enough good fortune for their nimble manipulators.

Sarawak Art: Visions from the Jungle

An unexpected eye-to-eye collision with a Sarawak painting is powerful enough to startle a goblin, and with subconscious determination, this is precisely what its creator had in mind. For thousands of years Sarawak's inland people have lived so close to nature that her awesome ways have fused with tribal life and ritual. Spirits animate the trees, birds, skies and rivers as the soul animates man. To live harmoniously with the invisible world one must first respect it.

Supernatural precautions were not the only inspiration for a vivid folk art. Pomp, ceremony, family pride and a dandy's vanity all contributed to high fashion in the jungles. Longhouse-dwellers lived in the midst of a verdant environment strewn with twisting vines, capricious butterflies and luminescent insects. Like the wild life around them, they primped their bodies in natural elegance. Warriors appeared at longhouse celebrations with exquisite hornbill carvings in their earlobes, eagles' feathers artfully arranged on multicolored beaded caps and tattoos adorning their skin with prestigious patterns. Women arrived in delicately woven sarongs trimmed with silver thread and jingling bells, their bodices and torsos smothered by silver jewelry.

Sarawak's decorative art lent a jubilant beauty, but never without a function, to tribal society. Painting popped up on everything from burial poles to bamboo containers but always as an addition rather than an end in itself. Tribal life demanded ceremonial masks to greet strangers, guardian spirits to protect hunters, "sickness figures" to draw out disease. These were finely carved when required by master craftsmen. "Art for art's sake" is an alien principle in the East where crafts either embellish daily life or enrich it with spiritual value. Now crafts are also a means of obtaining money through sales to souvenir shops, but here, speed is more important than precision.

Supernatural motifs decorate a longhouse in Sarawak. In the more modern setting of KL's National Museum, artists and audience ponder newer art forms (following pages).

Facts at a Glance

Official Name: The Federation of Malaysia
Land area: 330,000 sq km
  Peninsular Malaysia 132,000 sq km
  Sabah & Sarawak 198,000 sq km
Population: 13.250 million (1978)
Peoples: Bumiputras (Malays and other indigenous races) 53.5%, Chinese 35.3%, Indians 10.5%, Others 0.7%.
Religions: Islam (45%), Buddhism, Hinduism, Christianity.
Main languages: Malay, Chinese, Tamil, English
Birth rate per 1,000: 30.7
Death rate per 1,000: 6.3
Capital: Kuala Lumpur
Other major cities: George Town, Ipoh, Kuching, Kota Kinabalu
Political system: Constitutional monarchy with elected parliament
Head of State: Yang di Pertuan Agung (presently, His Majesty Sultan Haji Ahmad Shah Ibni Sultan Abu Baker)
Head of Government: Prime Minister (presently, Datuk Hussein Onn)

Independent since: 31 August 1957
Joined U.N.: 17 September 1957
Main exports: rubber (21%), petroleum crude (18%), tin (11%), palm oil (11%), timber (9%)
Main imports: machinery and transport equipment (36%), food (15%), manufactured goods (21%), mineral fuel (13%)
Main trading partners: U.S.A., Japan, Singapore, Australia, E.E.C.
Newspapers (In English): New Straits Times, Malay Mail
Per capita income: M$3,205
Currency exchange: US$1 = M$2.17
Electricity: 220 volts, 50 cycles a.c.
Highest point: Mount Kinabalu 4,100 meters
Climate: Daily average temperature range 21°–32°C
Time zone: Kuala Lumpur is GMT plus $7\frac{1}{2}$ hours; New York City plus $12\frac{1}{2}$ hours
Sports: swimming, fishing, soccer, golf

finding your way

Malaysia is no ordinary country. Visitors can literally travel any way they choose — via long-boat, helicopter, trishaw, mountain rope, funicular railway or Orang Asli jungle trail. Travel has so many dimensions in Malaysia that it becomes an end in itself. And there are more than enough opportunities to keep going.

Malaysia is a big country. Covering some 330,000 sq km, it forms a crescent which extends from the Thai border almost to the Philippines. Big, yes, but the paradox is that getting around in the Federation is remarkably easy. All sorts of transportation are available.

A modern, overnight train crosses the Thai border and follows the sweeping curve of the Malay peninsula to Johore Bahru in the south. Its counterpart, slower perhaps, chugs its way up the backbone of the peninsula, through seemingly impenetrable jungles to Kota Bharu in the north. A speedy riverboat with 100 passengers skims up Sarawak's wide Rajang River, from Sibu to Kapit. A motor launch with a party of weekenders cruises across the blue waters from Mersing to Tioman Island. An air-conditioned bus speeds from Kuala Lumpur through rubber plantations to keep its three-hour schedule to Malacca. A chartered light plane flies over the jungles from Kuala Lipis to Kuantan. A coastal steamer leaves Penang for Port Klang, Malacca, Singapore and then sails to Sarawak and Sabah. Aborigines belonging to the Senoi tribe paddle two sports fishermen up the Endau River to tributaries where no line has been cast before. Traveling in Malaysia can be as exciting and adventuresome as one wants to make it. Knowing how to get around is the secret.

Traveling reveals the charm that hides behind the masks of Malaysia. You may meet rural children at play (previous pages), or experience such contrasts as the National Mosque in a modern, fast-changing capital (following pages).

By Air

Malaysia's national airline, Malaysian Airline System, or MAS (*mas* in Malay means "gold"), has extensive domestic routes connecting all major points throughout Malaysia. These include many small townships in the more remote regions of Sabah and Sarawak which would otherwise be isolated from the mainstream of travel. At night, there are economy flights between Kuala Lumpur and Penang, Kota Kinabalu, Kuching and Singapore.

Malaysia Air Charter (MAC) and Wira Kris operate a fleet of light aircraft and helicopters throughout the country. Both have bases in Kuala Lumpur. The fare is between M$450 and M$750 an hour depending on the type of aircraft. Anywhere on the Malay peninsula is approximately an hour's flight from Kuala Lumpur. Anywhere in Sabah is approximately an hour away from Kota Kinabalu, the state capital.

By Train

The Malayan Railway operates over 2,700 km of track. Day express trains — the Magic Arrow between Kuala Lumpur and Singapore and the Golden Arrow between Kuala Lumpur and Butterworth — run daily. They have air-conditioned buffet cars for first-class passengers and fan-cooled buffet cars for second class. Night trains include the North Star between Kuala Lumpur and Butterworth and the Southern Cross between Kuala Lumpur and Singapore. Night trains consist of first and second class buffet cars. Air-conditioned sleeping cars are also available, but reservations are a must. In addition, the railroad operates an east coast service called the Sumpitan Emas (Golden Blowpipe) which runs daily between Gemas and Tumpat, via Kuala Lipis in the central highlands. A ride on the Golden Blowpipe

The small maps in the margin in Part Two indicate by means of a black dot the area covered in the text on the same page.

98

is a great change as it provides a view of the triple-canopied forest.

In Sabah, rail service is provided between Kota Kinabalu and Tenom (159 km) by the Sabah State Railways. For those who like to travel in style, railcars may be chartered anytime for a minimum of five passengers. This can be arranged through local travel agents or Sabah State Railways. The train passes through jungle terrain and along the famous Padus rapids.

By Sea

The Straits Steamship Company offers weekly sailing between Peninsular Malaysia and Sabah and Sarawak with stops at Kuching, Miri, Labuan, Kota Kinabalu, Sandakan, Lahad Datu and Tawau. A sea cruise is a very pleasant way to see Borneo's coastal towns. Prices are reasonable.

By Road

Because Malaysia's roads are good, one of the best ways to travel is to rent a car and set out on a spontaneous trip through the peninsula. (Note: driving is on the left-hand side of the road.) There are half a dozen dependable rent-a-car services in Kuala Lumpur and Penang. Rentals, without air conditioning, range from M$35, plus mileage and petrol, a day. Customers are required to have a valid driver's license. Because many of the country roads are dimly lit at night, it is advisable to drive during the day. Travel agents will also arrange for a private car and driver, who will also serve as a guide, for those who wish to go sightseeing.

In most countries, thrifty travelers would not consider traveling by taxi on a long journey. But in Malaysia "outstation" travel between cities is a favorite and inexpensive mode of transportation. A census would possibly reveal that more local people travel by taxi than by train or even bus. From Kuala Lumpur to the smallest village there are centrally located taxi stations, usually near the market place. Drivers call out their destinations to prospective passengers, and when a taxi has its full capacity—four passengers—it proceeds non-stop to its destination. Fares are rated per passenger, and it is possible to travel from the Thai border down the full length of the peninsula to Johore Bahru in the south for as little as M$30. But the driving is deplorable!

Bus routes connect all cities in Peninsular Malaysia. Fares on the public transport system are reasonable. Bus companies also offer charter services and sometimes supply guides. MARA's air-conditioned buses make daily runs to Alor Star in the north Kota Bharu in the east and Singapore in the south. In Sabah and Sarawak, Landrovers connect the rural towns. They are also available for private hire, with guide services.

Within City Limits

Taxis are available in all large towns and may be hired from authorized taxi stands or hailed by the roadside, with the exception of Penang where taxis are prohibited by law from cruising for prospective passengers. If a taxi is required at a hotel or private residence, it can be called by telephone, but the distance is calculated from the stand from which it is hired to the passenger's destination.

All taxis have meters. The authorized fares are 60 Malaysian cents for the first mile or part, 20 cents for each additional half mile, and 20 cents for each eight-minute detention. The normal taxi load, in terms of the meter rate, is two passengers and there is a charge of 10 cents for each additional passenger. Between 1 a.m. and 6 a.m. an additional 50 percent of the normal meter rate is added to the fare. There is no charge for hand luggage; 10 cents per piece for other luggage.

Taxis may also be hired by the hour. The fare is M$4 for the first hour or part and M$1 for each quarter of an hour thereafter. Air-conditioned taxis are available at about double the rate.

Many local people in Malaysia go by trishaw when traveling short distances. Foreigners may find it a novel means of transport. Trishaws are safe and fun. They cost about the same as taxis, although the rate must be established with the driver beforehand.

Accommodation

Throughout Malaysia there are all types of accommodation to suit everyone's pocketbook and taste. In Kuala Lumpur and other large towns there are fine modern hotels, offering air-conditioned rooms with private bath and telephone. Hotels range from minaretted Moorish-style buildings to towering skyscrapers with more than 600 rooms and suites. On the mountains there are resort inns with magnificent views of rolling hills and green jungles, and by the seaside are chalets overlooking uncluttered coastlines and distant offshore islands.

No town or village, irrespective of size, is without its Chinese hotels. These, of course, lack the luxuries of first-class hotels, provide only one sheet per bed and the skimpiest of towels, and you may have to share a bathroom and a telephone. But they are clean, well-lit, and inexpensive. They also express a mood of Malaysia you do not find in modern hotels.

Malaysia offers still another type of accommodation, and that is Government-owned Rest Houses. In many towns, they are on par with the best hotels, but they go one step further. They are a reminder of Malaysia's past when traveling officials relied wholly upon Government Rest Houses for accommodation. At the day's end, after journeying by horseback or bullock-cart over jungle tracks, the traveler eagerly searched the darkness for the glow of a hurricane lamp lighting the porch of the local rest house. On the veranda steps he was certain to be greeted by a white-coated Malay house-boy and led to his quarters. The sight was always welcoming — a spacious room with windows opened on to a veranda, a mosquito net draped over the bed, a porcelain jug filled with fresh water, sticks of smoldering incense burning in a pot beside the bed to keep the mosquitoes at bay. Air conditioning then was a turbaned youth who sat in a far corner. In a slow rhythmic motion he would pull the cord of the *punkah*, causing the enormous rattan fan to swing in pendulum fashion across the ceiling.

Quite a few such rest houses remain in Malaysia to this day, but hurricane lamps have been replaced by electricity, *punkah*-boys by five-speed fans or even air conditioning, and porcelain jugs by hot showers and baths. Chinese and Western food is usually available and the room rates are invariably reasonable.

Travelers who wish to "do" Malaysia on the rest house circuit, trading old-time horseback and bicycle methods for modern-day bus and automobile, would be well advised to make arrangements in advance through various state government officials responsible for accepting rest house bookings. There is a highly informative booklet entitled "Malaysia Hotel and Rest House Directory," published by the Tourist Development Corporation. It is a handy item for the wandering traveler in Malaysia.

Tourist Associations

Malaysia's principal cities and resorts have tourist associations with receptionists who offer tips on shopping, restaurants, hotels and local travel. Their offices usually have a supply of literature and maps which offer guidelines for several days of sight-seeing.

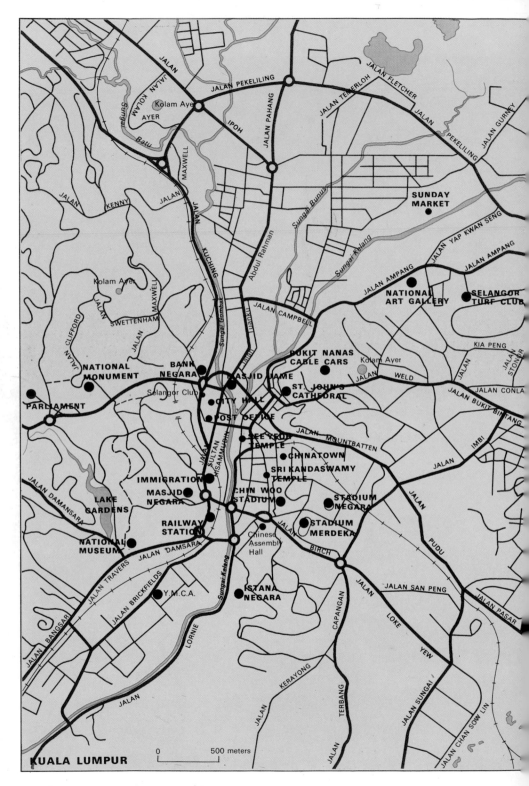

KUALA LUMPUR

An outpost one hundred years ago, a big city today, Kuala Lumpur is the capital of modern Malaysia and the brainchild of all Malaysians. To the newcomer she means something else. When the stranger first arrives he might suddenly think he is in a Muslim city, only to discover it is also very much Chinese, except it has a splash of Hindu color and flavor, with a British stamp of order and priority. A policeman on a street corner dresses down a traffic offender in four languages. There is a cricket match on the green of the *Padang* and the players include a British businessman, a Chinese bank clerk, a turbaned Sikh taxi driver and a Malay government official. A hospital in town announces: "Western medicine in the mornings, Chinese medicine in the afternoons." Marquees display signs in English, Tamil, Malay and Chinese. There is a post office with minarets; a great Victorian house with massive Roman columns and marble statues, turned popular restaurant. A city that celebrates New Year four times a year, and where no Asian is an alien.

Embracing Islam, Kuala Lumpur outwardly grew into a city of Arabian Nights magnitude — mysterious, daring. But this is only its facade, for, unlike some Arab cities that dwell in past glories, Kuala Lumpur has her eyes on the future. In the center of town, government buildings, banks and housing development flats crowd the skyline. Modern hotels and new stadiums stand side by side with the city's old Moorish architecture.

Kuala Lumpur — or KL as it is affectionately called — is a city of romance, a city that can play upon all the senses and stir the imaginations of citizens and foreigners alike. Drive along the river and look up, especially

True to the city's origins as a trading post, Petaling Jaya Street in the heart of KL's Chinatown bustles with shoppers (previous pages). The government today urges native Malays to fully join in the country's development.

at dusk when the buildings take on a special splendor. Lighted minarets are silhouetted against the soft grays of a night sky. Recently, with the curved ramparts of an elevated highway uniting all parts of the city, Kuala Lumpur has laid the foundations for a metropolis, yet she has too much character to adopt the stereotypes that go with it.

Unlike cities that developed without thought for the future KL was planned from the start. True, in her infant years she was a wretched town. Of the eighty-seven miner-prospectors who poled up the river to where the Klang and Gombak rivers meet, seventy died of fever within the first month. But they did discover tin. More miners arrived and other mines opened. Settlers and traders came. They built shelters and opened trading posts. They called the settlement Kuala Lumpur, "Muddy Estuary." It was an isolated outpost, surrounded by hostile jungle. But the mines produced and the town grew.

The early years were uncertain. Violence in its worst form accompanied quarrels over mining claims and water rights. Gang wars, feuds and murders went hand in hand with gambling farms and opium dens. And hanging over the Muddy Estuary was an ever-present threat of devastating fires and epidemics.

All that changed when heroes like Yap Ah Loy, Frank Swettenham, and Tunku Kuddin took control and decided to put KL literally on the map. In spite of overwhelming hardships, less than forty years after the first tin miners stepped ashore, Kuala Lumpur became the state capital. It was a bold move. The town was still a jungle outpost, unhealthy and crowded, built of wood and *atap* shacks packed close together along narrow lanes. Then came Frank Swettenham, the newly appointed British Resident. He put forth a plan to completely rebuild the town. He encouraged local businessmen to build brick kilns, and street by street the old town was pulled

Kuala Lumpur is a boom town showing influences from all the four cardinal directions.

down, widened and reconstructed with brick and tile buildings. Another scheme was to construct a rail line from Kuala Lumpur to Klang, connecting the capital to the sea. It was opened in 1886, and Sultan Abdul Samad, who made the inaugural journey, claimed it was "the best bullock-cart ride I ever had." Yap Ah Loy, Kapitan China appointed by the Sultan, warred against crime, built a prison and put down revolts.

Tin created Kuala Lumpur and when tin prices rose sharply in the 1880s, it gave rise to a prosperous middle class of businessmen, merchants and miners. They no longer had to live on their premises in the center of town. They began to build great houses along Jalan Ampang. In 1884 a Tudor-type building was erected in front of a cleared garden patch. It was named the **Selangor Club** and during the '90s became the center of the social life of Kuala Lumpur. Primped and plumed, ladies in crinolines huddled under their parasols to discuss the latest imported fashions, or to gossip about new arrivals and new faces. A band played twice a week out on the green. There were social and sporting events, musical evenings and fancy dress parties. Nowadays the long bar at "The Dog", as it is affectionately nicknamed, overlooks the padang and is a favorite watering hole for local businessmen.

Building and carving a new city out of the Malayan jungles a hundred years ago was a monumental achievement. Architects, designers, stone masons, sculptors and craftsmen had to be imported from abroad, at a time when it took three months for a packet ship to arrive from England. But the mammoth task continued, with its share of difficulties and unseen problems. For example, before construction of a new building could begin, the plans had to be approved by the home office back in the U.K.

Whether true or not, the construction of the **Secretariat** was unprecedented. "Too far ahead of its time," said Sir Charles Mitchel, Governor of the Straits Settlements, as he reluctantly placed a yen note, several Straits coins, a hunk of tin and a copy of the Selangor Journal in a niche below the foundation stone which was then cemented into place. The building, with its 40-meter central clock tower, was ready for occupancy by April 1897, two and a half years after the cornerstone was laid.

Ten years later **Jame Mosque**, constructed at the junction of the two rivers where the first miners stepped ashore, was completed. The mosque, built in traditional Arabian style, with its *kiblat*, or altar, facing Mecca, further intensified the daring Moorish design along Jalan Raja.

Like most mosques in Malaysia, Masjid Jame is open to all visitors. The only requirement is that one must remove one's shoes before entering.

Tin mining carved the city out of the Malayan jungle.

A cupola adorns the mosque-like railway station in the capital

Masjid Jame is surprisingly serene and quiet, a peaceful retreat from the bustling city outside its red brick walls. A pool within the courtyard, where adherents of the Islam faith wash themselves before entering the mosque proper, adds a subtle air of tranquillity to the place.

Masjid Jame's golden hour is at dusk, when soft light casts loose shadows across the river and food-stalls beyond. There, from Jalan Benteng, the fine silhouette of the minarets and domes are etched against the red sky of the setting sun.

Praises to Allah

A Rolls Royce with bumper flag unfurled brings a Sultan, his wife and their attendants from a distant state. A bus marked SEKOLAH stops at the gate and schoolchildren from Kampung Baharu file out, all smiles. The afternoon train from Ipoh and points north brings 3rd class passengers who make their anxiously awaited pilgrimage. A tourist bus unloads an Indian guide speaking Japanese to a hoard of camera-carrying tourists. Some of the women are dressed in traditional Japanese costumes; the others who are in miniskirts are given long, black robes to wear over their legs. An elderly Australian couple with a guide enter, hastily walk around and depart. All of them — Sultan, schoolchildren, pilgrims, tourists — have come to Malaysia's greatest shrine: **Masjid Negara**, the **National Mosque**.

Visitors pass a sign that reminds them that no shorts, miniskirts, loud talking or running are allowed within. They leave their shoes among the hundreds clustered outside. Muslims

and tourists alike silently climb the marble stairs and cross the tiled floor polished smooth by thousands of bare feet. At the entrance to the main prayer hall they separate. Non-Muslims must wait outside.

Prayers are held five times daily at the National Mosque, beginning at 5:30 a.m. Friday in Malaysia, as in the Muslim world of the Middle East, is the day of prayer, but generally it is not the day of rest. That is Sunday, except in the northeast states of Trengganu and Kelantan where banks, offices and stores close at midday on Thursday and reopen on Saturday morning.

The mosque, opened in 1965 after five years of construction, is the pride of the Malay population. From every corner of the nation young and old Malays alike come to pay homage to Prophet Muhammad. The marble building, with its minarets, reflecting pools and impressive galleries, is aesthetically one of the nation's finest edifices. The tiled walks, flanked by reflecting pools where water dances in thin columns, are cool and serene. The mosque's vast size absorbs the casual visitors who appear now and then in the distance as stick figures among the pillars. Even the children, with wide brown eyes, sit quietly beside the elders. As time draws near for worship the chambers fill up. Worshipers kneel in the main hall, as the Imam summons prayers.

The view from the mosque is as revealing as are its reflecting pools. The Moorish railway station lies to the south. Directly in front of the hill to the east is the National Stadium. To the north the highway carries traffic into the heart of Kuala Lumpur.

Islam binds Malays together, and links them to the world Muslim brotherhood.

Wearing sarongs and the songkok cap, the faithful bow to Mecca at Masjid Negara, the National Mosque.

hough Islam is the
fficial religion,
eedom of worship
s the keynote of
Malaysia.

he adorned altar at
ee Yeoh Chinese
emple (right). A
rahman priest at
ri Kandaswamy
indu Temple (left).

Memories of a Chinese Pioneer

You might walk down Jalan Rodger towards the Central Market a dozen times and not notice a narrow, crowded alley jammed with food carts and dining tables. But if you look again, you may see the sloped roof of a Chinese temple at the far end. Ducking so as not to slam your forehead into a low-hanging awning pole, you walk past the instant kitchens to arrive at a wall with a gate. It is the entrance to **See Yeoh Temple**, oldest and most venerable of the Chinese shrines.

When Kuala Lumpur was being rebuilt in the 1880s much money was spent on Chinese temples and clan association meeting halls. In honor of the god Sen Ta, protector of the pioneers, Kapitan China Yap Ah Loy

donated money and the land upon which the See Yeoh Temple stands. Since the Chinese worship a multitude of gods and goddesses, new deities have been added to the altars over the years.

A framed photograph of Yap Ah Loy sits on an altar in the rear of the temple. He looks more like a kindly saint than the powerful leader and social reformer he was.

Drumbeats at Dusk

Within a spacious courtyard incense burns near altars shrouded by silk curtains. Barefoot Hindu women soundlessly enter the premises, adding the colors of bright saris, bangles of gold and semiprecious stones. Men just off from work walk in wearing their street clothes. Quiet-mannered

children follow the guiding hand of an older sister. All is silent. A steaming sun yields to the evening coolness and a seemingly quiet temple becomes a controlled explosion of colors, sounds and smells.

In **Sri Kandaswamy Hindu Temple** on Jalan Scott the priest is conducting special prayers, called *poojas*, which are held three times daily. On Friday evening *poojas* at 6:00 p.m., the halls are most crowded. The temple orchestra plays the incredibly rhythmic spiritual music of India, as devotees offer their prayers at each altar in the temple. Two men wearing white *dhotis* chant in front of the main altar; they read from holy scriptures written in Tamil. Other devotees prostrate themselves face-down on the floor as a gesture of worshiping at the foot of God. After the services, worshipers mark their foreheads with white ashes — symbol of Lord Siva. The temple empties quickly and silence returns.

Parks and Gardens: Monument on the Green

While some cities struggle to keep their lawns green, Kuala Lumpur wages a constant battle to keep the dense jungle back. As one public works official put it: "Leave a seed unmolested on a pavement overnight, and it starts to grow through the concrete by next morning!"

Through planning and care, Kuala Lumpur is a pleasant garden city which has successfully transformed a threatening jungle into thirty-three public greens, varying in size from corner water fountains to the spacious Lake Gardens. At no point in the city, even in the down-

Viewing a cricket match on the Padang, facing the Secretariat building

110

town area, does one have that closed-in feeling. All one ever needs do to change the urban landscape is to raise one's head toward the green outline of the nearby hills.

The city's green heart is the **Padang**, flanked by a row of minaret-topped government offices.

There are cricket matches on the green every weekend and often the results, couched in esoteric jargon, appear in *The New Straits Times*: "The field he set for the paceman, who bowls an inswinger and is yards faster than the opposing paceman, was two slips, gully, third man, a deep fine leg (who was more a stopgap to the wicket-keeper), cover point, mid-off, mid-on and square leg."

The spacious **Lake Gardens**, near the museum, are more a picnic ground than a sportsman's venue. A twisting, hard-surface road snakes through the green lawns, past flowering shrubs and trees. The Gardens are not only Kuala Lumpur's public showpiece, they are its gathering place — the place where people go: old Malay couples who have made a pilgrimage to their capital city, girls in groups, fashion-conscious teenagers, girl watchers, discreet lovers. They stroll among the trees, sit on the grass or linger on the footpaths and bridges crossing the streams.

Monopolizing the view from the Lake Gardens is the **National Monument**. Tourists here are mostly Malaysians, wandering among the brick patios and waterfalls that surround the monument's base, occasionally stopping to pose for a "trick" photograph snapped by an industrious young man on his "odd" job. In his well-worn photo album there are pictures of school kids

he National onument in the ke Gardens mmemorates the ctory over mmunist urgency in the s.

balancing on one foot at the top of the tower of Parliament House, with the same dramatic impact that King Kong had on the Empire State Building. **Parliament House**, Malaysia's soaring symbol of national pride, is an eighteen-story tower block that dominates another corner of the Gardens. In these new, air-conditioned quarters the Senate and House of Representatives meet.

Mirror of Malaysia's Imagination

"Smile," says a student from the university as he poses his girl for a photo in front of the aeroplane that dominates the front lawn. Up and down the front steps Malaysians and foreigners alike stand smiling to have their pictures snapped in front of Kuala Lumpur's uniquely designed

Muzium Negara (National Museum). Situated at the south end of the Lake Gardens, the museum with its high, sloping roofs and two large mosaic murals looms up suddenly along Jalan Travers, the main thoroughfare leading into the capital. A visitor cannot miss it.

But the museum's attraction is not one of aesthetics alone. It serves as the mirror to Malaysia's imagination and history. On display are not only relics of the past but also whole scenes of Malaysian life. In one gallery is a complete Chinese house from old Malacca, with all the furnishings of the bridal chamber included. Another section is devoted to the Orang Asli, with various artifacts and models of their dwellings; another section displays a Malay *kampung*. The fineries of Malay culture which revolved around the sultanates are

The National Museum is a showcase of history and the many ways of life found in the country.

A giant mythical bir carries a sultan's palanquin at the National Museum.

preserved behind glass. Intricately patterned silver buckles, jeweled medallions, gold and silk headdresses and ruby-studded daggers conjure up the image of a monarch's splendor which still prevails in the royal courts today. Courtly dramas, folk dances and shadow plays fill the galleries. For travelers interested in history and art, there is a reference library with original manuscripts, charts and other data in the basement of the building. Although it is closed to the public, permission to use the facilities can be obtained from the curator.

One of the main features of the National Museum is the changing exhibits of local and national art, photo exhibitions, coin collections, and oftentimes collections of artifacts depicting a particular country or era. Each year a local newspaper sponsors a children's painting competition.

There are few better insights into a country than through the eyes and brushes of its youth. The paintings are for sale and are posted to buyers after the exhibition. Kuala Lumpur also has a **National Art Gallery** at Jalan Ampang with permanent displays of works by local artists.

The National Museum is about 800 meters from the railway station and is open from 9.00 a.m. to 7.00 p.m. except Friday when it is closed between noon and 2.30 p.m.

Something for Everybody

A connoisseur of exotic oddities could not feel more at home than in **Jalan Petaling**. Here are dry goods stores, music shops, street vendors, casket makers, optical houses, fortune tellers, Chinese medicine and

herb sellers, bridal dress boutiques, even a Chinese laundry. Walk down Jalan Petaling in the early morning or late afternoon with no purpose but to observe. Stand at the junction of Jalan Foch where the street begins and look down the 800 meters to where it ends at the **Chinese Assembly Hall**. Walk slowly. Stop to buy a souvenir, flag or a bowl of *mee* soup. Observe the alleys and side streets. Venture up a few. You might try turning up Jalan Sultan. There is a pet shop there, with cages of birds in front. In the darkened interior you can select a 4-meter-long python, a porcupine or a 150-kilo live dragon.

In Jalan Petaling anything is possible. Traffic is stopped, cars are lined up bumper to bumper. The late afternoon sun reflects upon their roof tops. Without warning a strange car appears, coming up the street against traffic, riding atop the roofs of jammed automobiles like a mechanic's apparition. You do a double take. Then you realize it is a life-size paper car, carried arm high by two youths, to be bought by a devoted Chinese next-of-kin and burned so that the deceased will have private transportation in the next life.

The end of Jalan Petaling changes as suddenly as it begins. Green lawns, a water fountain and a splendid Chinese temple with a massive wooden gate painted red appear. But there is also another large and unpretentious building covered with peeling, pale blue stucco.

The building serves as a venue for the many gatherings of the Chinese in Malaysia. When it was completed, there were sharp differences over the choice of name. Some wanted its name to commemorate one of the former Kapitans China, others favored Sun Yat Sen or Loke Yew who donated the bulk of the money for its construction. Finally, its benefactors settled on an all-inclusive name, and called it merely the "Chinese Assembly Hall."

When darkness falls, make another trip to Jalan Petaling. You might not recognize it, but the theme is the same: buying and selling — all for a song. Yet the aspect has changed. Vehicular traffic has halted. The street is blocked off at both ends. The sidewalks and pavements have become warehouses of vendors' goods on display. Anything. Everything. A galaxy of lights — neons, gas lanterns, naked bulbs — give daylight to the night and the curiosities of Jalan Petaling continue...

Shopping Tour:
Fortunes on the Sidewalk

Shopping in Kuala Lumpur is like rummaging through an Oriental attic stashed with valuables from half a dozen countries. And the best way to discover new items is to do the downtown area by foot. Visit the

The capital remain true to its origins as a market town a the junction of rive and roadways.

Young women enjo the search for bargains among clo merchants on Jalar Melayu.

114

t dawn the Central
Market bustles; at
dusk night vendors
all over the city
carry on the
bargaining.

small, unpretentious shops you would otherwise have missed. You can find everything there: bales of Indian silks, Persian rugs, hand-dyed bateks, Indonesian handicrafts, Malay krisses, Minangkabau antiques, Orang Asli carvings and plastic toys made in Red China.

A fine place to begin your walk-about is at Jame Mosque, where the first Chinese settlers stepped ashore more than a hundred years ago. Follow the river to the junction of Jalan Tun Perak, Melaka and Melayu. The mood changes from one street to another as rapidly as you can turn a corner. **Jalan Melayu**, for example, is known and visited for its Indian shops — silks, saris, jasmin, hand-hammered jewelry. The mood is further enhanced by incense odors that fill the air. Take a few steps from the curb to the taxi station and you

bathing a pewter
vase at Selangor
Pewter Factory on
Ipoh Road.

will be stopped by street vendors and medicine shows with snake charmers. Have your fortune told by a bearded, turbaned Sikh who rushes up and pins a flower on your lapel, emphatically stating, "I have something to tell you." Refuse, and the flower is taken away and pinned on another passerby with just the same urgency. Behind the taxi station is **Leboh Ampang**, also an Indian shopping center, where again the scent of incense pervades the air. Signs on shop houses reveal that the premises are occupied by a fortune-teller, a money changer or a second-hand paperback bookseller.

Jalan Melayu leads to KL's main thoroughfare: **Jalan Tuanku Abdul Rahman**, or "Batu Road," as many still call it. It is densely packed with a Chinese emporium, souvenir displays, many department stores and shopping arcades. Turn to the north and you discover a number of stuffy antique shops, and the multi-storey MARA building, a government-owned shopping center selling batiks and Malaysian crafts.

The early morning hours, before the town is fully awake, are a good time to see the local color at the **Central Market**. You can pick out vegetables that look like fruit or choose a snake from a bin and have it skinned alive for your lunch. Shoppers might find it interesting to visit the handicraft displays at Kampung Batek at 13-km-stone on Ipoh Road. The **Selangor Pewter Demonstration Center** on Jalan Genting Klang welcomes visitors.

Saturday Night's Sunday Market

Malays name their night for the coming day. Saturday night is their Sunday night and the Sunday market is their weekly bazaar, on our Saturday night. It is held in **Kampung Baharu**, an exclusively Malay section of town. Songkok caps, hand-printed bateks and curry mix are all on sale. Rows and rows of handicraft stalls offer everything from bird cages to conical hats. One man sells ashtrays, vases, jewelry boxes and flower pots, with flowers included, all made from tiny shells. A young boy tugs at the hand of his sarong-clad mother, imploring her to buy him a plastic cricket set. Teenage youths wearing the latest 'hip' fashions disappear into the market's small nightclub where a rock band plays slow music on a dark dance floor.

Meanwhile the laughter of children happy to be up so late can be heard above the bargaining sessions. Smells change from stall to stall as vendors offer fresh-cut flowers, tropical fruit or satay (tasty tidbits of meat served on skewers) grilled over an open fire. The market has an air-conditioned restaurant serving many popular dishes of the spicy Malay cuisine, including golden shrimp chips and fried fish the size of guppies.

A Punter's Paradise

Should you happen to be walking in the Ampang area on a Saturday or Sunday afternoon, enjoying the twittering of the birds, the far off hum of downtown traffic and perhaps the lazy drone of a light aircraft on a joyride from the Selangor Flying Club, you may be surprised to find the tranquillity of the afternoon broken by an outburst of excited cheers and roars. You are approaching the **Selangor Turf Club** and weekends are race days in Selangor. There are four associated Turf Clubs: Selangor, Ipoh in Perak, Penang and Singapore, and racehorses and jockeys travel the circuit throughout the year.

Petaling Jaya grew overnight from a small settlement to the country's major industrial center.

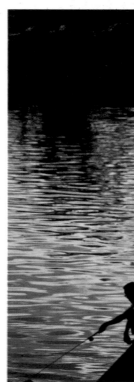

A food vendor at a Saturday night market, Kampung Baharu (left). A fisherman in Petaling Jaya (right).

Gambling is of equal, if not more, importance than form in Malaysia. Should the meet be as far away as Singapore, optimistic punters still gather in the grandstand to hear the odds and a live commentary relayed from the on-course club and to jostle for a place at the totalisator for a chance to win or lose their fortunes

There's an even faster track to be found at the motor racing circuit which draws International competitors to the annual Grand Prix races. Visitors need not miss the fun. They will find all racing events well-publicized in the local newspapers.

Wisma Loke: Paintings through the Moongate

One of the first wealthy men to move out of the ramshackle Chinese quarters of Kuala Lumpur was Cheow Ah Yeok, a close ally of Yap

A classical marble statue at the nouveau riche Loke Mansion.

Ah Loy. On the outskirts of town he built a fine house with sweeping archways, balustrades of glazed jade-colored porcelain from China, tiles from Malacca and a Chinese "moongate." After his death the house was taken over by Loke Yew, the most colorful of Malaysia's millionaires. A philanthropist, the Andrew Carnegie of the Orient, who arrived penniless from China at the age of 13, Loke Yew spread millions all over Asia. He had one personal indulgence, however, and that was the mansion, the first private house in KL lit by electricity. It became the showpiece of the community. "A first class repast was served at Towkay Loke Yew's house," wrote a journalist in 1897. "By the time that the champagne, hock, liquors and whisky had all amicably mixed, the company had exhausted all their vocal and oratorical powers."

Today the century-old house stands in the shadow of glass and concrete highrises on Jalan Medan Tuanku, a glamorous outcast restored and converted into an art gallery and museum-antique shop.

Le Coq d'Or—Love across the Street

Once upon a time there was a very poor Chinese boy who fell in love with a very beautiful and rich Chinese girl. He wanted to marry her but, of course, her father forbade it. The boy, who ran a bicycle repair shop, vowed he would make the girl's father regret his decision. From then on, he devoted his full energy to making money — from bicycle repair shop to garage to tin buying to tin mining. As can be expected, he became rich and famous.

He then built a house, a magnificent Victorian mansion with grand entrances, hallways and verandas. He hung 18th century paintings on the walls depicting the Italian countryside and Napoleon's march upon Moscow. He imported Italian marble statues to grace the high walls and installed an ultra-modern spray bath. He built the mansion on Jalan

Ampang, overshadowing the house in which the girl and her father lived, the father who once refused to let him marry his daughter.

When Chua Cheng Bok died in 1940 he left a will which stated that the mansion could never be sold from his estate, but it could become a restaurant on the condition that nothing inside would be changed. The mansion is now **Le Coq d'Or**, a favorite restaurant in KL.

Dining by Starlight: Mutton Soup and Lichee Juice

Because dining out, especially dining outside, is a habit and a hobby in KL, both sumptuous Chinese restaurants packed with wedding parties and tiny Malay satay stalls by the roadside do a brisk business after sunset. In the Mandarin Palace at the **Federal Hotel**, instant gourmets dine in elegance and join the round table tradition by selecting their choice of delicious, piping hot Cantonese tidbits served from push carts. Devotees of south Indian curries will find them at **Bilals** — try the chicken — while those who prefer north Indian cuisine should visit **Ranees Place**. If the company desires both south and north Indian cuisines, then **The Bangles** is the place. You will be surprised how alike most of their customers look; it is the mirrors. Beware! For a sumptuous Malay buffet served in elegant style then **Yasmin's** is the place.

For those who enjoy adventure in eating there are the many stalls and small shops which serve food that is often better than that found in large restaurants. Take **Jalan Benteng's** car park. Nightly, it is converted into an open-air food festival of Malay and Indian-Muslim cooking. There is no decor, but even the finest and most expensive restaurant in town could not offer a better atmosphere. Portable kitchens with tables and chairs are set up along the curve of the road that follows the muddy River Klang. On the opposite bank the Masjid Jame, with its towers and minarets, stands like a living mural.

The food at these stalls is as spicy as you like it. Mutton and chicken soup are the specialities. Noodles (*mee*) can be fried (*goreng*) or boiled (*rebus*). Satay, Malaysia's national dish, is also served, along with sugarcane or lichee juice, steamed cockles or crunchy peanut sweets. The stalls huddled along Jalan Campbell are patronized by a lively assortment of customers until 2:00 a.m. They are a delightful place for an informal Malaysian banquet at a round table.

A touch of old English can be found in places like **The Ship** and **The Coliseum** specializing in steaks and **Le Coq d'Or** famous for its flambés. All are owned and managed by Chinese families.

If Chinese cuisine is your taste and dining outside your pleasure, then

Kuala Lumpur offers fine examples of Indian, Malay and Chinese cuisine

Open-air food stalls crowd Jalan Benteng's carpark which each night is turned into a food festival.

118

he capital boasts
nly a modest
ightlife, with a
mattering of
ultural shows and
ightclubs.

the **Pines** at the far end of Brickfields is the place. It is an open-air restaurant with tables in a garden. Unlike most Chinese dining places, the lights here are low. There is also an air-conditioned "hut" with an intimate stand-up bar. The food is Cantonese with many European dishes.

Highlights after Dark:
Anyone for Coconut Champagne?

Yasmin's restaurant in Jalan Ampang has captured the music, costumes and dances of the traditional countryside and presented them on the strobe-lit stage. Each evening at 8.30 guests are welcomed by ebullient Raja Nor Jasmin — she really is a princess and related to the King of Malaysia — to this cultural happening. After an aperitif of coconut champagne, guests dine on satay,

spiced chicken, Bombay duck, fried rice, anchovy and cucumber, rounded off with local fruit. All the while, they are entertained by a lively sequence of native folk dances, village music and resounding gongs. It is a pleasant introduction to the inherent grace of the Malays, as young dancers sweep through ancient motions celebrating the universal delight in flirtation. Part of the happening is a wedding ceremony during which diners are invited on stage to bless the happy couple with scented water, rice and orchids. As the show concludes the audience is coaxed to join the popular *joget* dance.

Most other KL after-dark activities are found in the nightclubs of the large hotels with acts ranging from fire-eating to modern ballet. Those looking for discotheques can dance all night at the Merlin Hotel's To-

A Malay folk dance at one of the several nightclubs in Kuala Lumpur and Petaling Jaya.

side trips from
kuala lumpur

morrow, the Hilton's Tin Mine, the Regent's Regent Club or The Glass Bubble at Petaling Jaya. If strippers be your taste then there are the New Pacific and the Honey Cabaret at the Racecourse Nightclub, although the dancers are, by and large, second-rate imports from Australia.

Those sybarites looking for the pleasures of Bangkok and Manila will delight in the **Federal Hotel**, the first of KL's international class hotels. In this entertainment complex, five bands play in bars and restaurants and an international floor show can be viewed in both the Mandarin Palace and the Continental Sky Room. There is also a first-class Turkish bath —for bathing only. Not part of the hotel, but reached through it is the Latin Quarter with its 160 charming hostesses.

Tackling the Tigers

Among the greenest attractions around Kuala Lumpur is the **National Zoo**, 13 km from downtown on the road to Ulu Klang. Although the zoo boasts of a cosmopolitan animal kingdom, Malaysia's wildlife in captivity strikes the clearest chord. Staring a tiger in the eye from a distance of 3 meters is enough to elicit a surge of sympathy for the workers who had to clear jungles for the early railroads and the mines.

Living in this superb zoo is a cross section of Malaysia's wildlife. Plumed birds, 6-meter-long pythons, seladang (wild buffalo), tapir, crocodiles, and gibbons have found new homes in concrete enclosures, while only paces away the deep jungle broods over them. There is a white-

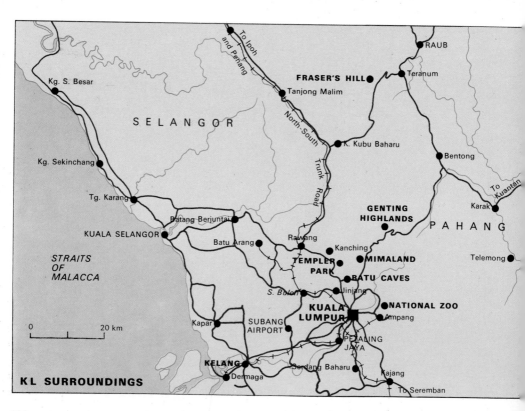

KL SURROUNDINGS

here are many interesting attractions a few hours drive from the capital.

feathered cockatoo that says, "Hello, Polly wants a cracker. Good-bye," to visitors absorbed in gazing at tiger cubs across the sidewalk. Then there are exotic marine exhibits, 81 species of fresh-water fish including the deadly and carnivorous piranhas. The quiet gardens laid around a peaceful lake are interrupted only by an occasional lioness' growl. The zoo is open from 10.00 a.m. to 6.00 p.m.

Sir Gerald Templer, British High Commissioner of the former Federation of Malaya, had an idea. As an outdoor man who loved the Malaysian countryside, especially the jungle, he put forth a scheme to open a vast jungle retreat for the general public, one close enough to the capital "so that the urban population can recreate after a hard and busy day in the city."

tiger prowls tamely the National Zoo.

A tract of land was set aside 22 km north of Kuala Lumpur and

Templer Park was officially opened.

Now city dwellers and foreign travelers can see the Malaysian jungle in miniature, all within one leisurely afternoon. There are well-marked hiking paths, lagoons for swimming and waterfalls. The only thing missing that would make the jungle complete is the tiger. But the National Zoo takes care of that.

Pilgrimage to a Limestone Cathedral

Tunneled deep into a gigantic limestone outcrop that rises like a perpendicular moon rock from the jungle floor are literally dozens of hidden caverns, some as large as cathedrals, while others, deeper and darker, remain unexplored to this day. Within these caves grow species

of plants seen nowhere else on earth. And in the largest cave stands a Hindu shrine where one day each year 100,000 Hindu devotees make one of the most bizarre pilgrimages seen anywhere. The place is the extraordinary **Batu Caves**, 11 km north of Kuala Lumpur on the road to Ipoh.

The mysterious limestone mountain was little known until 1878 when American naturalist William Hornaby, searching for new specimens of moth larva, stumbled upon it by accident. He was wandering around the area on horseback and came to the cliffs that tower above the trees. Hornaby started climbing. Centimeter by centimeter, he worked his way up the sheer face of the cliff. Halfway up he reached a ledge and there found the entrance to the now famous caves. He returned to Kuala Lumpur with news of his discovery. Years

later the local Hindu populace started an annual pilgrimage there to celebrate the festival of Thaipusam. Worshipers had to scale the steep, jagged cliffs to the Hindu shrine in the topmost grotto. As a sign of repentance for past sins, some devotees carried *kavadis*, wooden frames decorated with flowers and fruit and supported by long, thin spikes pinned into the carrier's body. Today the way to the top is paved with 272 concrete steps and is surrounded by hanging green ferns and tropical flowers. Hindu devotees still struggle up the precipice to seek forgiveness or to make pledges for future favors once a year (see pages 89–91).

Although the broken mass of limestone covers only $2\frac{1}{2}$ square km, it contains no less than twenty known caves, all of relatively easy access. Most interesting are those situated

The cathedral-like Batu Caves are the setting each year for the Hindu ritual of penitence, Thaipusam.

along the southern face, which bear such names as Hermit's Hole, Priest's Hole, Fairy Grotto and Quarry Cave. How they earned these names is anyone's guess, but the Cathedral Cave needs no explanation. Under a huge vault pierced by stalactites that tumble precariously for 6 meters spreads an empty hollow. Eerie shafts of light streak down from uneven gaps in the ceiling. Nearby are the illuminated "Dark Caves" with paths leading far into mysterious limestone grottoes. These can be reached by elevator. A couple of hundred meters from the lower elevator station, one of the relatively small caves has been made into an attractive museum with half-life-size plaster figures of the Hindu deities.

Fun for All

Eighteen km out of town and built on a verdant hillside of 120 hectares is KL's newest playground — **Mimaland.** Recreational facilities include fishing and boating, swimming and jungle trekking. There is also an amusement center and a children's playground. The free-form swimming pool, constantly fed by mountain streams, must be, if not the largest in the world, then at least the largest in Southeast Asia. There are good-sized fish in the 12-hectare lake and you keep what you catch. Beautiful gardens display a wide selection of Malaysia's rich heritage of flowers and shrubs. There is a minizoo with alligators and crocodiles, lizards and porcupines. No need to wander out of KL to watch the workings of a rubber plantation: Mimaland has its own active plantation.

Mimaland offers a wide variety of accommodations, much of it suitable for families. There are the comfortable native-style *bagan*, each with two bedrooms, standing on stilts in the lake; two-bedroom, housekeeping chalets; and a lakeside motel. For food, there is a wide range of restaurants to choose from.

It is best not to leave the beaten paths of Mimaland in the very early morning hours; the attendants at the swimming pool say this is truly "Malaysia in Miniature" — they have come upon a tiger obviously wanting to see what Mimaland is all about.

Wooing Lady Luck in Luxury

From a distance, **Genting Highlands**, shrouded in mists which blanket the dense jungle foliage covering the undulating peaks high above Kuala Lumpur, stand aloof — a mystical palace of pleasure. And that is precisely what it is for those with tall stacks of chips at their sides. Here, the rich and the hopefully rich woo Lady Luck in lushly carpeted, smoke-filled halls. Lovely Malaysian croupiers expertly flip Black Jacks while chip distributors, looking like clean-cut college boys, collect the bets. Those so inclined can also lose their money at roulette and baccarat or at the oriental games of keno and tai sai, besides literally hundreds of one-armed bandits. Shirt and tie or national costume is mandatory. Those who find this condition too demanding can still spend their chips in a room of one-armed bandits adjacent to the casino. At weekends, gambling continues round the clock but during the week the casino closes its doors between 4:00 a.m. and 10:00 a.m.

Perhaps the nicest thing about the casino at Genting Highlands is that "careful gamblers" can spend several enjoyable hours betting with Malaysian one dollar chips and still afford the taxi fare back to town. From Kuala Lumpur the serpentine drive to the glittering hideaway takes about one hour. Alternatively, there is a regular helicopter service from the Kuala Lumpur airport and from a helicopter pad at the fringe of the city. Even if you have no desire to gamble, the flight over the dense jungle is a great thrill.

There are five hotels at Genting Highlands, the newest, in which the

cated just outside capital, maland offers rdens, a zoo, ing, water sports.

e spirit of Wild st Malaysia lives genteely at the inos in Genting ghlands.

casio is located, being in the deluxe category. Another is first-class and three are economy. From the summit, a gondola cable car drops guests 750 meters in fifteen minutes to a height of 1,050 meters for the first tee of an excellent eighteen-hole golf course. Here, too, are an economy class hotel and a swimming pool.

Back at the 1,800-meter summit, those too young to gamble have not been forgotten. For them there is a $3\frac{1}{2}$ hectare man-made lake with row and paddle boats. In the lake a small island accommodates an aviary. Encircling the lake is a miniature railway. Then there is a funfair with its Ferris-wheel and the like. For the in-between child — too old for toys but too young to gamble — Genting offers a room filled with modern mechanical games, two bowling alleys and an indoor swimming pool.

Paradise on a Mule Track

At the outbreak of the First World War, Bishop Ferguson-Davie of Singapore thought it his duty to find a fellow countryman who was working as a mule train operator and inform him of world conditions. Rumor was that the man had a shack somewhere in the hills north of Kuala Lumpur. With the help of a local constable the bishop found his way to "The Gap" and from there struggled the last few kilometers up a steep trail, only to find that the mule skinner had fled. No doubt his decision came the moment he saw the church and the law coming. The hideaway, it seems, was more than a mere rest spot for weary drivers and tired mules. The bishop found a shack all right, called "Gambling Farm Number

Genting Highland glow enticingly in the twilight.

they did in India,
: British
ablished several
l stations as
reats from
pical weather.

One," and another den called "The Keys of Paradise" which capitalized on the local opium trade. The story is that adventurer and opportunist Louis James Fraser was never seen again, having vanished in the more glamorous byways of Singapore. But **Fraser's Hill** is still there, even if the gambling shack is gone, and what was once the Keys of Paradise on the mule track is now a relaxing weekend retreat for business executives escaping big cities.

Scattered over the seven hills, accommodations include a new 100-room hotel which, unfortunately fails to blend with the landscape; many greystone bungalows with their neat English gardens blooming with roses and hollyhocks; and innumerable bungalows of all shapes and sizes. For recreation there are an easy nine-hole golf course, three tennis courts, excel-

lent playgrounds for children, pony rides and a large fresh-water swimming pool under a waterfall.

There's a wealth of jungle flora awaiting the nature lover who explores the well-kept jungle paths. Maps are available and guides can also be hired to show you the trails.

Unfortunately, for those without private transport, Fraser's Hill is difficult to reach. It is a one-hour bus journey from KL to **Kuala Kubu Bharu**, which is just off the main trunk road between KL and Ipoh. From Kuala Kubu Bharu, there is a twice daily bus which, in one and a half hours, climbs 1,700 meters to Fraser's Hill. From "The Gap," a distance of 8 km, one-way traffic operates.

A good 240-km road leads from Fraser's Hill via Raub and Bentong to Kuantan on the middle of the East Coast.

*ngalows and
ilets provide a
ekend retreat at
aser's Hill.*

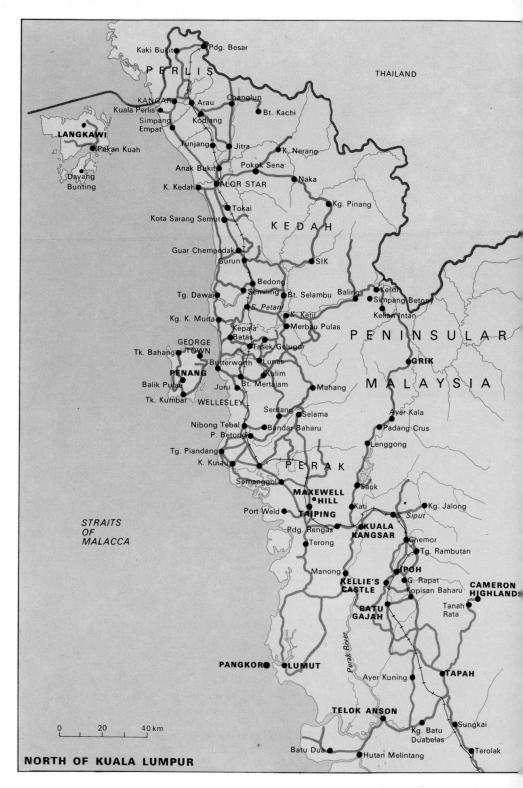

NORTH OF KUALA LUMPUR

128

beaches and mountain retreats

mountain
rts north of
ala Lumpur feel
rly alpine,
le the beaches on
hore islands
r the best of the
ics.

Cozy fireplaces and air-conditioned beach cottages; warming hot toddies and tall iced drinks; sweaters over saris and sarongs around bikinis; mists rising from green valleys and sun filtering down through palms. Malaysia is a land of delightful contrasts, from cool, quiet mountain retreats to sunny beach resorts. The mountain retreats, called "hill stations," are patterned after their British counterparts in India. Malaysia has several, including Fraser's Hill overlooking Kuala Lumpur and Cameron Highlands near Ipoh. Even Penang Island boasts a hill station with all the prerequisites—cool air, a panoramic view and accommodations. Penang Hill goes even a step further: it has a funicular railway to carry visitors to the top.

Owing to the presence of mangrove swamps and mud flats, bathing beaches along the coast north from Port Dickson are few and far between, but the several offshore islands compensate for this. Pangkor, Penang, the Langkawis (there are ninety-nine in the last group) all have good beaches and are accessible from the mainland. And all have accommodations. For the adventurer, there are other islands, of sorts. On "Crab Island," off Port Klang, you can catch your dinner with a hook and bait; or farther north, on Song Song, you may be fortunate enough to see 4-meter-long lizards, much like the Komodo dragons of Indonesia. RAF pilots claim to have spotted them from the air but no brave soul has yet ventured ashore to investigate.

Island beach resorts and mountain retreats are all within a few hours' drive of one another. A visitor can awake in the alpine breezes at Cameron Highlands, have a round of golf or hike a marked jungle trail, and bask in the sun on a beach in Penang that same afternoon.

Jungle-smothered hills and vales unroll beneath secluded lookouts on Malaysia's hill stations (previous pages).

From Ipoh, the tin mining capital of Malaysia, northward to Taiping there is a spectacular stretch of road. In the valley along which the road unwinds are small rubber and coconut plantations with proud Malay houses, some carved and decorated, appearing helter-skelter among the trees. In the distance are the ever-present limestone mountains, rising one behind another, each in a diminishing shade of gray until the very last is almost imperceptible and faintly blends with the equally gray sky.

No drive northward from KL need be without points of interest between destinations. Leave the main trunk road and explore. You will find quaint towns like Telok Anson that might meet your fancy; you might stumble upon a Malay festival or a Chinese opera in a small village; or you might wish to explore caves in the many limestone outcrops that dominate the Malaysian countryside.

It was in caves in these limestone hills which rise perpendicularly from the jungles that the distant ancestors, still ages away from discovery of the wheel and perhaps even fire, sought shelter during their migration down the peninsula. Generations passed as they moved from cave to cave, leaving stories etched on cave walls in the form of pictographs, perhaps man's first graffiti. Near Ipoh there are fourteen such hills with caves. In many, instead of the picture-writing of old, is scribbled "Tony Woo loves Mary Tan" in three languages. Undignified, perhaps, but 10,000 years from now today's graffiti may puzzle some future scientist. Many of these caves have been transformed into elaborate temples, with limestone walls polished smooth and painted. Here Chinese and Hindu devotees keep their images of gods and goddesses underground.

The peaceful drive past timeless villages, gentle green hills and shaded valleys was not always so serene. Perak and Kedah have witnessed their share of bloodshed and hard times. Sir Andrew Clarke, the Governor of the Straits Settlements a hundred years ago, described the area as a place "where nothing but fighting and murder and violence and piracy goes on." The major problem was the clan wars among the Chinese miners at Larut. In one skirmish alone, more than 1,000 men were killed on the first day of hostilities. The agreement that finally settled the dispute was the Treaty of Pangkor, which marked the beginning of British intervention in the Malay States.

In the town of Kroh near the Thai border you can sit in a coffee shop and listen to some of the elders spin yarns about the period. One story the older folk like to recount is about Captain Hubert Berkley, the District Officer at the time when the Boundary Commission was hammering out details of the treaty. It seems Berkley and some of his men sneaked into the jungle and moved the boundary stones farther north. They say that Berkley used an elephant to drag the stones and, as a tribute, the town folk erected a statue of an elephant near the new rest house.

Gone are the days of Rajahs and District Officers, yet the past is still part of the north. Taiping has the oldest museum in Malaysia, but on the other hand George Town in Penang is almost a museum itself. And while some old-timers complain that "old George Town" is being torn down and replaced by the new, 96 km north of Penang are the Langkawi Islands that know no changes at all. Their landfall seen across the Indian Ocean is no different from what it was when Hindu traders came looking for gold and tin and new markets 2,000 years ago.

Steep and seeming impenetrable, the fine plateau of the Cameron Highlan was discovered in 1885 by a British surveyor.

Golf Clubs and Blowpipes

At Tapah, on the trunk road joining Kuala Lumpur and Ipoh, a road shoots off toward the hills and for 90 km, the first 72 of which are excellent, winds and twists its way to Peninsular Malaysia's rooftop, the **Cameron Highlands**. As cool air funnels down the mountain pass, the temperature drops almost immediately. Palms and banana trees give way to deep jungle growth. Thick ferns seem to fan the road, and clusters of bamboo add the living touch of a Japanese ink drawing. Orang Asli wearing breech cloths and carrying blowpipes amble incongruously along the roadside.

Cameron Highlands is actually three districts in one. For the newcomer it can be confusing, and perhaps somewhat disappointing, especially when, after 45 km, he arrives ar Ringlet, the first district. Best to push on! Four km later, the pleasant Sultan Abu Bakar Lake is passed and then, after a further 15 km, he comes to Tanah Rata, the region's principal village. The scenery becomes superb — cool and clean air, streams, lakes, and a view of rolling, green mountains that fade into distant grays on the horizon. Deep shadowed valleys are filled with fluffy clouds. Darkened rain squalls pile up on a distant ridge. The scenery was not always so charming. Steep, hostile, seemingly impenetrable, infected with spirits and demons of the underworld, Cameron Highlands was a mountain jungle unknown even to the Malays until 1885 when a government surveyor on a mapping expedition reported finding "a fine plateau with

ged limestone
crops and hidden
leys characterize
landscape north
KL (facing page).
a plantations
im the rolling
's of the
meron Highlands,
r Tanah Rata
ght).

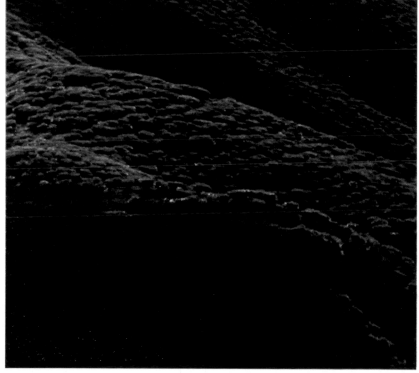

gentle slopes shut in by mountains."
The surveyor was William Cameron.

Tea planters hastily claimed the plateau, and before long the Chinese discovered that the high altitude was excellent for growing vegetables and began farming the valley floors. To carry their produce to market, they built a road. A wealthy rubber planter came looking for a place of leisure, discovered the route and built a house which his family could use on weekends. Cameron Highlands, the mountain resort, has never stopped growing since.

Along **Tanah Rata**'s single street are several Chinese hotels and stores which sell some of the products of the Camerons — fresh strawberries and cream; mounted butterflies, 15-cm scorpions and thick-legged, furry spiders; Orang Asli blowpipes and poison arrow containers. Nearby are the ubiquitous Government Rest House, a couple of moderate hotels and the agricultural research institute. The latter can be visited, as can several tea plantations in the district where the traveler can marvel at the magnificent foliage which looks like monochrome tesserae of a mosaic, watch the tea being processed and become intoxicated on its aroma.

Three km above Tanah Rata is the Cameron's famous eighteen-hole golf course with a cozy pavilion equipped with bar and restaurant. Through the dense foliage of the jungle beyond, you occasionally catch a glimpse of an Orang Asli village on a distant mountain ledge. Many Orang Asli prefer the simple, outdoor existence near the wilderness which their ancestors knew. The 20th century passes their doorstep with apparently little effect upon their way of life: no more than they have upon the contemporary golfer in tartan bell-bottoms.

Golf clubs and blowpipes raise no eyebrows at Cameron Highlands. Visitors go to relax, and while relaxation to some might be a game of golf or tennis, to others it is a hike along some of the jungle trails. These lead to tea plantations, waterfalls, Orang Asli settlements and, for the energetic, to the summit of the surrounding mountains of which Gunong Brinchang, the highest, reaches 2,000 meters. On clear days Ipoh and other towns and the Malacca Straits can be seen.

The jungles around Cameron Highlands are deceivingly dense. Several years ago a well-known American named Jim Thompson, who founded the Thai silk industry in Bangkok, came to Cameron for a holiday. He went for a walk, supposedly got off the track, and was never seen again. Search parties spent weeks combing the surrounding jungles, without success. Now information booklets cautiously advise travelers hiking into the hinterland to tell someone which way they are going

Jungles in the area are untamed and still claim on occasion their victim.

Cameron's well-known 18-hole golf course at Brinchang.

to and to stick to the paths which, unfortunately, are poorly marked. Maps are available at most hotels.

Tanah Rata resort has now blossomed into the holiday destination for Malaysian college students and diplomats alike. Local Boy Scouts with knapsacks on their backs thumb rides up the winding hills, while expatriates from Singapore lounge on colonial verandas, munching fresh strawberries and cream. Ingenious engineering, careful planning and profound craftsmanship have obviously contributed to the mountain resort. It is the largest and best organized of Malaysia's hill stations.

Riches Underground

Ipoh, the tin center of the world, is on the trunk road and rail line about midway between Kuala Lumpur and Penang. It is an industrial town, populated mostly by Cantonese whose ancestors helped build a city out of a tin miners' camp. With admirable foresight, they decided to leave plenty of green for breathers — the largest being Taman D.R. Seenivasagam Park in the center of town.

Both north and south of Ipoh, along the trunk road, are sheer limestone outcrops. At their base are what appear to be some odd-looking buildings, constructed flat against the cliffs. Most of them are painted white and have red tiled pagoda roofs. They are, in fact, the facades of caves converted into temples, both Chinese and Hindu. Ipoh is rich in such shrines, many reminiscent of those found among the hills of distant Tibet.

One of the largest shrines is **Perak Tong**, 6 km north of town. It also has the biggest statue, 67 meters

e Smokehouse, a
tel at Tanah Rata
the Cameron
ghlands.

high, that of Lord Buddha in a sitting position, his half-a-meter eyes gazing down from above. Water-lily ponds, ornate decorations in bright colors, as well as ornamental gardens with tortoise pools are common to all the temples. In the natural coolness visitors can wander about from chamber to chamber, studying the many deities, marveling at nature's unmatched architecture. The smell of incense, the smoke curling up from brass burners and hushed voices all lend an air of serenity to the caves.

Do not hesitate to explore. Go beyond the main altars and visit the 54-meter-high Laughing Buddha and the painting of Kuan Yin, Goddess of Mercy. Then, in semi-darkness you can climb a stairway (ask the caretaker for the key) to the upper reaches of the cave. The climb is arduous. Follow a thin shaft of light from above and finally, 355 steps later, you reach Nirvana. Here Kuan Yin, seated atop an elephant, gazes out on Ipoh and the surrounding countryside — a splendid view which is, unfortunately, marred by industrial scars in the foreground.

Sam Poh Tong, the biggest of the rock temples, is 6 km south of Ipoh. Its origin dates back to the turn of the century when Ipoh was gradually changing from a mining center to an industrial town. A monk passing through found the cave and decided to make it his abode and a place of meditation. He remained in the cave for twenty years until his death. Other monks followed his example. Today, five monks and a half dozen nuns who have dedicated their lives to Buddha have made this cave their home.

A stiff climb of 246 steps leads to the open from where there is an excel-

Ipoh is the tin capital of the world and its cavernous limestone hills contain the shrines of Chinese miners.

Another of the numerous caverns around Ipoh, capital of Perak State.

134

ddhist statues
wd Perak Tong
rine, in a
estone cave near
h.

lent panorama of the mountains and the countryside surrounding Ipoh.

In contrast to the tearing pace on the trunk road close by, life at the temple goes on as it has done for centuries in Buddhist shrines throughout the East. Temple life has few interruptions. Chief priest Choong Kam sometimes visits Ipoh to tend to business matters, but the others rarely go into town. Several of the priests have been at the temple more than thirty years and the only break in events they recall is the Japanese Occupation. "Those were hard times," said the chief priest. "We can look back and smile, but the Japanese had one objective—to close our temple." They succeeded. The Japanese turned the cave into an ammunition and fuel dump until the end of the war.

A fantastically moody place is the hollowed-out center of the out-crop, which forms an almost perfect circle of perpendicular cliff 70 meters high. There stands an old, dilapidated stone house with a garden pond containing turtles, symbols of longevity among the Chinese. All is silent here. "When we want to be completely alone," said chief priest Choong, "when we want to forget the world . . . then we come to this house encircled by cliffs." Apparently the privacy of the inner chamber has lured other people besides the clergy. On deserted walls carved out of cliff face is enough "I love you, etc." graffiti to fill a book. But few people enter now.

Other attractions in Ipoh are the racecourse—the best of many in Malaysia—the handsome colonial style railway station with its hotel, the architecturally pleasing neocolonial government offices and law courts and the modern state mosque.

Kellie's Castle: Almost Came True

Roots of wild figs and banyan trees, like tentacles of an octopus, have spread themselves out over the brick fabric, splitting the walls. Ceilings have crumbled. Arches have been lifted upwards, entwined in a claw-like grip of gnarled tree trunks. When you enter, brushing aside creepers and thorny vines, you get the feeling you are treading on a grave. In a sense you are, for here died a dream, the brainchild of a wealthy, eccentric rubber planter who long ago began constructing a castle in the jungles. And a true castle it is, with great dining rooms, grand entrances, archways, winding staircases, dank cellars, ramparts and even a towering watch tower. But as mysteriously as the construction began, it halted, and a

man's dream fell into ruin. The only record shows the land was deeded to a Mr. Kellie-Smith, a rubber planter who lived near Ipoh about sixty years ago. When his house was near completion he left on a brief trip to England and never returned. Now a young Indian cowherd may serve as guide, bravely leading daring visitors through a barricade of barking dogs guarding an old gate in front of a new tin mine. Kellie's castle, or Kellie's Folly as it is sometimes called, is on the turnoff $6\frac{1}{2}$ km from Ipoh to Batu Gajah.

Why Fight Tropical Traffic?

Twelve km long and four km wide, **Pangkor Island** is fairly readily reached from Ipoh or Taiping. In either case a drive of about one and a half hours leads to Lumut from where there are excellent ferry services to the island.

Legend tells that once a young Sumatran warrior fell in love with a beautiful princess, and to win her favor he sailed north to distinguish himself in battle. When he failed to return after many months, the princess set out to find him. She searched high and wide and upon reaching Pangkor Island learned the tragic news that he had died in battle and was buried there. The villagers led her to his grave, whereupon, distraught and heartbroken, she climbed a cliff and flung herself onto the rocks below.

The Beach of the Beautiful Princess is named after her, as is a new beach hotel that can be reached only by ferry from Lumut on the coast.

Pangkor has changed little over the years. Primarily an island whose economy depends on the sea, it is dotted with fishing *kampungs*. The two main villages — Pangkor and Sunghai — extend on stilts far out over the bay, looking like scenes on picture postcards. A few kilometers to the south are the island's only

From Lumut a fer leaves several time daily for Pangkor Island, little changed over the years.

angkor, with
veral hotels and
st houses, is a
vorite weekend
ating for
Malaysian students.

relics of her eventful past. Standing in ruins covered with jungle growth are the stone foundations of a Dutch fort, dating back nearly 300 years to the time when the Dutch captured the island. Chiseled on a boulder close to the ruins is the Dutch East India Coat of Arms.

In the mid-1800s Pangkor was a pirate stronghold, a menace to shipping in the straits. In a move to liquidate the pirates, the Sultan of Perak ceded Pangkor Island to Britain in 1876, along with a narrow coastal strip to the north and south called the Dindings. With control of Pangkor and the Dindings, Britain was able to combat the pirate problem.

Pangkor's two hotels are on the west side of the island. Four times a day a ferry leaves Lumut for the **Princess Hotel**'s quay which is located on idyllic Oyster Bay. The journey takes thirty-five minutes. The ferry slides down the Dindings River through the kilometer-wide channel where thick jungle growth enwraps the banks. Occasionally, a 1-meter-long lizard scampers for cover in the undergrowth. From Oyster Bay a wondrous, antediluvian bus transports guests the 1,000 meters to the hotel situated on Telok Belanga.

To reach the **Seaview Hotel** you board the ferry at Lumut for Pangkor village, a voyage of twenty-five minutes. There, one of the island's eight taxis or two buses takes you the 3 km to the hotel at Pasi Bogak. Here, too, is the spacious, but run-down, Government Rest House.

For the energetic there is a splendid 4-km jungle walk from the Princess Hotel across the top of the island (966 meters) to, first, Sunghai village and then Pangkor village.

illie's castle now
ruins was once
e dream of a
t-rich-quick
lonial planter
icing page). A
all launch anchors
Pangkor Island
low).

(Twice daily — in early morning and late afternoon — this trip may be taken by ferry.) For the less energetic a 4-km path along the shore joins the Princess and Seaview hotels. Midway is the primitive *atap* hut **Minivillage**, much favored by impecunious Malaysian students.

The **Lumut Government Rest House** contains a museum with an excellent collection of seashells and corals, ancient weapons and items of historical interest. In August there is a sea carnival (*Pesta Lumut*) which includes sporting and cultural events, the latter featuring Malaysian music and dances.

Gold Dome in a Royal Town

Until 1888 the wheels of transport had either wooden or iron rims, with the exception of a few motorcars that used solid rubber. Driving on rough roads then could be extremely uncomfortable. The man who changed this was John Dunlop, when he designed "hollow rubber tyres filled with air." His invention created a great demand for rubber and attention turned to Malaysia, and a town called **Kuala Kangsar** in particular. A dozen years before, several rubber trees had been planted as an experiment in the gardens of the agricultural station there. From these trees were to come the many thousands of young shoots that turned Malaysia into the world's leading rubber producer. One of the original rubber trees can still be seen in front of the old Residency and another close to the government offices in the center of town.

About 3 km out of town, overlooking the Perak River, is Malaysia's finest mosque — the golden,

Ubudiah Mosque at Kuala Kangsar is considered one of the country's finest Muslim shrines (left). A lofty silence settles upon Tasek Chenderoh, a lake formed by the Perak River (facing page).

onion-domed **Ubudiah Mosque**. One km further on is the **Istana**, the sultan's palace, which can be visited with special permission. Another 1 km brings you to the brightly painted 19th century ceremonial hall with exquisite gingerbread carvings on its eaves and facade.

Halfway to the mosque is an excellent Government Rest House located in a commanding position overlooking the Perak River.

Side Trip via Grik:
Malaysia by the Backroads

Leaving Kuala Kangsar, the traveler journeying northward to Penang can deviate from the main route and take a less traveled backroad which provides a change in scenery and mood. Beginning in the lowlands in lush, green rice fields, the backroad becomes a causeway across a lake, then snakes through deeply jungled mountains near the Thai border, and swings west again through old rubber plantations to the coast.

The lake is **Tasek Chenderoh**, formed by the waters of the Perak River. It is magnificently silent. Lofty mountains in the background, with an ever-present halo of clouds, are mirrored in the still waters. Beds of lilies grow lavishly in the water. Fishermen in frail boats glide across the lake, tossing nets that make radiating ripples. Above the lake there are deep ravines and gorges. The jungles seem incredibly deep. Nearby, at a town called **Grik**, are several Orang Asli settlements, but these can be visited only in the company of a government ranger. At **Kroh** there are customs and immigration offices for those wanting to enter Thailand. The

villages en route are predominantly Malay but in the countryside Indian rubber tappers cluster in plantation quarters. It is a one-day trip from Kuala Kangsar to Penang.

Graceful, Tree-lined Town

Taiping, which admits to the heaviest rainfall in Peninsular Malaysia, is a reflection of its name: "Town of Everlasting Peace." The name was acquired at a treaty which ended the Chinese Clan Wars in 1874. Taiping seems to have been left undisturbed ever since.

In the 1890s, long before the word "ecology" was bandied about, an abandoned tin mine on the fringe of the town and in the lee of Maxwell Hill was landscaped to create the magnificent **Taiping Lake Gardens**. The architect's name, Captain Akwhi,

an Indian inspector of mines, should be high in the annals of the history of Malaysia. Situated in the gardens is a zoo which covers an area of about 50 hectares. Here, too, is the new Government Rest House whose architecture, a mixture of Sumatran and classical Roman styles, shows that the Malaysians are determined to continue the improbable architectural styles the British introduced in Kuala Lumpur. Another architectural gem is the neocolonial town office best seen from the rear. Just beyond the far end of the Lake Gardens is an Allied War Cemetery.

The **State Museum**, the oldest in the country, displays a wide variety of exhibits assembled at the beginning of the century. A gallery of weapons, pottery and agricultural implements illustrates the life of the aborigines nearby. Malaysia's first railway, built

in 1885, covered the 13½ km from Taiping to Port Weld.

Taiping has an exciting *pasar malam* (night market) at the side of an enormous area of covered eating stalls, one of which serves "Bird's Nest Water — Hot or Cold."

Privacy in a Rose Garden

Up at 1,020 meters on **Maxwell Hill**, Malaysia's oldest hill station, there are no golf courses, Swiss-type restaurants, swimming pools or even jungle walks, but there is a badminton court. The cool air and moist clouds hanging low over the jungles below, the changing view when the clouds wash off the Straits of Malacca from Penang to Pangkor, and the comfortable bungalows with warming fireplaces give Maxwell Hill the simplicity of a natural hideaway that sets the

rishaw cycles
n Taiping's
e-lined street
ght). An Indian
endant works
Maxwell Hill,
country's
est hill station
ich lacks extensive
reational
ilities, but is
owed richly by
ure (facing
e).

mind and heart delightfully at ease.

Before the Second World War, the immaculate lawn in front of **Speedy Bungalow** was a croquet court. During the war, the Japanese used it to house carrier pigeons. Here, too, at Maxwell Hill, Asian "Quislings" were trained.

The first road to the top of the hill was constructed after the war with the "help" of Japanese prisoners and was finished in 1948. Before that anyone who wished to reach the top but did not fancy hiking had the choice of going via pony back or sedan chair. In the early years the trail was lined with porters carrying heavy loads of fragrant tea down the hill. Now tea growing is no longer practiced and only a handful of Indian laborers remain to keep the all-powerful jungle back and the gardens neatly manicured.

Although there is a paved road today, access is prohibited to private automobiles. The government-owned Landrovers which operate from the far end of the Taiping **Lake Gardens** serve as mountain taxis departing every hour between 7:00 a.m. and 6:00 p.m. daily. The one-lane road is steep and narrow, and the drive to the summit is awe-inspiring. At bends in the road the jungle suddenly parts and below appear green lowlands divided in a pattern of roads and fields. The air turns brisk and the sun becomes lost in a bow of mist and clouds. At the **Half Way House** traffic halts until Landrovers coming down the mountains pass by. The 12-km journey takes forty minutes. Landrovers will deliver a traveler to the front step of his bungalow and leave him to the privacy of a Malaysian retreat. If he be energetic then, at the foot of the hill, within a stone's throw of the Landrover station, is a large freshwater swimming pool fed constantly by a waterfall. In addition, the Lake Gardens has a sporting nine-hole golf course.

From Malaysia's cool hills we descend to Penang scrape.

penang: island
of many dimensions

Like most cities of Asia that juxtapose the glass and concrete of the new with the tile and teak of the old, Penang has several dimensions. A newcomer can arrive by ferry, be transported by trishaw to a Chinese hotel on Jalan Kimberley or Jalan Chulia in the heart of Chinatown, eat his meals in the small restaurants and foodstalls, walk the waterfront and visit the village on stilts, and after two weeks leave Penang not knowing there is a tourist complex. On the other hand another visitor may have cocktails served at the poolside overlooking the Penang roadway and later dine in a revolving restaurant sixteen stories above the flickering lights of the city and never really know that an exciting, vibrant Chinatown exists.

A sight-seeing trip round the island by motorcar or bus takes half a day; one of exploration could take several. Road maps reveal dozens of roads that end at seaside villages. Each one proves interesting in its own special way. And there are areas where roads do not go—only footpaths. One of the loveliest secluded beaches, where a lighthouse guides ships at sea, can only be reached by hiking down the sand when the tide is out. There are offshore islands to visit, mountains to climb, and temple sanctuaries to see. Penang is Asia unveiled.

On arrival, visitors are usually intrigued by the narrow, congested streets of **George Town** and its pulsating waterfront. It is here, on the waterfront, that Penang is linked to the 20th century by the flotilla of freighters and steamers anchored in the harbor, which cause the ferryboats from Butterworth to zigzag a 4-km course to reach the landing at Weld Quay. The voyage from the mainland to Penang is free but on traveling in the reverse direction you pay a nominal fee.

Sailing junks and Rhio traders (previous pages) bring back the old days in Penang Harbor.

George Town is unmistakably a Chinese town, from crowded streets with Chinese characters spelling out mystic logos, to the thriving port from where Malaysia's rubber and tin find their way to the world's markets.

As predominantly as the port is Chinese, the countryside is Malay. A few kilometers out of town, you leave the hustle and bustle of commerce, the noise and the crowd for an agrarian, quiet and thinly populated society—the peace of a gentle, unhurried life.

But Penang is also Indian. When the British arrived from India, they brought a number of Indians with them. Some were sepoys; others were members of the new police force; and a few were merchants. In 1824 Indian convicts were sent to build roads and fill in the swamps along the waterfront. The practice stopped in 1873

With secluded beaches, Chinatown, and Malay villages Penang Island offe the visitor an excellent chance to unveil Southeast Asia.

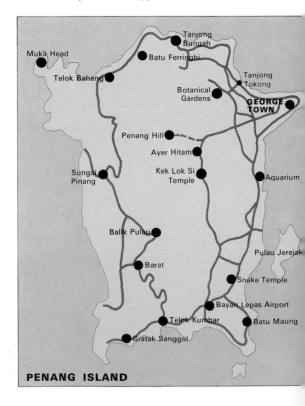

PENANG ISLAND

Tanjong Bungah
Muka Head
Batu Ferringhi
Telok Bahang
Tanjong Tokong
Botanical Gardens
GEORGE TOWN
Penang Hill
Ayer Hitam
Sungai Pinang
Kek Lok Si Temple
Aquarium
Balik Pulau
Pulau Jerejak
Barat
Snake Temple
Bayan Lepas Airport
Telok Kumbar
Batu Maung
Gratak Sanggol

but Penang continued to see the flow of Indian laborers. In 1910 some 80,000 Indians arrived in Penang to find work in Malaya. Not all of them stayed, but they did leave their stamp upon Penang. The spicy scent of curry dominates the older section of George Town; a taxi driver speaks Tamil as well as Malay, English and some Hokkien. A Hindu temple stands on top of Penang Hill and a small Hindu shrine stands next to a Buddhist image on a rocky promontory in the south.

Throughout history Penang has changed names like the seasons. Early Malays called it Pulau Ka Satu, or Single Island. Later it appeared on sailing charts as Pulau Pinang, or Island of the Betel Nut Tree. The British renamed it Prince of Wales' Island, and finally, with Malaysia's independence, it reverted to Penang. There are still many appendages

attached to it—"Pearl of the Orient," "Gateway to the East," "Isle of Temples." When you come to know Penang you discover they all aptly apply.

Traces of Old Penang

Probably the most costly "cannon ball" in history was shot at **Kedah Point**, near Fort Cornwallis. After Francis Light had concluded the negotiations for a British settlement at Penang with the Sultan of Kedah, he arrived at the island with three sailing ships carrying 100 sepoys, 30 lascars, 15 artillery men and 5 British officers. The site he chose for the settlement was thick with jungle. The work of clearing away the undergrowth proved arduous and the sepoys complained of hardships. To induce them into action, Light loaded

1786 the British de Penang a air station for st India Company ps sailing the y of Bengal.

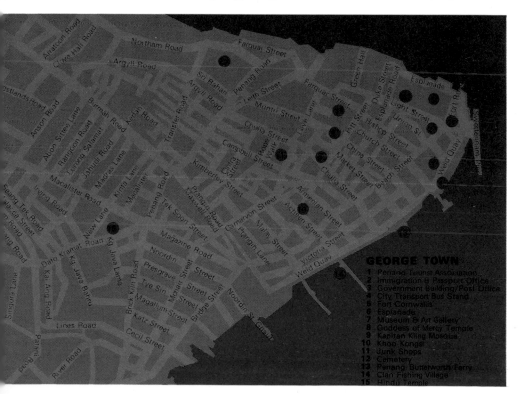

GEORGE TOWN
1 Penang Tourist Association
2 Immigration & Passport Office
3 Government Building/Post Office
4 City Transport Bus Stand
5 Fort Cornwallis
6 Esplanade
7 Museum & Art Gallery
8 Goddess of Mercy Temple
9 Kapitan Kling Mosque
10 Khoo Kongsi
11 Junk Shops
12 Cemetery
13 Penang-Butterworth Ferry
14 Clan Fishing Village
15 Hindu Temple

a cannon with silver dollars and fired it into the jungle. Before long the land was cleared and the first camp was established.

On 11 August 1786, a flag was raised and the settlement was named Prince of Wales' Island. Light's dream had been fulfilled, but not easily. Light had long seen the need to establish a base to repair British ships damaged by rough winds in the Bay of Bengal. He thought Penang was an excellent choice but it took him sixteen years to convince the East India Company that he was right. And even then, after the settlement began, there were those who had doubts about its success. Also, Penang was obtained under false pretences. The Sultan of Kedah, whom Light had befriended, agreed to let the British settle Penang under two conditions: that they pay a small yearly tribute and that they protect the Sultan against his enemies. The Sultan never did get the protection he needed, and several years later he went to war against the British to reclaim the island. But by that time, it was too late.

When Francis Light took possession of the island, there were less than 1,000 Malay fishermen in scattered *kampungs* near the sea. To encourage trade and commerce, Penang was made a free port, which means no taxes on imports and exports. "Only this way", Light said, "could trade be attracted away from the Dutch". His strategy worked. In eight years the population increased to 8,000, comprising many immigrant races: Chinese, Indians and Bugis, among others. Today the island boasts of more than 500,000 people, over half of whom are Chinese and over a quarter Malays.

To promote trade, the British adroitly made Penang a fre port, which has ke the island prosperous to this day.

An old cannon at Fort Cornwallis points blankly to it eventful past.

during historic
es in Georgetown
ovides at a quick
ance an overview
recent Malayan
story.

The East India Company gave Light little support. He started the colony with a staff of one clerk, no police force and no established system of laws. Then abruptly the feeling changed from lukewarm to wildly optimistic, and in 1805 Penang was made a presidency with a full governor, giving it equal status with Bombay, Madras and Bengal. The tragedy is, Francis Light had died the year before.

Originally, **Fort Cornwallis** was a wooden structure. Between 1808 and 1810 it was rebuilt with convict labor.

Now the inner part of the old fort is a garden and playground for children and there are future plans to turn it into an amphitheatre. Where guards once stood along ramparts and where cannon balls were neatly stacked next to the embrasures, young boys play follow-the-leader as they

nimbly balance atop a wall or swing out hand-over-hand on the barrel of Seri Rambai, known to many Penang residents as 'the traveling cannon'.

Seri Rambai was presented by the Dutch to the Sultan of Johore in 1606. It was later captured by the Portuguese and somehow turned up in Java where it remained for a hundred years until pirates captured it and tossed it into the Malacca Straits. In 1880 it was hauled up, taken to Selangor and eventually brought to Penang. It is believed that women who desire children should place flowers in the barrel of the cannon and offer special prayers.

Traces of old Penang still linger in George Town. Just next to Fort Cornwallis, traffic circles the city **Clock Tower** which was presented to Penang by Cheah Chin Gok Esq. in commemoration of Her Majesty

mbstones at
nang's Christian
netery read like
ges of an early
ry.

Queen Victoria's Diamond Jubilee. In **Penang Museum**, two blocks away, visitors can peer into a Chinese bridal chamber created in the lavish style of the 19th century when Malaysian-Chinese girls took great pride in the quality of beadwork on their slippers. One room, dedicated to a glimpse of yesteryear, is hung with old paintings and etchings from the days when Fort Cornwallis was the center of town. Another is an opulent showcase of bejeweled krisses, the dagger-like weapons Malays used for protection and for prestige. There is a rickshaw that rambled through one-lane streets forty years ago, and beautiful vermilion "birthday tapestries" stitched with gold embroidered dragons and phoenixes. **Penang Art Gallery** upstairs displays *batek* paintings, oils, graphics and Chinese ink drawings. Most of the techniques are new but the solemn, moody sea scenes and village portraits reinterpret a way of life that is little changed from the pioneer days.

Early Penang had its share of hardships along with the silver dollars. The lovely, old **Christian Cemetery** shaded by frangipani blossoms reveals a silent drama from the olden days. Penang's natural enticements were already well known in 1805 when a British officer wrote: "Prince of Wales' Island is universally allowed to be one of the most healthy situations, and invalids are frequently sent in from different residences and their health is speedily restored." As epitaphs tell, many died at sea before reaching Penang. Others contracted fever as the jungles were cleared, or were murdered by gangs of robbers.

Streets of George Town

Penang is a Far East warehouse for everything imaginable, from electronic gadgets to plastic toys. There are silks from Thailand and India, fabrics from England, cameras from Germany and Japan, textiles from America and from Malaysia, brocade and sarongs. **Jalan Pinang** is the main

shopping bazaar. Shops open in the early morning and do not close until the bars are empty and the late moviegoers have cleared the streets.

Jalan Campbell, just off Jalan Pinang, is the main "Chinese" shopping center where you can buy nylon shirts and fake alligator-skin shoes, laughing jack-in-the-boxes and precious stones, which are guaranteed to cut glass, from Nepalese street vendors.

Perhaps the most exciting shopping in Penang is in the many "junk" shops along **Rope Walk**. Here, shoppers must literally climb over mounds of discarded gear. "What you might uncover will astound you," gleamed a contented antique dealer from Sydney, holding a sandalwood jewel box with the lid hanging hopelessly to one side. "But this can be fixed," she added. She had already found a

Penang Museum has exhibits on the life-ways of Straits-born Chinese who blended Malayan elements with their own traditions.

Trishaw lanterns flicker furtively on George Town's nighttime winding streets.

148

orge Town is
all enough to see
foot; but
shaws are a
asant alternative
unhurried
ring.

British army bugle dated 1890, and a dusty tray filled with Buddhist votive tablets. If you do not mind getting your hands dirty, you are certain to discover a dusty thing or two. One London boutique salesgirl found a Chinese emperor's robe salvaged from the local opera stage.

Penang has an unusual night market called **Pasar Malam**. One Italian tourist returned to Penang after visiting in the south for a week and was greatly disappointed to discover the market had closed down. It was only by accident that she learned it had moved. But then that is what makes it unique: every two weeks the hawkers pack up and move to another location. The areas, wherever they might be, are well lighted and the bargains range from tiny trinkets to cheap Kelantan batek sarongs and plastic sandals. People-watching here

is one sure attraction everyone enjoys.

George Town is not so large that getting around is a problem. Walking is a delight and distances pass unnoticed. Taxis are plentiful and inexpensive but they are not allowed to "cruise" for customers. The easiest and most enjoyable way to get around is by trishaw. That way, the city passes by in a kaleidoscope of changing colors, the way it should be in George Town. Even a trishaw ride in the monsoon rain can be enjoyable. The driver zips his passengers into a plastic covering, and with the rain falling on the canvas he pedals slowly through the misty streets. At night there is a special romance about riding in a trishaw. Then the driver lights small lamps that adorn both fenders. The tiny lights flicker in the darkness like glowworms in a field.

Leaning over the railing of a

*ffic jams Jalan
mpbell, part of
nang's Chinese
p house district.*

hotel balcony, standing on top of Penang Hill, walking along the waterfront, riding through the crowded streets of George Town in a trishaw — no matter where you are at sunset, you are certain to be awed by the spectacle. The light of day fades, the horizon is streaked with shades of red, mist gathers in the distant hills and day passes. Lights in town begin to come on, the ferries mark their zigzag course and trishaw drivers stop to light their lanterns.

The streets of George Town are made for night life. The Chinese never seem to go to bed. Their open-front restaurants are noisy gathering places where waiters shout your order to someone in a back room. A juke box, if there is one, is turned on full volume. Hawker stalls on Gurney Drive and the Esplanade do a thriving business, whilst brightly-lit stores cater to late night shoppers. At the fashionable hotels, latecomers wait in line at the discotheques. There are roof-top restaurants where diners look down over the city lights, hills and harbor, and dark cellar cabarets with no view at all.

Those who prefer their entertainment in bars can find a few around George Town and on the northern outskirts of the city. Some small and friendly establishments, like the Hong Kong Bar, keep a 'family album' of snapshots showing just about every traveler who walks in and buys a drink. They provide juke boxes for dancing, game machines for entertainment and good-looking barmaids for conversation. Others are more consciously sophisticated, like the Den in the **E & O Hotel,** where there is a resident band. Penang is undoubtedly a place that makes evening walks fond memories. The weather is perfect for being outside, where the most spontaneous night life always is.

One does not have to look for excitement on the streets of George Town. If you take a room in a Chinese hotel you will understand why. Early morning might begin with a funeral procession through the streets: there are drums and gongs and mourners. In the afternoon it might be a lion dance, a noisy affair with more drums and gongs, where mobs of youngsters follow the lion, taunting it with shouts and screams. Come evening and it could be a Chinese opera, where people sit for hours and watch highly painted faces pantomime classical tales of old, or a rock band playing pop tunes on the Esplanade. You can never tell what you might find — a bargain or a baritone.

Dragons on the Rooftops

For a city with few skyscrapers, George Town has the most cosmopolitan spiritual world this side of the hereafter. People worship in Malay mosques, Anglican churches, Burmese shrines, Thai wats and Chinese temples. Most bedazzling among them is not even a temple but a clan house built by the **Khoo Kongsi,** or mutual benefit society of the Khoo clan, whose ancestors migrated to Penang from Fukien before the days of Captain Francis Light.

Khoo Kongsi is so elaborate that it almost exceeds celestial proprieties. The clan house was designed to capture the splendor of an imperial palace with a seven-tiered pavilion, wondrous dragon pillars and hand-painted walls engraved with the Khoo rose emblem. The original design was so ambitious that conservative Khoo clansmen cautioned against it lest the Emperor of China be offended. The night after the building was completed in 1898, the roof mysteriously caught fire. Clan members interpreted this as a sign that even the deities considered the Khoo Kongsi "too palatial" for a clan house. The Khoos rebuilt it on a smaller scale and the result was one of perfection.

Khoo Kongsi appears at the end of a labyrinth of tiny streets near Cannon Square which is at the end of

Hunting for bargains goes on morning, noon, and after hours at the night market, which shifts location every two weeks.

Though Penang has its share of nocturnal diversion it is "undoubtedly a place that makes evening walks fond memories."

eople from the
ame town or region
China banded
gether into clans
hich still play an
aportant role today
the life of Chinese
alaysians.

he dragon-shaped
of of the Khoo
ongsi clan house
Georgetown, the
est of its kind
Malaysia.

Jalan Pitt. Arriving there by trishaw is like being guided out of time to a heavenly abode where dragons dance on rooftops and fairies play lutes among the clouds. Sagging eaves are transformed into enamel mosaics of celestial kingdoms. Gilded beams become curvilinear gardens where saintly immortals dwell. The outer walls are a pageantry of legendary episodes carved, painted and polished by experts from Cathay. Giant guardian gods on the main doors prevent the intrusion of evil spirits, while stone lions chiseled from green granite help keep guard. Behind the altar's facade of glistening gold leaf and red lacquer stand statues of the gods of longevity, wealth, prosperity and happiness. On either side of the central shrine are ancestral halls honoring the patron saints of the clan. Surrounding their images are "sin-

choos," wooden tablets remembering deceased clansmen. On the walls are gold plaques inscribed with the names of distinguished members who have earned a high academic degree or who have attained a position of leadership, such as Justice of the Peace.

Khoo Kongsi is one among many Mutual Benevolent Associations that serve Penang's Chinese community. Clan houses are scattered all over town, but none ever aspired to such lofty proportions as the miniature imperial palace built by the Khoos.

Joss Sticks for the Goddess of Mercy

Of all the Chinese temples, **Kuan Yin's,** Penang's oldest temple in Jalan Pitt, is the most humble and the most crowded. It belongs to the people in the street: the noodle hawkers, the trishaw drivers, the housewives who

do the daily marketing, the old shopkeepers who count abacus figures, the workers who build cupboards, repair bicycles or sell sundries. Kuan Yin personifies mercy. She hears all prayers and helps anyone who asks her. She is often portrayed by the illustrious image of a serenely composed woman with eighteen arms. "Two arms are not enough to help the suffering in the world," explains the old temple caretaker who ceaselessly totters about, dusting altars and emptying incense urns. Kuan Yin's temple always has a well-worn look. The halls are heavily laden with scented smoke. The floors are littered with joss stick wrappers and discarded shopping bags. The altar looks like a plebeian banquet table with roasted chickens, sweet cakes, oranges, pineapples and cookies neatly placed as humble offerings to the goddess.

On the eve of Chinese New Year, when good luck is in highest demand, Kuan Yin's temple catches fire. Hundreds converge at her altars to burn joss sticks, light red candles, and invoke her name. Smoke billows from furnaces set up in the courtyard, as a billionaire's fortune in paper "joss money" is sent to Kuan Yin via the fire. Everybody from businessmen to beggars jam the front gates, carrying a stream of glowing joss sticks that flows into the temple. An apparition appears amid the smoke. It is a human face transfigured by colored goggles and a kerchief over the nose. It looks like a space-age bandit or an air-pollution survivor behind a makeshift gas mask. Actually, it is a boy hired by the temple to collect the plethora of burning joss sticks and dump them in the furnace outside. One bleary-eyed foreigner, witnessing the

The Goddess of Mercy, Kuan Yin, is probably the most popular and most worshiped of the Chinese gods, revered by Taoist, Buddhist and Confucian.

The smoke of joss sticks burdens the air at the temple of Kuan Yin, Goddess of Mercy, in George Town.

crowded scene, moaned: "I never cried so much in church in my life."

Kuan Yin is a Buddhist deity, a Bodhisattva who refused to enter Nirvana as long as there was injustice on earth. She is ever-present on Chinese altars, whether the worshipers be Taoist, Buddhist or Confucian. Throughout the day, people visit her temple to burden her with problems they cannot solve or to thank her for the blessings which ended their worries. The clicking of "divining sticks" ricochets throughout the halls as devotees ask her advice for the coming week. Men and women on the streets of George Town know that Kuan Yin will reply. She is perhaps the most beloved divinity in the Chinese altars of Penang.

The worshiping of Kuan Yin is a meeting ground between traditional Chinese belief and Buddhism.

Penang Buddhism

The eve of Chinese New Year at the **Penang Buddhist Association** is a more formal affair than the mad rush of devotions at other temples. Women arrive in modern and simply-cut sam-foos or store-bought Western dresses, conscientiously fashionable. A teen-age girl patiently leads her dignified grandfather across the wide marble floor where a seated congregation chants praises to Lord Buddha. The Association organizers busily arrange patterns of bright flowers, fruits and colored cakes on a large, shiny table carved out of blackwood imported from Canton. Enthroned on the high altars are six white marble statues of Lord Buddha and his disciples. Over-head hang crystal chandeliers from Czechoslovakia and on the walls hang

fine-lined paintings depicting Buddha's path to enlightenment. As temple bells ting, the chanting rises to usher in the new year, to celebrate an eternal rebirth for all generations. Outside the front door, beggars sit quietly chatting among themselves. They know benevolence is a precept of the Chinese New Year and they receive it passively.

Ordinarily, the large, luminous hallway that dominates the Chinese Buddhist Association is the most serene sanctuary in Penang. The building, completed in 1929, reflects the desire of a Buddhist priest who wanted to indoctrinate his followers with orthodox rites and ceremonies. Here you will not find joss-stick hawkers or paper-money burners. Prayers are considered the essence of Buddhist worship, and the Penang Buddhist Association cherishes the simplicity

inherent in its Buddhist faith.

The variety of Buddhist worship in Penang is so striking as to make sight-seeing a new experience in every temple. One can enter the gigantic meditation hall at **Wat Chayamangkalaram** and find a workman polishing the left cheek of the 32-meter-long Reclining Buddha, third largest statue of its kind in the world. Wat Chayamangkalaram, in Burmah Lane is a Thai Buddhist monastery. Gigantic Naga serpents, mystical creatures that link earth to heaven, form the balustrades at the entrance of the meditation hall. Fierce-visaged giants tower over the doorways in the role of otherworldly bodyguards who leave little to the imagination. Monks with shaven heads and saffron robes soundlessly tread over lotus blossoms patterned on the tiled floor. All around the monumental image of

Kek Lok Si temple, largest Buddhist temple in Malaysia on a hill in Ayer Itam in Penang.

slumber are smaller statues of lesser Buddhas with donation boxes on their pedestals. Inscribed on one box are the words: "To devotees who worship this god, your wish will come true, what you wish will come to you."

Inspired by a Vision

High above the bustle of George Town looms the "10,000 Buddhas Precious Pagoda" which dominates a bucolic landscape of rock gardens and tortoise ponds. The temple complex is named **Kek Lok Si** or "Monastery of the Western Paradise of the Pure Land Sect of Buddhism." Its creation was inspired by a vision in 1885. A visiting Buddhist abbot, Reverend Beow Lean, gazed up at the chain of hills above Ayer Itam village and saw that they formed a flying crane with white wings spread out across the land. The crane is a Chinese symbol for immortality. The Reverend heeded the good omen and built Malaysia's largest Buddhist temple, the pride of Penang.

Kek Lok Si is split into three tiers spread over a rocky incline. The three "Halls of the Great" honor Kuan Yin, goddess of mercy; Bee Lay Hood, the Laughing Buddha; and Gautama Buddha, founder of the faith. It is here that the monks pass their hours in prayer.

On Sundays Kek Lok Si witnesses a holiday parade as Chinese families spend their free afternoon strolling among the opulent gardens on the threshold of paradise. The spiritually-oriented playground has an informal give-and-take atmosphere, free from the solemnity of secluded shrines. A tunnel of souvenir shops and knick-knack stands leads to the pagoda.

Pilgrims entering the "10,000 Buddhas Precious Pagoda" find a painted cardboard cut-out of a man in a gray-flannel suit pointing out "Way to Pagoda." His directions, in fact, lead to a red and green ticket booth manned by a bald priest in gray

robes. The sign above says (in five languages): "May the visitor to this Buddhist Pagoda be so good and kind to put some money into this charitable box as a holy contribution to the worshiping and praying purposes." Inside the pagoda a spiral staircase twists up through chambers adorned with thousands of Buddhas: in niches, in paintings and on the walls. Perhaps the pagoda is a cool contemplation tower overlooking the coconut palm-shaded township of Penang. "It's a very complicated structure," says an amiable Chinese climbing his 152nd step. "Very, very complicated," re-joins his friend. But the mystical purpose of the pagoda eludes most of its pilgrims. "It's a tourist attraction," the man offers, "its original purpose, I wouldn't know."

Botanical Gardens:
Bliss below the Waterfall

"Another very important consideration in a place proposed for a Colony is fresh water," wrote Lt. Popham of the Royal Navy. "No country can be better supplied with this valuable article than Prince of Wales' Island. Water descends from the hills and is collected into several small rivulets, the two principal of which empty themselves into the harbor, the one near, the other 2 km from the town; and in the latter of these the ships' casks may be filled in their long-boats at low water."

After nearly 200 years the fresh-water springs in the hills above George Town continue to lure visitors up from the lowlands. Although they are labeled Waterfall Gardens, they are actually Penang's **Botanical Gardens** in the grounds of which grow some of Malaysia's most beautiful tropical plants. Monkeys inhabit the trees and delight visitors when they come down to the lawns to be fed, especially in the early mornings or late afternoons. The waterfalls start over a hundred meters above the gardens and come tumbling down

ilt by a visiting estern Buddhist bot, Kek Lok Si a leading raction for both votees and sitors.

e salubrious nosphere of nang bursts forth the Botanical rdens.

through the green, where there are footpaths and small wooden bridges, much like a Japanese garden. On holidays, families round up distant relatives for a picnic lunch by the stream while barefoot children romp on the rocks or play "follow-the-tourist." Benches are scattered throughout the Gardens and provide pleasant resting spots in the shade. And, like other similar places in the world, lovers come to take advantage of blissful nature.

One of the most scenic spots on the island is **Ayer Itam Dam**, with a 18-hectare lake reflecting the lush green foliage of the surrounding jungle. A 3-km road from Kek Lok Si Temple winds its way up to the dam. The air becomes cool, especially in the evening when the breezes blow across the lake.

Beyond the dam, atop a hill and reached by a long flight of steps, is the Indian shrine of **Nattukotai Chettiar**. Here, as well as in Kuala Lumpur, is held the awe-inspiring festival of Thaipusam (see page 79). There are those who claim that the Thaipusam festival in Penang is even more dramatic and interesting than the one in Kuala Lumpur. Certainly, it does not suffer in comparison.

Apart from Ayer Itam Dam, Penang has a wealth of small reservoirs, most of them constructed not only for their utility value but also with an eye on aesthetics. **Guillemard Reservoir** sits atop a hill on Mount Erskine. Its dazzling reflection is one of the first things arriving passengers see when flying into Penang. Around the reservoir are casuarina trees planted in rows and trimmed to match the landscape.

Penang has numerous streams and waterfalls. Early Malays believed the water came from springs connected to Lake Toba in Sumatra. In fact, it comes from rainfall, which averages 325 cm a year. Nonetheless, it remains a "valuable article" as Lt. Popham said, particularly when it runs through the gentle gardens behind the town.

Penang Hill

Despite the first impressions one might get about George Town being a busy place, beneath its facade it is a town of leisure. People who live there enjoy their city and island. They frequent the parks and gardens, take trips around the island and visit the many temples. Penang Hill is one of their favorite spots. As far back as 1897 people were struck by the scenic beauty and "the desirability of Penang Hill as a health resort." There was only one problem: getting there. Someone finally came up with the idea of building a railway to the summit. After years of arduous labor the line was completed. Two passenger cars mounted on tracks were attached to a thick cable, which passed through pulleys. Steam power was ruled out

Penang has a wealth of reservoir such as Ayer Itam and Guillemard.

A couple enjoy Penang's Botanica Gardens, also calle the Waterfall Gardens.

156

cending Penang
ll culminates in a
ta of sea and
ind, mountains
d valleys.

in favor of a Pelton wheel, propelled by water power. "An ingenious method," was the remark of the time. Everyone awaited the day when the railcars would start rolling. But when it finally arrived, the water wheels would not work. They did not even sputter. The Penang Hill railway passed into oblivion.

In the next twenty-five years, science progressed. After studying the funicular railway systems in Switzerland, Penang residents opened the present line on 21 October 1923. It has been in operation ever since. The ride to the summit is one of the highlights of a visit to the island. As the cars rumble slowly up the steep incline a panorama of sea and island, mountains and tropical valleys continuously unfolds. From each small substation along the way, paths disappear into the cool forest or gardens of private

bungalows on the terraced slopes. One of the most pleasant experiences a visitor can have is to spend a day or two in the hotel at the summit. The 500 people who live on the hill have built a small Hindu temple and a mosque. There are usually several enterprising schoolboys eager to earn some pocket money by guiding visitors around.

Apart from funicular railcars, Penang has much to offer in the way of recreation. George Town is Asia's Monte Carlo where, once a year, racing cars from all over S.E. Asia career around the winding roads and along the sea front to compete in the Malaysian Grand Prix. Horse racing is also popular and races are held five times a year at the Penang Turf Club. There is an eighteen-hole golf course and the green fees are M$20 a day.

Penang has its share of cinemas

with some showing the latest English language films. Anyone who has not seen a Chinese swordsman of old on the silver screen, wreaking vengeance against great odds, and usually winning, might find it a memorable experience. There is always one or two good sword-fighting films playing in George Town.

Round-the-Island Trip: Beginning with a Double Take

Beyond the outskirts of George Town another Penang begins. By starting at the waterfront in the morning, the visitor can head south, follow the winding and sometimes mountainous road for 74 km and by evening return to the same spot from which he started. He can visit a temple where poisonous snakes hang from the rafters, watch tropical fish swim in an aquarium, see an alleged foot-print of a heroic Chinese admiral, swim in a pool beneath a waterfall, meet Malay fishermen in remote villages, have lunch in a polished teak restaurant and lounge away the afternoon on a soft, white beach that is equal to the best in Asia.

Travelers have a variety of ways to make a round-the-island tour. Hotels and tourist offices can arrange for group tours in air-conditioned buses with guides. Private chauffeured cars with or without guides can be hired through the tourist office. There are also rent-a-car services, offering sedans for M$32 a day. Or you can make the trip by public bus transport. For less than a dollar it will take you anywhere you want to go. The only difficulty is that unless you want to hike you cannot leave the main road. There are no trishaws in the country and taxis in Penang are not permitted

Sight-seeing round the island can be completed in a half day, or you can linger and forget time.

Sampans, launches and junks crowd the Chinese clan piers in Penang harbor.

h Chinese clan
ns a pier and
ctly controls its
n territory.

to cruise for passengers.

George Town has one of the most unusual waterfronts in Asia. Visitors arriving by ferry usually do a double take when they first see it. The area is what locals call the **Clan Piers**. It consists of villages built on stilts over the sea. The people who live there are either boatmen or fishermen and each group belongs to a clan. On Lim's Pier only members of the Lim family can live, while Chew's Pier is the sole property of the Chew Clan. The houses extend far out to sea, and at low tide the fishermen's boats rest high on the mud banks. On tiny docks that consist of no more than a few narrow planks on the sand and a ware-shed, laborers unload heavy burlap sacks stuffed with cargo brought in by the lightermen. No one minds if a visitor strolls along the often shaky wooden piers, provided he is

not a Chew in Lim's territory.

On the outskirts of town are the mills and factories, which are soon passed, and the Malay countryside. The roads are well marked with kilometer-stones indicating the distances from George Town. A road map is helpful but not necessary. You cannot really get lost. There are a number of side roads, some worth exploring, but most of them end at remote villages on the coast. Where there is little traffic, the fishermen have the habit of drying their *ikan bilis* (a very small fish) on the pavement. Oftentimes there may be a half-kilometer of fish laid out to dry, with only tire room left on the road.

Aquarium and Snake Temple

Those interested in tropical marine life should visit Penang's

sonous vipers are
ywhere in the
ke Temple of
an Lepas,
ang.

Tunku Abdul Rahman Aquarium and Laboratories at km-stone 6 — on the road south of George Town. Winding one-way corridors lead past huge tanks with glass fronts in which swim some of Southeast Asia's most interesting sea life. There are giant Indian carp from the inland rivers and spotted eels from the coral reefs offshore. Each display tank is provided with captions giving illustrations, scientific and common names of the specimen and brief notes. In a marine museum are exhibits, models and charts showing the early development of fish and crustacea, poisonous and venomous aquatic organisms, and fishing gear and fishing products used in Malaysia. On holidays and weekends the aquarium is usually crowded. The aquarium is open every day except Wednesdays from 10:00 a.m. to 6.00 p.m. A restaurant is nearby.

* * *

"Not worry, no bite," a Chinese lad insists as he probes at a small tree. Interwoven among the branches slithers a 1-meter-long, green and yellow viper. The jaws open and red fangs hiss. "See," the boy repeats, "no bite."

The viper lives in the famous **Temple of Azure Cloud**, more popularly known as the Snake Temple. The road south from the aquarium passes the Science University of Malaysia and km-stone 14 marks the serpents' shrine. When you climb the steps to the ornate temple, you may think there is nothing unusual about it. Even when you see a few snakes curled up, it does not seem too extraordinary. But then you begin to notice that poisonous pit vipers are everywhere — on altars, shrines, incense burners, candlesticks, vases, tables, under foot and over head. There is even a "maternity" tree where many new-born snakes, the size of earthworms, slither along the branches. In an adjoining room a photographer stands by to take your photo, if you care to pose with a snake or two curled around your arms and neck.

These vipers, the photographer guarantees, have no poison fangs.

The snakes are venerated because of their kinship to the mythical dragons of Chinese folklore. It is claimed that, during the day, burning incense in the temple keeps them doped. At night they drop down from the ceiling and branches and suck the chicken eggs left for them by worshipers.

Malay Fishing Villages: 1,000 Years of Hand-Me-Down Experience

Having no luck with lotteries? Do you suffer from poor health, or need business success over rivals? Or is it one of the opposite sex you wish to conquer? If so, you might try joining the multitude of believers who pay their respects at a small shrine on a rocky promontory at **Batu Maung**. The shrine marks the sacred footprint of Admiral Cheng Ho, the Chinese "Columbus" of Malaysia. Villagers believe that Cheng Ho called at this spot on one of his seven voyages to Southeast Asia. On Langkawi Island, 96 km to the north, is a similar footprint. The two are believed to be a pair and anyone who lights joss sticks and places them in the urns beside the footprint will have good luck, great fortune and all his wishes come true. The shrine is on the southeast tip of the island about 3 km from the Bayan Lepas Airport, a short distance beyond the fishing village of Batu Maung.

When it is high tide at Batu Maung, fishing boats are run up on the beach, and left high and dry when the waters recede. Ships' joiners take advantage of nature's drydock to make repairs on vessels before the next tide ends their work day. These skilled carpenters use tools that should be museum pieces, as ancient as their trade, but their finished product is the result of a thousand years of hand-me-down experience. It was in vessels such as these that their distant ancestors explored and traded

At the Snake Temple, snakes a venerated as relatives of mythi dragons of Chine folklore.

Outside the city a towns in Penang Island, Malay fishing villages ar agrarian kampung carry on the way they have for generations.

in the islands of the Malay Archipelago. They have perhaps turned from traders to fishermen but their art remains the same.

Near the fishing village and Cheng Ho's footprint you can see a mermaid and a dragon on the beach and the world's most photographed horse. The mermaid and dragon are plaster; the horse is real. Batu Maung Garden Photo Studio is a miniature fantasy land reminiscent of the Tiger Balm Gardens. There are concrete dolphins, a giant frog, a meter tall ostrich, an elephant and even a helicopter. A sign says: "Only Customers (Who take Photo From Studio) are allowed to Snap our Self-decorated Views." The display is the stock-in-trade of Garden Photo Studio.

Several small roads in the south branch off to the coast. Usually they are the commercial link between a fishing village and the trunk road. It was in small villages such as these that the few Malays lived when Francis Light established the first settlement.

Malaysian architecture in cities and towns changes constantly with the times but the *kampung* houses look much the same as they did a hundred years ago. Malays take pride in their homes, the interior of which can often be glimpsed from the road. The furnishings are simple and each house will have a framed photo of the King and Queen. Houses are elevated, making the life style within cool, dry and clean. There are fruit trees in the neatly swept courtyards, bearing rambutans, mangosteens, bananas and papayas. Outside each house is a water basin for washing the feet before climbing the stairs. Malays always leave their shoes outside to keep the interior of their house clean. Cleanli-

*h countryside
lds in southern
ang.*

ness is one of the prime virtues laid down in the Koran and most women sweep their home several times a day. Often the scene along Penang's south coast is like one's childhood image of a neat little house with flowers growing outside the doorstep. Only the Imam's chant from the *surau* (village mosque) distinguishes the moment.

The road skirts around the southern end of the island and turns north. The scenery changes from flat rice land to rolling hills. Cultivation gives way to dense, damp jungles. The road twists upward and where the foliage clears there are striking views of the island dropping to the sea far below. Here, too, are spice plantations of pepper, cloves and nutmegs in search of which Arab, Spanish, Portuguese and other Western traders came long ago to this part of the world. At **Titi Kerawang** there are waterfalls in the

hills, with a serene view of the Indian Ocean. The natural fresh-water pool that is filled from the waterfalls is suitable for bathing, though a big water pipeline mars the scenery. The falls make a good rest spot en route round the island.

Finally at km-stone 21 the road reaches the northern end of the island and the beach resort area begins. Before starting on the final leg of the drive back to George Town, visitors who want to try something unusual might want to hike down the beach to **Muka Head** where there is a lighthouse jutting out on a rocky promontory. There is no road and the only access is via the long isolated beach or by a small jungle track. For anyone seeking solitude there is no better place in Penang. The many small coves and sandy beaches make excellent camping grounds.

Penang's south coast is pastoral, along the north coast Muka Head juts out of a rock promontory.

Typical Malay kampung *house in Penang village.*

penang's beaches and enroute to langkawi

Batu Ferringhi whets the appetite beaches more secluded and untouched, then it via Alor Star and Kuala Perlis to Langkawi Islands.

The road on Penang's north coast follows the curve of the land, twisting up and around a hill or skirting the fringe of the sea. Rocky promontories jutting out into the sea divide the shoreline into small bays and coves, each with a different character and charm. All are excellent for swimming and sun bathing and you will find one appealing.

Most activities are centered around **Batu Ferringhi,** one of the most popular beach resorts in Southeast Asia. Here are the large luxury hotels of **Rasa Sayang, Casuarina, Golden Sands** and the **Holiday Inn.** They provide a variety of facilities including waterskiing, sailing and pony or horseback riding. Smaller and older, but comfortable and reasonably priced, are the **Palm Beach** and **Lone Pine.** There are also small inns and motels. Many villagers in this area, especially at Telok Bahang, also offer accommodation.

These beaches are readily accessible from George Town — the road is good and the distances are short. But taxis in Penang do not cruise. The bus journey involves a change of buses and takes more than one hour.

Sandwiched between the Hotel Rasa Sayang and the Casuarina on Batu Ferringhi beach is the **Yahong Art Gallery.** The gallery is a storehouse of some of the finest arts, crafts and antiques of Malaysia and China. It is also the home of Mr. Chuah Thean Teng, Malaysia's foremost batek artist, whose work has won international recognition at a number of one-man exhibitions in the major capitals of the world.

There are restaurants galore, from the beginning of the beach area at Tanjong Tokong stretching the 11 km to Telok Bahang. Often they consist of nothing more elaborate than a collection of rickety, wooden tables set on the sands overlooking the distant shoreline of George Town to the south. Waiters approach the tables casually dressed in whatever

best suits them for the day. But the dishes they suggest are something else —delicious, fresh seafood soup with sharks' fins, big, round, crisp spring rolls and chicken baked in seasoned black sauce. At **Tanjong Tokong,** the **Sayang Masmera Restaurant** serves excellent Malay food. At **Tanjong Bungah,** two of the better restaurants are the **Hollywood,** offering Muslim, Chinese and European cuisines, and the **Seri Batik,** serving Malay dishes.

Secluded between rocky promontories, shaded by stately palms and lace-like casuarinas and washed by the blue waters of the Indian Ocean, the northern beaches have made Penang renowned as a premier holiday island in the sun.

The Sound of Drums

Situated amidst a sea of rice fields is **Alor Star,** the capital of Kedah, Malaysia's rice bowl. The main attraction here is the enormous *Padang* (town square), enclosed by an interesting hodgepodge of buildings. Dominating them all is the **Zahir mosque,** one of the most beautiful in the country. Facing it, on the north side, is the olive-green, yellow and egg-shell blue **Balai Besar,** the great hall where the Sultan of Kedah still holds audience on ceremonial occasions. Between these two buildings is the three-story octagonal **Balai Nobat** which is topped by an onion-shaped dome. From this building, according to legend, the sounds of drums could be heard at dawn, just before morning prayers. Next to the mosque is a baroque clock tower. To the west of the Balai Besar are ultra-modern, white Moorish-style government offices while to the east is a squat, unattractive, "between the wars" government building. The square is completed by beige-colored, neo-renaissance government buildings on the west and east sides.

Those with time and a spirit of adventure might wish to visit **Gunong Jerai** (Kedah Peak), the highest mountain (1,202 meters) in northwest

Peninsular Malaysia. Situated on its slopes are more than forty archaeological sites — the most significant is Pengkalan Bujang — which attest to the occupation of this region by Hindus from India.

The Sea Is a Secretive Labyrinth

Tucked into the northwest corner of the peninsula and literally a stone's throw from the Thai-Malaysian border are the **Langkawi Islands** — ninety-nine of them. Unlike the other islands on the west coast the vast majority of the 30,000 persons who live on these islands, only three of which are populated and two of these but sparsely, are Malays. You would be told how difficult it is to reach these islands, but do not believe it. Fifty minutes get you from Alor Star to Kuala Perlis from where there is a regular ferry service to the islands. You would be more comfortable in the nonair-conditioned boats. The crossing takes two hours. (Incidentally, there is an irregular but frequent boat service from Kuala Perlis, which has customs and immigration facilities, to Thailand. The voyage takes one hour.) For those that prefer a faster mode of travel, Malaysia Air Charter operates daily flight services (except Wednesdays) from Penang, Alor Star and Kuala Lumpur.

When the islands are first seen from the ferry they appear as one, spread out along the horizon in a jagged and uncertain silhouette. But, as the ferry nears, the view changes. Shadowed cliffs, topped by dense virgin jungle which, in places, reaches a height of 600 meters, drop abruptly into the sea to form channels and narrows, inlets and bays.

The Moorish style mosque at Langkawi's main village of Pekan Kuah.

ries leave
ularly each day
m Kuala Perlis
the two-hour
ssing to
ngkawi Islands.

More islands and passageways appear. The sea route becomes a labyrinth like the fjords of Norway, deep and secretive. It soon becomes obvious why pirates and buccaneers who preyed upon the trading ships in the Malacca Straits used these islands as a place of refuge. It was impossible for the British men-of-war to hunt them down.

Finally, the ferry edges through the last channel and the granite cliffs give way to the sweeping curve of a wide bay fringed by coconut palms and dominated by a Moorish-style mosque. Looming in the background are the serrated fingers of Gunong Raya (Raya Mountain). A concrete jetty, where small trading boats unload their cargoes, reaches out into the bay. Here is **Pekan Kuah**, Langkawi's main village. It has the peace and quiet of a slumbering town in the tropics.

Accommodation is no problem. There are three small Chinese hotels in the village center; a pleasant Government Rest House splendidly situated midway between the quay and the village; the Government-run Sri Samudra bungalows and chalets; and the Langkawi Country Club, located 800 meters south of the quay. The latter offers horse-riding and speed-boating, a below-average tennis court and an inchoate golf course. There is, however, a delightful nine-hole golf course 8 km from the village center.

Ornithologists and lepidopterists will delight in these islands, which have species of butterflies not found anywhere else in Malaysia. For the others the main joys are the desolate, sandy beaches of the islands and the waterways which they flank. Many of

e labyrinth of
erways once
cealed pirates
o preyed upon
os sailing through
Malacca Straits.

the beaches are a mere ten minutes from Pekan Kuah and transport to them can be arranged with local fishermen or the country club. The main island boasts some beautiful coves rich in corals and marine life and splendid beaches like Tanjong Rhu, Pantai Tengah and Pasir Hitam (Black Sands).

From Tanjong Rhu fishing boats can be hired to go round the cape to the gray limestone cliffs beyond, which are approachable only from the sea. There is a cave there called Gua Cerita or Story Cave inscribed with ancient writings from the Holy Koran which, like so many places on Langkawi, has its legend. A rickety bamboo ladder, hung from stalactites, leads to the entrance.

Another legendary spot is the hot springs of Telaga Air Panas, 13 km by land from Kuah. Story tells how two of the island's leading families became bitter enemies. The quarrel culminiated in a violent fight whereby a jug full of hot water was spilt on this spot and the unfortunate feuding fathers were transformed into the two mountain peaks of the island.

You can reach Telaga Tujoh, Langkawi's famous waterfalls by a jungle trek from Kuah or an hour's boat ride from **Kampung Pantai Kok**. Telaga Tujoh means Seven Wells but it is really a fresh water stream that cascades through a series of seven pools forming natural slides from one to another.

Langkawi has 120 km of paved roads and getting around is no problem. You can hire taxis, minibuses, motorbikes or bicycles. There are also organized tours. The tour passes through rubber plantations, rice fields and coconut groves to distant fishing *kampungs* and isolated beaches. En route, the

The main island a country club, g course, and government rest house, making one's visit no hardship at all.

These Langkawi fishermen are Malays, as are th majority of nearly 30,000 inhabitant. the islands.

tour stops at the hot springs, the tomb of Mahsuri - an island beauty who was involved in court intrigue and falsely accused of adultery - and Padang Mat Sirat where black rice grains can be scraped from the soil. These grains remain from the scorched earth policy adopted by the islanders when they were attacked by the Siamese over 200 years ago.

Another delightful tour, this time by sea, is to **Dayang Bunting Island**, the second largest of the group. Here, set in dense jungle and separated from the sea by a narrow strip of land, is a fresh-water lake with a legend — the lake of the pregnant maiden. The maiden was a Kedah princess forbidden to marry her young Malay lover. They fled to Langkawi but were followed by angry relatives. The Kedah princess flung herself into the lake and drowned. It is believed that women who are barren and desire to

have children need only bathe in the lake, or drink its water, and they will conceive. The voyage through the island channels, at times a mere 800 meters wide and flanked by towering 300-meter marble cliffs, is memorable.

There is a mystery about Langkawi that puzzles historians. When the British were looking for a naval base, they considered these ideally situated islands. An entire fleet of ships could safely anchor within the sheltered waters. But for some unknown reason, East India Company agent Francis Light chose Penang.

The Chinese came to Langkawi as long ago as the 6th century, when they called it "Lung-yu Kiao-yi," from which the present name derives. In 1407 the famous Chinese Admiral Cheng Ho visited the area. But there are no historical landmarks today. Langkawi is simply islands of beauty — pristine, untouched by the world.

ats can be rented
tours to the
aller islands.

traveling south
through history

About 20 km south of Kuala Lumpur and **Kajang** is reached. If you are hungry — or even if you are not — stop awhile. Kajang boasts the best *satay* in all Malaysia. It is not that the meat is better in Kajang than in other parts of the country, but Kajang makes the best sauce.

Satay is the hamburger of Southeast Asia. Chicken, mutton or beef is cut into bite-sized pieces, mixed with spices, salt and sugar and marinated for at least six hours. The meat is then threaded on skewers and grilled over a charcoal fire. From time to time it is basted with oil. The sauce for *satay* is made from peanuts, chilis and coconut milk with salt and sugar to taste. When it is served, the plate of *satay* will also contain slices of raw cucumber and onion.

Rubber plantations and tin mines dot the landscape heading south.

Seremban: True to the Past

Along the road to Port Dickson, travelers pass out of the state of Selangor and into **Negri Sembilan**. The name Negri Sembilan means "Nine States" and alludes to the loose federation of Malay chiefs who ruled these lands before they were united under British administration. Much of the countryside — small clapboard homes with batik on the clotheslines and papaya trees in the front yard — is reminiscent of the quiet Malay villages that were sprinkled over Negri Sembilan centuries ago. And **Seremban**, the state capital, could not be more typical of the Malayan-Chinese town that sprang out of the tin-mining boom eighty years ago.

Seremban's city planning was probably nothing more complex than a spontaneous expansion of shop houses along the main road. Though the pattern has since disappeared into a maze of cluttered arcades and tiny alleys, Seremban is essentially a one-street town splashed with signboards advertising innumerable trades. Above the din of trishaw bells and bargain sessions, government clerks mill over their paperwork in colonial buildings set on the hills behind the town. True to Negri Sembilan's past, the impressive state mosque is designed around nine pillars.

Seremban is in Minangkabau country, largely settled by Malays from West Sumatra. Minangkabau means "buffalo horns" and many of their houses have roofs that sweep to two horn-like peaks. The state museum is a fine example of the Minangkabau architecture of the 19th century. A high building on stilts with an *atap* roof, it was formerly the re-

Just south of Kua Lumpur lie severa history-studded places and excelle beaches.

Candles like a sea of stars engulf Malacca's 18th-century St. Peter's Church on Good Friday (previous pages). A 19th-century Minangkabau house contains Seremban's state museum (right).

sidence of a Malay prince and had to be dismantled at its original site at Ampang Tinggi and brought piece by piece to the state capital to be reconstructed. Although Minangkabau in design, its carved wooden panels show European and Malay influence. On display are ceremonial krisses, a collection of Minangkabau and Dayak swords, and royal headdresses.

From Seremban, there is a railroad sidetrack to Port Dickson. Although the route itself is flat, the track twists and curves aimlessly.

By the Blue Lagoon

Thirty-two km south of Seremban, 96 km south of Kuala Lumpur, lies the lovely seaside town called **Port Dickson**. Those who cannot find time to spend on the superb East Coast beaches might make do with Port Dickson and its blue lagoon.

Do not expect a bustling port, for it is not. Nor is Port Dickson much more than a one-street town. But the 16 km of sandy beach to the south, which terminates at the old Rachado Lighthouse, is something else indeed. That first view of the lonely sea, seen through the coconut trees, is a silent spectacle. The sea is deep blue and seems to merge with the sky in the distant horizon. There is a sweeping curve to the shoreline, with palms, some so bent with age that they practically touch the water, stretching to the water's edge.

The drive southward along the uncluttered coast is so exhilarating that you will be tempted to park and dive into the inviting water. The red sands are soft yet firm and this, together with the gently sloping bottom, make Port Dickson ideal for children.

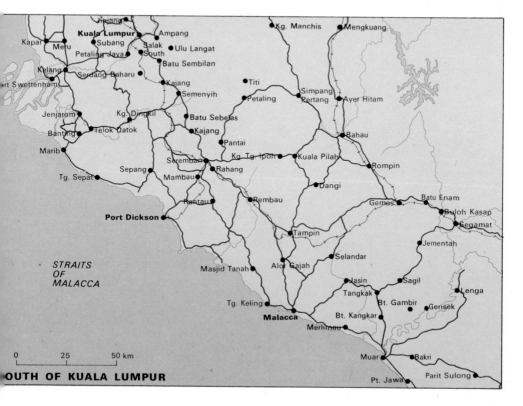

STRAITS OF MALACCA

0   25   50 km

OUTH OF KUALA LUMPUR

It is also very popular with the boating fraternity.

The **Yacht Club**, 7 km out of town, encourages travelers to use its facilities but you must be introduced by a member and its four pleasant bedrooms cannot be booked in advance. There is a swimming pool and four good, hard tennis courts, but no boats for rental to nonmembers. Across the road is the nine-hole **Garrison Golf Club**.

Boats can be obtained, however, at the **Si-Rusa Inn**, 12 km from town. When Mr. Chelliah, the Malaysian Indian who owns and manages this hotel, came to Port Dickson in 1949, the hotel had but a few rooms. Gradually, when he had accrued the necessary capital, Mr. Chelliah expanded his hostelry until today it boasts of 176 rooms with accommodation as varied as simple rest-house type rooms, air-conditioned caravans and a new 52-unit block whose rooms have such amenities as wall-to-wall carpeting.

Mr. Chelliah's views are interesting — no building should be taller than the trees which surround it; no building should be within 100 meters of the beach. It is fascinating to chat with him over his favorite refreshment — Scotch and water.

Soon, the Si-Rusa will have alongside it the first-class, 250-room **Federal Hotel** complete with swimming pool, discotheque and other amenities.

The **Fairwinds Hotel**, 5 km from town, is in sad shape, with yellow stucco peeling in places, the ceiling slumping here and there and the grass so dense that one wonders if it shelters tigers and elephants. But, it is a great reminder of bygone days when plan-

Children enjoy snorkeling in Port Dickson's clear waters.

172

tation owners sipped sundowners on the spacious verandas and talked about labor problems, rubber prices and the Saturday dinner menu. It would be an ideal location for a movie based on one of Somerset Maugham's short stories.

* * *

Sixteen km out of town, in the shadow of the **Rachado Lighthouse**, is the **Blue Lagoon Village**. Here, six beach cottages can each accommodate six adults in three bedrooms (one air-conditioned), with all the niceties to make a stay in Port Dickson most enjoyable. Clown fish, stick fish and live coral compensate for the murky waters of the blue lagoon. Reef shrubs undulate with the tides which flow over jagged submarine landscapes sprinkled with star-like and prickly sea urchins.

A half-km winding drive from

...ound Port ...ckson's blue ...oon is a popular ...ort with a good ...ection of ...ommodations.

Blue Lagoon Village and a climb of sixty-three steps through thick jungle lead to the 16th-century Portuguese lighthouse. It was built to guide sailing ships toward the historical port of Malacca, then the most important trading station in Southeast Asia. Far below, swirling currents mark the ancient meeting place of South China Sea and Indian Ocean tides, causing a small whirlpool effect beyond the coral reef. Turtles can frequently be seen.

Although the lighthouse is closed to the public, a smile and a nice word will generally, or a pass from the Malacca Tourist Office, 90 km away, will always, gain you entry. The lighthouse keeper leads you up a narrow spiral stairway to the light chamber above. The sudden view is striking. Across the 38-km channel lies Sumatra. Along it, freighters leave their wakes upon the sea, junks and sailing ships beat upwind, small fishing boats hug the coastline, seen in shades from bright greens to somber grays. Like tentacles reaching out to sea, precipices of land silhouette the coast. After the visit an exciting jungle walk down to the beach can be made from the lighthouse gate.

* * *

Twenty-three km south of the lighthouse, at the far end of the small village of **Pengkalan Kempas**, is a site which will delight antiquarians. Next to the tomb of Sheikh Ahmad Majnun, dated 1467, is a group of three stones — the Sword, the Spoon and the Rudder — each about 2 meters tall. They are of uncertain provenance although thought to predate the tomb of the sheikh. The Sword might be of Hindu origin but is now supposed by some to be linked with early sun worship. There is also an "ordeal" stone, with a hole through it, which is reputed to tighten around the arm of any liar should one be brave enough to make the test. From Port Dickson it is a ninety-minute drive to Malacca, where the past of the southwest coast seems very much alive.

malacca: history's sleepy hollow

History is everywhere in Malacca, peeping out from odd corners, hinting truths from epitaphs, yet never really telling it. It is a town with a glorious past, reflected in a letter a seaman wrote home to Portugal 300 years ago: "Malacca is the richest seaport with the greatest number of merchants and abundance of shipping that can be found in the whole world."

For centuries Malacca had been a rendezvous for every seafaring nation. Indians, Javanese, Chinese, Arabs, Siamese, Portuguese, Dutch and British all ventured to the harbor town in search of profit through trade, piracy or plunder. And each in turn left something of its own culture behind to be forged and blended into what had never been before.

Geography was responsible for it all. Located at the mouth of the Malacca River, astride the maritime route linking the Indian Ocean with the South China Sea, Malacca stood where the monsoon winds met. As tillers of soil depended upon monsoons to bring them rain, so trusting sailors relied upon the winds to move their ships. A Bugis, two-masted, square-rigged trader from the Celebes with the riches of the East in its hold — camphor, cloves, nutmeg and sandalwood — let the northeast monsoon drive it through the narrow straits between the Malay peninsula and Sumatra to the port of Malacca. Here the cargo was discharged and new precious wares from India and the Middle East were loaded — cargoes of silks, carpets and porcelain. When the winds changed, the southwest monsoon assisted the same vessels to return to their home ports. European merchants needed only to call at Malacca to fill their ship holds with

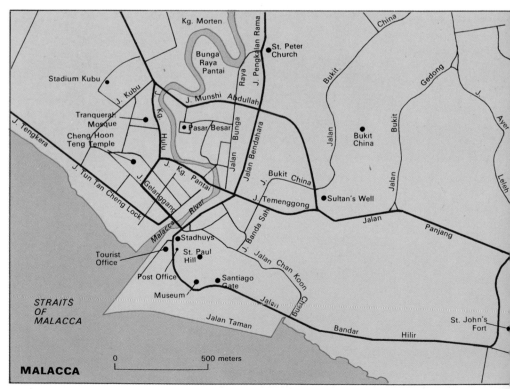

MALACCA

town in
alaysia evokes the
st as strongly as
alacca, which was
ce one of the
eatest seaports
Asia.

the fabulous riches of the Orient.

It was the rich port of Malacca —the key to controlling the spice trade — that caused some of the early East-West power struggles. In 1511 Malacca fell to the Portuguese and for more than a hundred years it was their fortress. In 1641 the Dutch took over and held the port for 150 years, until they ceded it to the British in exchange for Bencoolen in Sumatra.

Under the Portuguese, Malacca was to see colossal changes. At first, when the town fell, Sultan Mahmud withdrew to Muar in hopes that the invaders would plunder the city and move on. But the Portuguese had other ideas.

Much of the history of Malacca is housed in a 150-year-old Dutch building that was once a private residence overlooking the port. The **Malacca Museum** contains a unique

collection of old coins, stamps, a rickshaw, Portuguese costumes from the 16th century, Dutch weapons, old Malay krisses and shields, British cannons, gold and silver filigree jewelry and framed, sepia-tone photographs of sailing ships anchored in the Malacca River.

Malacca's history began long before Europeans made the scene. Early 14th century Chinese accounts speak of it as "a large trading station" and as far back as 1360 the port was paying tribute to the Siamese. But it was not until Parameswara, ruler of Tumasek (later known as Singapore), came to settle in Malacca and establish the beginning of a Malay Empire that Malacca entered the pages of written history. The Malacca Sultanate flourished in a golden age of Malay culture. Monarchs commissioned their scribes to compile

the Malacca
useum an old
inting depicts the
n during the
tch period of the
th century.

The CITY *of* MALACCA *in the East Indies.*

chronicles which have since become classics in Malay literature. The court elite carried golden krisses studded with jewels, a weapon which has come to symbolize Malay royalty. Through the museum exhibits, the visitor can trace Malacca's history from the ancient Malay kingdom, through Portuguese and Dutch rule and British occupation to its present status as a state in Malaysia.

Walking through History

The story of Malacca, and all Malaysia in a sense, need not come from a textbook. A 1-km walk or a leisurely trishaw ride through town can reveal the past. Trishaws are an excellent means of getting around in Malacca. The drivers know the sights and many of them speak understandable English, in which case they make fine guides. You might not only learn that the Portuguese came "a much long time ago" but also that along the seafront there is a great soup stall that sells the best *mee hoon* (very thin noodles) in Malaysia.

The visitor to Malacca may find it difficult to visualize life behind the medieval fortress 400 years ago. But, as he walks the narrow streets, visits old temples and mosques, lingers among ancient ruins and epitaphs, Malacca's history begins to fall into place.

It is easy to get around and although there are many things to see Malacca can, except for the expert, readily be "done" in one day. However, those who wish to linger awhile and absorb the atmosphere of "sleepy hollow," as the inhabitants of Malacca love to call it, will find that they can intermingle their sight-seeing with sunning and swimming. **Shah's Beach Hotel**, 8 km to the north, on the main road to Port Dickson, has tastefully decorated chalets and a swimming pool.

Off the coast is a group of small islands. At weekends, there are regular boats to the largest island, **Pulau Besar**. But be warned! Legend has it that should one eat pork within forty-eight hours of visiting the island, one's boat will sink.

* * *

The best place to begin is right downtown at the **Cheng Hoon Teng Temple**, the oldest Chinese temple in Malaysia. The building is a beautiful example of Chinese architecture. The carved roof, ridges and eaves are elegantly decorated with exquisite Chinese mythical figures, animals, birds and flowers of colored glass and porcelain. Step through the massive hardwood gates, and you have stepped back through Malaysia's time machine. The temple, dedicated to the city's earliest Chinese pioneers, marks the 1406 visit of Admiral

A one-kilometer walk through Malacca's narrow streets takes one, through the towns many periods: Malay, Chinese, Portuguese, Dutch English, and mode Malaysian.

Malacca's main street is a hodge-podge of buildings.

1405 the emperor
China made the
en Malaccan ruler
ng of the city and
hinterland.

Cheng Ho, an illustrious envoy of the Ming Emperor.

Monks in yellow robes move silently among the gilded pillars while Chinese worshipers with lowered heads walk from image to image, holding smoldering joss sticks firmly in their hands. Shiny tables and beams are lacquered black with panels of inlaid mother-of-pearl. Gold lions standing guard at the entrance have the yellow worn off their heads from countless devotees rubbing them for good luck.

No single name in history was so widely known and respected throughout the East as that of Admiral Cheng Ho, the jeweled eunuch of the Ming Court. His personal and single-minded leadership had so established the prestige of the Ming Dynasty that the story of his seven voyages to the southwest were repeated for centuries

afterward. Parameswara, the Sumatra-born Malay ruler of Malacca, gladly welcomed the envoy of the Ming Emperor of China, whom he hoped might give protection against the Siamese who were moving southward down the peninsula. In 1405 the Emperor did that and more. He appointed Parameswara King of Malacca, under Chinese protection, and marked the occasion by giving him a written commission, a seal, a suit of silk clothes and a yellow umbrella — the emblem of Malay royalty ever since. Cheng Ho was later deified by the overseas Chinese and given the religious name of Sam Po. In the Cheng Hoon Teng Temple there is an inscription cut in a stone commemorating his visit to the cemetery on a hill behind the town known as "Bukit China."

Just around the corner from the

alacca's Cheng
on Teng Temple,
oldest Chinese
nple in Malaysia,
rks the royal visit
Admiral Cheng
.

Cheng Hoon Teng Temple is **Jalan Gelanggan**, Malacca's main thoroughfare. It was formerly Jonker Street, but by any name it would still remain one of the town's most interesting streets. Much like Kuala Lumpur's Jalan Petaling, it is a hodgepodge of every shop house imaginable: spirits importer; hairdressing salon; wooden shoe cobbler; rattan shop; sporting goods store; coffin maker; apothecary with Chinese herbs on display; sign printers; acupuncture clinic; furniture factory; dental hospital with office hours printed in English, Chinese, Malay, Tamil and Thai; photo studio; a half dozen temples squeezed between commercial enterprises; and three antique shops. Amidst the cacophony of honking horns and bullock carts thumping over hard pavements, fez-wearing tailors pedal sewing machines in open front shops, furniture makers hammer a table leg into place, and vendors and shopkeepers call out to passersby, "Come look around."

The antique and junk shops are a mirror to Malaysia's past. Heavy brass irons with receptacles for hot coals, ornate oil lamps hanging from the ceiling, pearl inlaid nightstands, opium benches, brass urns and a Chinese wedding bed are what a typical shop offers. The Pakistani shopkeeper points to a carved, wooden jewelry box. "I saved it for a prime minister," he tells you, "but I don't know when he'll be back." You study the box with a very unconvinced look on your face. "No matter," he continues, "I like you. You can have it."

Continuing through Malacca takes one past Dutch-built houses and to Portuguese descendants.

Malacca hides a treasure trove of antiques.

Malaysia's past is the stock-in-trade an antique shop on Jalan Gelanggan.

178

Architecture from Holland

When you cross the Malacca River bridge and come face to face with a neat, little square with a clock tower surrounded by salmon-colored government buildings and a towered church, you almost expect to see tulips growing in the gardens or a passing cyclist wearing up-pointed wooden shoes. The square obviously was built by the Dutch, and architecture is Holland's main contribution to Malacca.

The Dutch arrived in 1641 as conquerors, having driven out the Portuguese after a siege that lasted eight months. But what they found was not a rich and prosperous port of the fabulous East, as they had expected. The city they struggled so hard to conquer lay in near total ruin.

The walls of the fortress were broken down, the castle and its towers were tottering, and the wooden churches were rotting. Hardly one building was left undamaged by the powerful bombardment.

But the industrious and fastidious Dutch lost no time putting things in order. As soon as they were in control, they began to rebuild the city with a Dutch flavor. The walls of the fortress were repaired and the bastions renamed. A moat was dug around the fortress and a drawbridge built. Protective ramparts were laid round the suburbs and heavy brass cannons mounted on all the walls. In a short time Malacca became a well-defended port again. Unfortunately, the only surviving parts of the Dutch fortifications are the Santiago gate, bearing the date 1670, and the small fort on St. John's Hill.

Next came the construction of the **Stadhuys**, with incredibly thick walls and massive hardwood doors supported by studded, wrought iron hinges. After 300 years, the old Stadhuys is still being used as government offices. The only difference is that today officials sit writing their memoranda under electric fans that hang from beautiful, old paneled ceilings. As they have always done, clerks sit at their desks noting down complicated figures in thick ledgers. Time does not change bureaucracy as quickly as it does power.

If the clock in the tower at the Stadhuys strikes noon when you cross the bridge, chances are the town will be at siesta. Things move slowly in Malacca, and her leisurely timetable is part of her charm. The small square is empty at noon, the museum closed and traffic almost at a standstill. The only excitement occurs among the rows of foodstalls that cover an entire block and face the sea. It is cool there in the shade. Local cooks whip up Malay, Chinese and Indian dishes with astounding speed and serve noodle snacks or curry lunches with great gusto.

The River: Ever Constant

At the end of the street, before the bridge crosses to the Stadhuys, a narrow lane leads to the quay along the left bank of the river. Time seems to have passed by this section of town. Great, ancient junks, high bows and raised poop decks — reminiscent of their distant cousins that once brought Admiral Cheng Ho's dragon court entourage to Malacca centuries ago — float side by side against the wooden pilings of the dock. Their romantic cargoes of spices, silks and camphor have been forsaken, for these battered, unkempt vessels now carry bulky sacks of charcoal that fire the kitchens of Malacca. The laborers, wobbling up and down the narrow planks that join ship to dock, strain under the heavy loads, and like the sturdy junks they unload, they are part of Malacca's timeless past.

Yet once the Malacca River was different. When the Portuguese colony was at its zenith, the river was a deep, bustling waterway jammed with ships of a dozen nations. Great sailing vessels, loaded to the scuppers, vied with each other to maneuver up the river to tie up at the quay, while countless smaller vessels, anchored in the roads, depended upon flat-bottom scows to load and unload their valuable wares. Ships chandlers did a thriving business selling stores to captains, and there is a story that the town was so vast that it took a cat walking over the tiled roofs a year to make the circuit. Maybe the story-tellers exaggerated but we do know that when the Portuguese captured Malacca, d'Albuquerque sailed his warships upriver to beseige the town.

Malacca River is today but a subdued reminder of its bustling past.

A tombstone in St. Paul's Churchyard dating from the Dutch period.

he Portuguese
ere the first
estern power to
vet Malacca,
izing it in 1511.

Santiago: Gate without a Wall

When the Portuguese captured Malacca, they were determined to make it one of the mightiest strongholds in the Orient. D'Albuquerque immediately ordered the construction of a formidable fortress. Hundreds of slaves and captives were put to work. Stones from demolished mosques and elaborate tombs were used to build the thick-walled fortress, which was called A Famosa. When it was completed, with cannons on the walls and soldiers standing guard, it filled the townspeople with both fear and respect.

Later A Famosa was enlarged to enclose the entire hill, including the European settlement. The city walls enclosed a castle, two magnificent palaces, a hall for the Portuguese

e Santiago Gate,
that remains of
alacca's once great
rtuguese fort.

Council of State and five churches. This fortress withstood attacks for 150 years, until it was finally breached in 1641 by the Dutch. The walls and gates were badly damaged by the Dutch artillery and all that was left of A Famosa was the Porta de Santiago — a gate without a wall. The fortress was restored by the Dutch in 1670 who engraved their coat of arms above the gateway. In 1807, when the British ruled Malacca, the fort which the Dutch had rebuilt was destroyed. But Porta de Santiago was preserved through the intervention of Sir Stamford Raffles who was in Malacca at that time.

Churches

Both the Portuguese and the Dutch came to Malacca looking for spices, but the Portuguese left behind

their blood and their faith. In 1521, only ten years after they captured the city, the Portuguese built **St. Paul's Church**. St. Francis Xavier conducted mass in the church during his several visits to Malacca. After his death on the island of Sancian, his body was interred in St. Paul's for nine months before being taken to Goa in India. In 1557 Malacca became a bishopric. The diocese included Burma, Thailand, Malaya, Indonesia, China and Japan. Jesuits, Dominicans, Franciscans and Augustinians had their headquarters in the city.

The Dutch discontinued services in St. Paul's Church when their own Christ Church was built. However, they used the ground around St. Paul's for the burial of their noble citizens. Lining the inside walls of St. Paul's are engraved tombstones reminding all future generations that "Angarieta Roberts Alma, aged 29, wife of merchant Davidt Verdonch, died and was buried here in 1652."

Early morning or late afternoon is the best time to climb St. Paul's Hill to the church. The beauty of St. Paul's is the fact that it is a ruin. No restoration could make it more attractive.

When the Portuguese garrison was forced into submission the Dutch gave safe conduct to the soldiers and amnesty to the Portuguese descendants, many of whom chose to remain behind rather than take up a new life in Goa. In 1710 the Portuguese Eurasians of Malacca built another church a short distance from the center of town. They named it **St. Peter's**. Unlike its richly decorated counterparts in Goa, it is simple and relatively unimpressive. Throughout the year, except for an occasional wedding or funeral, not much goes on. Good

St. Peter's church built in 1710 by the Portuguese still hosts a thriving congregation of Portuguese descendants.

Friday, Easter and Christmas, of course, are the big exceptions.

Good Friday services at St. Peter's Church are the most elaborate in Malaysia. Thousands of people — Chinese, Eurasian and Indian — crowd the church to attend the services and take part in a candlelight procession. A life-sized statue of Christ, crowned with thorns and draped in deep purple robes with gold embroidery, is solemnly borne above the devout Catholic congregation. The churchyard becomes a sea of flames ushered in by the mournful sound of hymns. Malacca Chinese and Portuguese Eurasian Catholics living throughout the country try to return to their home town every Easter weekend and attend the ceremonies at St. Peter's which they knew so well as children.

Despite the solemnity of a staunch Catholic mass, the crowds that gather outside the church after the service meet friends and cast flirtatious eyes as if it were carnival time in spring. Children, looking most reverent and pure in their Sunday clothes, romp around the lawns or negotiate coins with the Indian peanut seller. Everyone laughs, including the priest and the young girls selling religious literature, which appropriately includes a biography of St. Francis Xavier.

Christ Church, built a hundred years after the Stadhuys, had its pink bricks shipped from Holland, then Malacca masons faced them with local red laterite. The church is full of old, engraved tombstones, many of which tell a grim tale about the hardships the early settlers faced. Captain E.L.M. Evans of Her Majesty's 51st Regiment, for example, lost his beloved wife, aged 24, and his three children during a diphtheria epidemic in 1856. The immense rafters within the nave were each carved from a single tree and date back to the founding of the church. The original solid, heavy wooden chairs for Sunday worshipers still remain in use, and

above the altar a wooden crucifix hangs from iron hoops fastened to the wall. The story is that when the church started there was no pulpit. The pastor would sit in a chair that had ropes running to the hoops. When he was ready to preach, his sextons would winch him halfway up the wall. Thus, he gave his sermon.

In front of the church is a small water fountain. At the end of the little square, professional scribes with ancient typewriters pound out messages to distant loved ones for those who never learnt to read or write. The pace of the town is easy. No one rushes. Even trishaw drivers, reclining in sleepy repose in their trishaws, cannot get excited when strangers amble down the street and ask for their services.

Portuguese Eurasian Settlement: A 350-year-old Heritage

The legacy the Portuguese left behind is far greater than their ruins. Proud descendants of Portuguese soldiers bearing such names as Sequiera, Aranjo, Pinto, Dias, D'Silva and D'Souza cherish the traditions of their European lineage. "I gave to each man his horse, a house, and land," wrote d'Albuquerque in 1604 when he reported with pride to Portugal that 200 mixed marriages had taken place. On direct orders from the king, d'Albuquerque encouraged men of the garrison to marry local girls, whom he called "his daughters." Such intermarriages flourished and girls were even sent out from Portugal to marry local men. The Portuguese were instructed to treat local folk as equals and it has been noted that d'Albuquerque would courteously escort local women to their seats in church as though they were noble Portuguese ladies.

As can be expected, a strong Eurasian community grew up with loyalty to Portugal through its ties of blood and religion. After 400 years the Portuguese Eurasians in Malacca, as

s in several former colonial lands, Christianity has taken root with unabashed fervor.

The Portuguese encouraged intermarriages, and this day a Eurasian community thrives in Malacca.

well as in other towns of Malaysia, continue to speak Cristao, a medieval dialect once spoken in southeastern Portugal. "It is pure 16th-century Portuguese," remarked Father Manuel Pintado, a local parish priest, when asked how closely the language spoken conforms to that in his homeland. "Remarkable, but it is spoken nowhere else."

Today, the descendants of the early Portuguese live in a community of their own, 3 km from the center of Malacca, near the beach. There are about 500 Eurasians, mostly fishermen. The name "Portuguese Eurasian Settlement," as it is called, is misleading. There are no cobblestone streets, white stucco walls or red tiled roofs as one might find in towns in Portugal. Instead, the dwellings resemble Malay *kampung* houses with clapboard walls and tin roofs. They are all painted in pastel blues and greens, are small, unpretentious and identical with one another. "They are proud people who live within the walls," Father Pintado explained. "The Dutch occupied Malacca much longer than the Portuguese and were here after the Portuguese were expelled, yet little is left of the Dutch occupation."

Pass through the Portuguese Eurasian Settlement quickly and you will be disappointed — there is not that much to see. But linger and meet the people. Young boys still sing beautiful ballads in Portuguese and their sisters can show you a dance which their grandmother learnt from her grandmother. An old man at a fruit stall tells you about a hidden tunnel from St. John's Fort to St. Paul's Hill, in which the Portuguese had hidden all their treasures before the Dutch overran Malacca. Almost a hundred years ago, a friend of his uncle had looked for the tunnel and was never seen again.

The Festa de San Pedro, held each year in June, is a happy time for these remarkable people. Then, the fishermen elaborately decorate their boats with bunting and sacred texts. A mass is conducted in the open and after the boats have been blessed by the parish priest the evening is spent in merrymaking.

Another unusual custom is called "Intrudu," meaning "Introductions," celebrated on the Sunday preceding Ash Wednesday. Then the residents wear fancy costumes and throw water over one another. Even those at home are not spared. The merrymakers make a point of visiting and drenching them with water as soon as they open their doors. To show there are no hard feelings they are invited in for refreshments. Later in the day the men dress up as ladies and the ladies dress as men, and go around selling cakes and fruit.

* * *

St. John's Fort is a convenient stop on the way back to town. After a short but tiring climb to the top of the hill where the concrete fort stands, you can ponder the most likely location for a tunnel entrance, while recovering your breath and enjoying a panoramic view of Malacca. Apart from the absence of cannons, the fort is much like the Dutch left it when the British took over after Malacca was exchanged for Bencoolen in Sumatra. Fearing that Malacca might fall into enemy hands, the British had all the strongholds, except St. John's Fort and Santiago Gate, destroyed. Now the old, vacant fort is sandwiched between a very strange-looking water tank on one side and Malacca's tallest building, a ten-story block of flats, on the other. No matter how hard it tries, 20th-century Malacca is still an incongruity.

Sumatra Comes to Malaysia

In Malacca there are few Malay relics of her distant past, the reason being that to provide building material for their forts and defences, the European invaders tore down the ancient Malay tombs and mosques. There is, however, 2 km along the

184

Port Dickson road, the **Tranquerah Mosque**. Built 150 years ago, it is of typical Sumatran design. In the graveyard of the mosque is the tomb of the Sultan of Johore who signed the cession of the island of Singapore to Stamford Raffles in 1819. The Sultan spent his last years in Malacca where he died in 1835, at the age of 59.

Malacca's history goes back much further, when it was a small, inconsequential fishing village. In 1376, Parameswara arrived after fleeing from his own invaded domain of Tumasek, later called Singapore. Parameswara proclaimed himself ruler of Malacca and proceeded to unite and mold the fishermen into a powerful nation, which by the end of the 15th century held undisputed claim over the entire southern portion of the Malay peninsula.

It was through Malacca that the Islam faith came to Malaysia. All Malays have been Muslims since the later part of the 15th century, when rich Moorish merchants from Pasai in Sumatra settled in Malacca. From here Islam spread by conversion and by force throughout the peninsula.

A Princess and a Magic Well

On a hill at the back of the town, weeds smother Chinese tombs left unattended by relatives for generations. Hills are auspicious burial grounds, according to the Chinese geomancer, for the mass of land blocks the winds of evil and offers the spirits of the ancestors a good view over their descendants. But on **Bukit China**, "China Hill," most names and dates have been eroded by the rains. What remains is an old, half-forgotten cemetery and the story of a Ming princess.

In ancient times, Malaya and China carried on a diplomatic war of wits which grew to be legendary. Around 1460, when Sultan Mansur Shah ruled Malacca, a Chinese ship sailed into port with special orders from the Son of Heaven. The entire interior of the ship was delicately pinned with gold needles, and the message sent to the Sultan read: "For every gold needle, I have a subject; if you could count their number, then you would know my power."

The Sultan was impressed, but not dismayed. He sent back a ship stuffed with bags of sago with the message: "If you can count the grains of sago on this ship you will have guessed the number of my subjects correctly, and you will know my power." The Chinese Emperor was so intrigued that he sent his daughter, Princess Hong Lim Poh, to marry the Sultan. She arrived with no less than 500 ladies-in-waiting, all of great beauty. The Sultan gave them "the hill without the town" as a private residence and promised that the land they occupied would never be taken away from them. To this day, Bukit China belongs to Malacca's Chinese community. Several of the graves there date back to the Ming Dynasty; they are among the oldest Chinese relics in Malaysia.

Princess Hong Lim Poh's followers built a well at the foot of the hill, whose waters soon became as legendary as her marriage contract. The Chinese say that after Admiral Cheng Ho drank from the well, its water attained an extraordinary purity. It never dried up, even during the most severe drought, and many believed that if a visitor drank from it he would return to Malacca before he died.

Now, the Perigi Rajah, or Sultan's Well, is protected by wire mesh. It has not dried up and its purity has entered history. Young Malaccan students of Chinese descent come to see the landmark and perhaps snap some pictures, but few tread the paths up the hill where their forefathers lie buried. Malacca is changing, leaving its secrets behind.

After leaving Malacca one could continue south to Johore and the tip of the Malay peninsula, lying on the doorstep to Singapore.

any of the settlers the Malacca ;ion are scendants of matran migrants.

y Malacca ntained relations imperial China, in the late 1400s Chinese munity of acca was granted for their own called to this Bukit China.

the green heart

Boating through swirling rapids, fishing for giant carp, shooting game with a camera, climbing mountains, watching birds, exploring caves, swimming placid river waters, going on safari through jungles 100 million years old, visiting Orang Asli settlements — and getting away from 20th-century traffic and pollution. Malaysia has what few countries in the world have — a great, undisturbed outdoor world waiting for discovery. With two-thirds of the country under jungle, where lush greenery begins at the edge of the sea and rises to high mountains, there is certain to be adventure.

Topping all jungle haunts is the **Taman Negara** that spreads over the northern interior of the Malay peninsula. Within this area around the mountain massif of Gunong Tahan, the highest peak in Peninsular Malaysia, there are countless limestone hills thickly covered with forests, fast running streams and an abundance of wildlife. Travel within the park is chiefly by water although visitors, should they choose to, may make a land trip inland from any of the posts on the Tembeling River with equipment, guides and porters supplied by the Park Service.

To discover the "green heart" of Malaysia our writer and photographer team made a lengthy expedition with the chief game warden and his rangers through the northern reaches of the National Park and floated on bamboo rafts down the Lebir River into Kelantan state. Much of the area was unexplored and known only to the Orang Asli Negritos who live there. They report ...

"We set out from Park Headquarters up the Tembeling in three longboats driven by 40 h.p. outboards. Each boat had a helmsman and a lookout, the latter standing on the bow with a long pole and guiding the boat through the rapids. The first night we camped on a sandbank at the tributary of the Sok River. Early the following morning we continued upstream. By afternoon we had traveled as far as we could by river. The boats turned back, leaving our ten-man expedition completely on its own. We had only one way to go now and that was to cross the unexplored jungles in search of the headwaters of the Lebir River, where we would build rafts and pole our way back to civilization.

Tapping the unlimited potential of Malaysia's outdoor world, a proud fisherman (our intrepid author Harold Stephens, left) shows off his main course for a campsite dinner.

The main difficulty of such an expedition is logistics. Clothing, first-aid kits, bedding, tents, food all add up and so no luxuries were permitted, for every gram of extra weight would slow us down. Our diet was the same as our guides': rice, dried vegetables, coffee, tinned sweetened milk. We had curry to flavor the rice, and fish from the streams provided protein.

Our three Negrito porter-guides carried the bulk of the supplies in hand-fashioned pandanus sacks with pencil-thin strips of rattan for shoulder straps. When we finally started off, they each carried a staggering load of 55 kilos.

The ability of Negritos to maneuver in the jungles is astonishing. Our first encounter after leaving the river was to scale a steep bank, slippery and muddy, with only thin roots for support. However, they ascended it with the ease of riding an escalator.

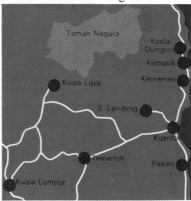

The first hour or two in the jungle are always the worst. Everything is magnified. Each shadow lurks like some terrifying, unseen demon. Each overhead branch holds a slimy creature ready to drop. Each turn brings you face to face with a monster of the deep. But this soon passes. You forget, when your clothes become wet from perspiration, when you are more concerned with a sure foothold than what might be there, when you are panting in desperation to keep up with the Negritos cutting the trail and

moving at almost a run.

There are things about the jungle that cannot be learned overnight. You look down to step over a tangled root and a thorny creeper knocks off your hat. You look up to cut away a vine and you trip over a log. And yet these guides (barefooted and swinging knives) move without ever faltering. Soon, a python sleeping on a branch does not alarm you; an elephant rushing through the reeds is just another passerby.

The curse of the jungle are the leeches. No one is immune to them. The Negritos' legs became reddened with blood, especially about the toes. We had our boots laced up, socks tucked into trousers, belts tight. A blotch of red appeared on our leg. A leech had gotten in. A little creature that an hour before was the size of a red ant was now fat as a golf ball.

The first night or two are the most difficult. The ground is hard and damp. But then when muscles tone up, when rice with a little curry is an epicurean delight, and when you can sleep on a log, the jungle takes on new dimensions of meaning.

The sounds of insects and birds are ever present. Gibbons call cryptically to one another. A muddy stream bed reveals that elephants had passed that morning. The Negritos scale trees and bring down ripe rambutans and other fruits. And there are fish. A cast with a spinner brings the evening meal.

The evenings, after tired bodies have bathed in the river and darkness closes in, are the most delightful. There is something intimate about the jungle then. The world is a simple sphere that encompasses the circle of light around the campfire. The light is like a cage, not sealing you in but keeping out the jungle.

Around the warming fire, back to the jungle, everyone sits. The game warden translates the tales our Negrito guides tell. They are great stories, fired with imagination. A rogue elephant that repeatedly des-

Our writer and photographer traveled the unexplored north part of the Natio Park, accompani by the game war and Negrito guid

You get used to python overhead and the elephant rushing by, but t leeches forever a curse.

190

troyed a *kampung*; a tiger that trailed Muda as he walked along a river, seeming to know that Muda had a spear and was prepared for him. Muda is the oldest of the Negritos. You ask him his last name. He looks abashed, then raps his chest and says, 'Muda.' He has no other name. You ask his age. He does not know. Is he married? He lives with two women. How many children? He has to count. Four. You begin to ask their ages, then realize that the concept of time has no meaning here. What is a year when there are no seasons. What is one day when it is like every other one. Life simply moves on.

Talk grows weary and then, singly or in pairs, everyone wanders back to his tent, mosquito nets fall into place, the fire dies and the noises of the forest become more intense. You lay there looking up through the open flaps of the tent at the sky of unhelpful stars. A shrill cry raises you to your elbows. All sounds stop. An animal has made a kill. Nothing more. Lazily, you drop down again. Soon you forget that an elephant trail runs through the camp. Your mind erases the tiger prints you saw in the sand. You no longer think of the jungle; you see it in visions. The stars, the fire, the stories, all melt together into one concept of a night unlike any other.

We learnt a lot from the Negritos. They pointed out fruit and wild berries which we could eat. They showed us game trails and knew almost to the hour when game had last passed. Every turned leaf, every bent twig, every disturbed vine had a meaning. They were unwritten signs in their jungle that are as clear as traffic signs on our city streets. And like city signs, they too had to be obeyed. Certain leaves we could not touch, certain mud holes we did not cross, certain shortcuts we had to avoid.

The days turned into a week. On our best day we could do perhaps 9 km. It seemed like twenty. When we followed game trails we moved faster, but most often we had to hack every centimeter of our way through the jungle. Then, what we feared might happen occurred: the monsoons started early. We saw elephants cross our trail but when we reached the spot where they had been, there were no tracks. At first the rains were refreshing. They kept us cool. But when they turned into a tropical downpour, in a time-worn jungle, things did happen. We were in a column descending a slope when a loud crashing sound brought us to a halt. It sounded like the roar of an avalanche. One hundred meters ahead a gigantic tree, perhaps 3 meters in diameter and 60 meters high, splintered in midair, as if struck by high explosives. The unbelievable might of nature. The sheer weight of the rain upon the overhead foliage became such a destructive force that mighty trees began to collapse around us. The trunks would splinter, and then bullet-like they would come shooting earthward, pulling other trees, interwoven with vines and climbers, with them. They gave off terrific explosions, sending debris and showers of rain and mist in every direction. We dropped packs and equipment and began running. But where? There were no openings. Suddenly ahead was light; there was sky. It was a river. We reached the safety of the Lebir River. When the rains stopped, we returned to retrieve our gear.

Now came the gigantic task of building four rafts. We felled bamboo from the forest, some of the pieces 10 meters long. These we brought to the river and lashed together with thin strips of rattan. Each raft consisted of nine logs and was about three-quarters of a meter wide. In the center we constructed a raised platform for our gear. Each man cut his own 4-meter-long pole. We shoved off, using the poles to avoid rocks and big trees which were floating downriver like ourselves. Then came the thrill of the first rapid. All stood gripping their poles. The current picked us up, the

night the world simple sphere by light of the npfire.

tropical npour broke ny softwood s, turning the st into an osion of wood debris.

Negritos shouted out a warning. White water was everywhere. In moments it was over. The gushing ended as suddenly as it started. Our rafts moved among the strange wreckage of the jungle in the slow motion of the stream. The sun revolved around us. Banks slipped by, new and yet unchanged. We stayed close to the bank to take full advantage of the swifter currents. Occasionally, the sky disappeared behind a vault of virgin forest.

We drifted round one bend and came face to face with Orang Asli Negritos — a man, his wife and a small child. His only clothing was a breech cloth. She was naked. They were traveling upriver on a three-log raft, laden with ripe fruit.

We wanted to buy several durians. Willingly the man handed them over.

We spent some time after that with other Negritos. Here truly were Rousseau's 'noble savages.' It was the French philosopher who wrote in the 18th century that the ills of civilization could be cured if man returned to his primitive state. Their secret, we learned, is one of adjustment to their environment. They have fears, certainly, but they know how to cope with them. There is nothing complicated about their existence. Life is simple. A man who goes into the forest takes his wife and child with him. They share pleasures, as well as problems.

The Orang Asli are not driven by ambition or obsessed with objectives. Happiness is measured by the amount of leisure it brings. The people of these quiet jungles do not crave excitement. We learned they have no craving for outside civilization. They could, if they wished, float downstream to a government settlement, and the Malaysian Bureau of Aboriginal Affairs would provide for them. But they lead their own lives and they are contented.

After ten days on the river we came to a grass house, and more houses a few kilometers later. Finally a settlement, then a town."

A jungle trip through the National Park is the closest anyone can come to the green heart of Malaysia, and conveniently it is flexible enough to range from a leisurely two days of fishing to a two-week tropical safari. Outboard motorboats of the National Park Service carry visitors the 120-odd km from Kuala Tembeling Halt on the Malayan Railway to the headquarters of the park at Kuala Tahan on the Tembeling River. Although the mail train "Golden Blowpipe" does not stop at Kuala Tembeling Halt, visitors who wish to alight there can do so if sufficient notice is given the station master in Kuala Lumpur or at Gemas. By pre-arrangement also, the south-bound train may be stopped to pick up visitors at Kuala Tembeling Halt for the return trip to Kuala Lumpur. There is now a small airstrip in the park for helicopters and light aircraft, but permission to land must first be sought from the park's offices in Kuala Lumpur.

Visitors can stay at the headquarters at **Kuala Tahan** in various accommodations that range from a luxury rest house to a youth hostel and tents. Western and local food is obtainable at the rest house. Outlying lodges are equipped with all the basic essentials but visitors must undertake their own cooking. Provisions can be bought at the local store.

Short jungle trips can be made to **Jenut Tahan** and **Jenut Tabing,** two salt licks just a short walk from the headquarters. Further afield but still in a day's walk, or a short boat trip away, are the high hides of **Belau** and **Kumbang.** Here hides have been built among the trees and fitted out so that an observer may remain there for a week without descending. Occasionally, a wide variety of animals visit these licks — elephant, wild buffalo, tapir, deer, wild pig and tiger. However, big game is more often heard than seen. For the less active, river trips are a relaxing way to spend

The Orang Asli se like Rousseau's noble savages, uncorrupted by th selfishness and ru of so-called "civilization."

The Malayan Railway goes fro Kuala Lumpur to Tembeling Halt, whence boats tak visitors to Natio Park headquarte

e park's rivers
d streams are
ll stocked for
cellent angling.

*ouacking for the
*ht in the heart of
* National Park.*

a morning or a day equipped with swimsuit, picnic lunch and a fishing rod.

The rivers of Taman Negara offer excellent fishing for the angler. But for the most successful fishing it is best to be further from the headquarters. It is a day trip up-river to **Lata Berkoh** or **Perkai** where Fishing Lodges are available for those that wish to linger. The rivers are usually clear and cold and well stocked with fish of the carp family. The *kelah* is the most sought after and can weigh as much as 7 kilos. The *sebaru*, a voracious predator, is the fish most frequently caught. It weighs up to 5 kilos or more. Any spinning rod and reel can be used — a light nylon line and either a fixed spool or ordinary spinning reel.

For those who wish to stay longer in the park, there are many more adventurous trips that can be undertaken still further up river and beyond the marked jungle trails for which it is required to take a guide. The climb to **Gunong Tahan**, W. Malaysia's highest peak at 7174' is an exciting nine days adventure trip.

Whatever the choice of activity in the park, binoculars are invaluable for spotting wildlife and particularly the multitude of beautiful birds; a powerful torch is essential equipment for a night spent in a hide, and a warm jacket a wise investment against chilly mornings. Taman Negara is closed between November 15th and January 15th because of the monsoon rains.

Enquiries about travel to the park should be directed to the Director General, Department of Wildlife and National Parks, Block K 20, Government Offices Complex, Jalan Duta, Kuala Lumpur. Telephone 941272 and 941466.

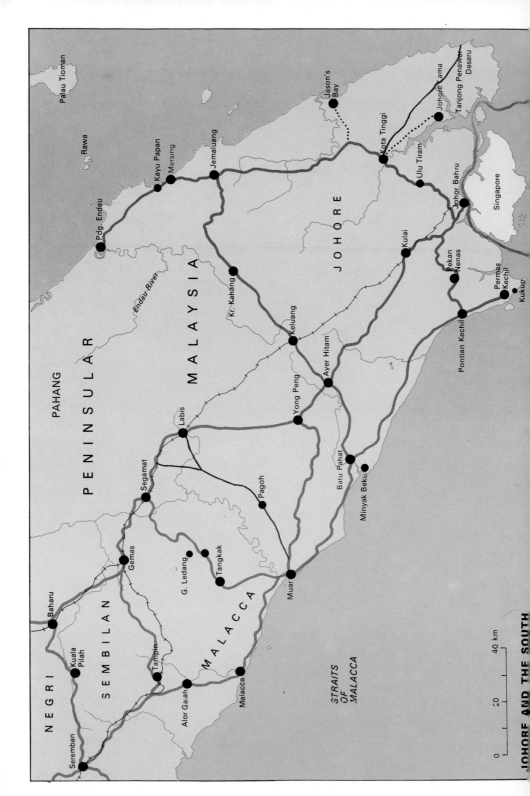

JOHORE AND THE SOUTH

Johore State occupies the entire southern tip of the Malay peninsula, and has many pineapple and oil-palm fields. Johore has over 1,000 km of good roads and just about every kilometer is serviced by Mercedes taxis. Its hotels and rest houses, if not luxurious, are conveniently located.

One can, for example, dine at a ramshackle restaurant on stilts that lures motorists to fight traffic and drive 80 km over pot-holed roads to feast on chili crabs. He can hire a fishing boat at Mersing to carry him to the many offshore islands, some the size of a city block and uninhabited. He can cruise down the historic Johore River to Johore Lama, one of the earliest capitals of the Malay Kingdom, or he can peer inside a camouflaged pillbox built before World War II.

There is plenty for the history

buff. Near Kota Tinggi were found beads from the Mediterranean, establishing the date of the earliest trade with the West at several centuries B.C. But Johore evolved its own identity only after the fall of the Malacca Sultanate to the Portuguese in the 16th century. Malacca's Sultan refused to capitulate and fled to Johore. Soon Johore was to emerge as a major power in the Malay archipelago. The Portuguese, seeing the Johore Sultanate as a dagger pointed at their throat, were determined to destroy it. In 1536 they sent an armada up the Johore River and sacked the existing capital at Johore Lama, but the Sultan merely moved his capital 30 km further upriver. Other attempts likewise failed to destroy Johore.

Although Johore today rings with a strong Malay culture — its people are known to speak the best

...usk descending on ...nosque in Muar ...ings a tranquillity ...ically Malaysian.

Malay in the peninsula and wear the *baju kurong*, the national dress, on everyday occasions—it also has an air of Western influence. History attributes this to Sultan Abu Bakar, who took over the reins of government when his father died in 1862.

Abu Bakar was educated in Singapore by English clergy. He spoke fluent English and came to know influential Europeans in the business world. It was during his rule that the foundations of modern Johore were laid. In 1866, he moved his capital to Johore Bahru and within a few years had transformed a humble fishing village and trading port into Malaya's newest city and one of its largest. He took a keen interest in planning the capital, particularly the Istana. Unlike many of the Moorish-style palaces throughout the country, the Istana was furnished with the impeccable taste of an Englishman.

Although Abu Bakar established close ties with Britain—he was the first Malay ruler to visit England and was a personal friend of Queen Victoria—he never accepted a British Resident. In 1868, to show his independence, he took the title of Maharaja and went on to regain the land between the Muar River and Malacca, and to extend the borders of his state from the Indian Ocean to the South China Sea. A treaty with Britain in 1885 allowed British control over Johore's external affairs, but not internal. Sultan Abu Bakar's power remained steadfast, and because of it Johore is now a rich state.

With its relatively low cost of land and ready labor, Johore is beginning to make impressive gains in luring foreign industry and tourism to its region. Several industrial estates

Early Johore State resisted encroachment by foreign powers, gaining an identity of its own when Malacca fell to the Portuguese in the 1600s.

Gunung Ledang n Sagil on the w southi is the legend abode of a fa

have been established, plans are underway to build new luxury hotels on the virgin east coast beaches and designs are in progress for an international airport capable of handling jumbo jets.

Sulphur Springs and Sultans' Tombs

Johore's west coast road zips through dozens of small towns and *kampungs*. En route to Muar, approaching from Malacca, a detour on the road to Segamat leads to some beautiful natural waterfalls cascading 2,500 metres down the rocks to the crystal clear pools below. Picturesque and unspoiled, the **Sahil** waterfalls have no tourist facilities. Weary travelers may want to refresh themselves before they reach Muar at the hot sulphur springs of **Sungei Kesang**, three miles off the main road. Simple changing rooms are provided. At Pagoh, twenty-six km from **Muar**, there is an old fort containing the tombs of two Malacca sultans. Situated atop a small rise, it was constructed to protect the sultans from attack by pirates. Nearby, in the graveyard at **Kampung Parit Pechah,** lie ninety-nine tombstones, marking the graves of an entire village which was wiped out by a single spear about 500 years ago. According to legend it all happened at a wedding party. The spear was tossed by a jealous lover into the chest of the bridegroom, removed and tossed again, eventually also killing the bride and all the wedding guests.

Batu Pahat, notorious for its floods at high tides, is a conference centre for Johore. There is a small beach and a legendary well nearby at Minyak Beku. Nineteen km south of Pontian Kechil, which has a comfortable Rest House, the road ends at Kukup on the southern tip of the peninsula.

Pots and Chili Crabs

You can't miss the **Aw Potteries** situated as they are on the main trunk road to **Ayer Hitam**, 93 km from Johore Bahru or 32 km from Batu Pahat, and proclaimed by two colossal earthenware genii. The Menangkabau showroom displays all sorts of pottery in the distinctive Aw glazes. Behind the showroom is the studio itself where you can watch craftsmen at work through every stage of the process. The most spectacular feature is the immense snake kiln. Fifty-three yards long, the brick-built kiln of traditional Chinese design, is the very womb of the potteries giving birth regularly and unprotestingly to some 2,000 individual pieces of pottery at each firing. Mr. Aw Eng Kwang, the founder, came from China in 1940 finally settling in Kampong Machap where there is an abundant supply of clay and firing wood. From a simple beginning manufacturing latex cups and flower pots, the Aw family, representing four generations of potters, have built up a thriving business of international repute.

The west coast road terminates at **Kukup**. Built on stilts, the houses are linked to one another by plank walks and look as though they might topple into the sea. Late afternoon is the ideal time to arrive, when the sun is low over the sea and the evening breezes begin. But it is not to watch the setting sun that people go to Kukup. It is to eat chili crab. Kukup, with its unpretentious clapboard restaurants, is famous for its spicy chili crab. The restaurants do not have fancy decor, not even walls. But they do have atmosphere, and great food.

Along a railing facing the sea in one restaurant is a huge square net, lowered and raised by an ancient, wooden crank. Boys wind the net up from the sea and scoop out the daily menu — eels, fish, crabs, lobsters. Chili crabs, the speciality, are eaten with fingers; it is messy, but delicious. Choose your own style of cooking: chili prawns, steamed fish, sweet-and-sour fish, chili mussels. The food is guaranteed to be fresh!

Like a Stage Curtain

Johore Bahru is the mirror of everything that is Malaysia. The approach from Singapore across the causeway is no subtle introduction to the vast, mysterious and partly unknown country beyond. A newcomer's arrival to Johore Bahru comes suddenly, like a stage curtain opening. From the old tower dominating the skyline and shoreline there is a magnificent view of the Malaysian mainland, Singapore and the Indonesian islands. Looking west from this vantage point you can see the **Istana Gardens** enclosing the sultan's palace. Adjoining these gardens, which include a replica of a Japanese tea house, is the famous **Johore Zoo**. It was once the sultan's private animal sanctuary but since 1962 it has been opened to the public.

The **Istana Besar** — the sultan's palace — is open to visitors between 9:00 a.m. and 12:00 noon, except on Fridays and public holidays. However, prior arrangement should be made with the Controller, Royal Household, Istana Besar, Johore Bahru. The palace is not to be confused with **Bukit Serene**, the sultan's private residence. Perched on high ground overlooking the river, its 32-meter **Tower** is a city landmark. Another landmark standing high on a hill overlooking the Johore Straits is the **Abu Bakar Mosque**. The spacious building, with marble colonnade lining the interior, can accommodate 2,000 worshipers.

Johore Bahru is connected to Singapore by a causeway carrying vehicular traffic and a railroad. Its proximity to Singapore makes it a gateway for urban vacationers at the

At Kukup, beside sheltered waters, food is guaranteed fresh.

...om the old tower ... Bukit Serene, a ...norama of Johore ...hru unfolds below.

...hore Bahru is ...pically Malaysian, ...ith gardens, a zoo, ...e sultan's palace ...d residence, and ...osques.

weekend. Then, traffic slows down to a snail's pace. Timber lorries, tourist buses, outstation taxis, motor scooters and Singaporeans escaping city life in their Holdens and Mercedes vie for positions at the immigration gates. Whether it be to see an X-rated film banned in Singapore, to find a sandy beach, or to try the roulette wheels at Genting Highlands, the crowds flocking from Singapore to Malaysia create traffic jams equal to those found on any highway connecting a busy metropolis with its green lungs.

An interesting introduction to Malaysia's wealth awaits you at **Ulu Tiram Estate**, which is 26 km from Johore Bahru. Here you will see rubber trees being tapped and the various processes which the latex passes through before it is ready for export as either sheet or crepe rubber. The

oil palm is also cultivated here and you may visit the estate factory and observe how the oil is extracted from the fruit for subsequent refinings which provide the base for soap, margarine and cosmetics.

Spectacle for the Dinner Guest

Kota Tinggi is a small, quiet town with a loud splash. Fifteen km northeast of the town center are the famous Kota Tinggi Waterfalls which thunder down 36 meters to the polished rocks below. Swimming is permitted to anyone having enough courage to plunge into icy waters. Ten well-furnished Swiss-type chalets face the falls, inviting visitors to spend the night. These have cooking facilities with utensils, gas range and refrigerator. An open-front restaurant serves both Chinese and European dishes.

In the evening the falls are gaily illuminated, making a lively, dancing spectacle for the dinner guests.

Three km beyond Kota Tinggi, at **Kampung Makam**, is the old Royal Mausoleum where past sultans of Johore were interred. Boats can be hired in Kota Tinggi for a cruise along the historical Johore River. About 20 km downriver is **Johore Lama**, once the state capital and now the site of archaeological excavations. Under restoration is **Kota Batu**, one of the oldest forts in Malaysia. It stands at the crest of a steep, rocky promontory and commands a clear view up- and downstream. For 400 years the cannons have remained in their embrasures, forgotten, overgrown by the jungle. A few cannon balls still remain embedded in the stone walls. If you wish to stay in Kota Tinggi to explore further, Bunga Raya is a friendly hotel.

Suntans on the South China Sea

Looking for a spot in the sun? 54 km from Kota Tinggi there is a glorious twenty-five km stretch of golden beach on the edge of the South China Sea. The sea is generally clear and calm but during the monsoon months in December and January the waves tumble down the beach in a froth of crashing surf. The excellent road terminates at Tanjong Penawar at a holiday resort called **Desaru**. Here you can rent beach chalets, some equipped with cooking facilities for families. There are ponies to ride, canoes to row and tennis courts for the energetic. There is also a restaurant and at weekends hawker stalls on the usually quiet beach cater to the influx of guests and day trippers. Plans are afoot for

A guard stands before the sultan's palace, Istana Besar, in Johore Bahru (left). Chilly waters cascade down Kota Tinggi's waterfall (facing page).

this stretch of beach. Three new hotels are going up in the next few years and an 18-hole golf course.

At one time **Jason's Bay,** or Telok Mahkota as it is now signposted at the turnoff from the Mersing road 13 km from Kota Tinggi, was once the most popular of Johore's beaches. But now the long sandy beach has silted up and there are mud flats at low tide. There are no facilities at the beach but those who wish to get away from it all will find their solitude interrupted only by sea birds, sandflies, and no more than an occasional visitor.

In Search of Mythical Islands

Mersing, situated on the right bank of the mouth of Mersing River, is a quiet, pleasant town, except for the river mouth. Here is a large, bustling fishing fleet and all the excitement one associates with a fishing port. Accommodation is available in a splendid Government Rest House sitting on a bluff above the sea and separated from it by a simple nine-hole golf course. There are also several simple Chinese hotels, notably the Mersing Hotel with an excellent restaurant. If you are in Mersing around the first of May don't miss the annual festival at **Kayu Papan** where you may be lucky to see the **Kudang Kepang,** a trance dance seldom seen outside Johore.

Mersing is the setting off point for a group of sixty-four idyllic volcanic islands in the South China Sea. One of these, **Pulau Tioman,** was mentioned 2,000 years ago in what was perhaps the first guide to Malaysia. Arab traders then made note in their "sailing directions" that Tioman, lying some 56 km off the east coast

of the Malay peninsula, offered good anchorage and a freshwater spring for filling their casks. Centuries thereafter, the twin peaks called "Ass's Ears" at the southern tip of the island guided ships at sea. Ming pottery found in caves reveals that early Chinese traders also made Tioman a port-of-call.

Gone are the Arab and Chinese traders, their place now taken by lotus-eating sybarites. They are fortunate in that Tioman, 20 km long and 12 km wide and devoid of vehicular traffic, has the very pleasant **Merlin Hotel**. In addition to normal rooms, the hotel offers dormitory accommodation at reasonable prices. However, this will interest groups only because if an individual arrives and there is nobody in the dormitory he must pay for all the beds. The hotel is well provided with scuba and fishing equipment and a glass-bottomed boat: the corals are beautiful and fishing excellent. The hotel launch leaves Mersing daily and takes two and a half hours to reach the island. Alternatively, the crossing may be made in twenty minutes by plane from Mersing. Tioman is everybody's dream of a tropical island. When Hollywood was looking for a mythical island to photograph in "South Pacific," it chose lovely Tioman to portray the legendary Bali Hai. There is a Government Rest House on the island and permission to stay there can be obtained from the District Officer in Rompin.

Smaller, but just as beautiful as Tioman, is **Pulau Rawa**. Accommodation here, which consists of bungalows and chalets (shared facilities in both cases) is simpler than on Tioman. Scuba-diving equipment is available.

Mersing is the starting point for junkets to sixty-fc islands just off the coast.

Pulau Rawa island of Tioman, setting the movie South Pacific.

The hotel launch leaves Mersing at high tide each day for the sixty-minute, 16-km journey to the island.

Another interesting island is **Sibu**, the "Island of Perilous Passage," inhabited by aborigines.

The Endau River: Known to Few

Imagine your campsite on a secluded sandbank of the Endau River. A log fire burns, creating a circle of light in the dense foliage. Apart from the din of insects, an occasional cry from the forest disrupts the silence, reminding you that across the river on the opposite bank are footprints of tigers and rhinos. You recall being awakened that morning by the trumpeting of an elephant. You fought a dozen rapids to reach your present camp. But it was worth

gotiating rapids the Endau River ere an angler ds the big ones.

it. When you cleared the last rapid, Bujong, your Orang Asli guide, storyteller and jungle master, handed you a fishing rod. You cast into waters where seldom, if ever, had a spinner been cast. A carp weighing 15 kilos swam cautiously in the deep shadows of a log and in a lightning jolt took your bait. Bujong cooked your evening meal over an open fire.

No river in Asia is more remote and yet so close as the Endau, which separates the states of Johore and Pahang — mangrove swamps and mud flats at the lower reaches, Orang Asli settlements farther up, and the first rapids which often deter the casual visitor. But beyond are the headwaters and a beauty known to few men. For guides and information check with the Tourist Information Center in Mersing or Johore Bahru.

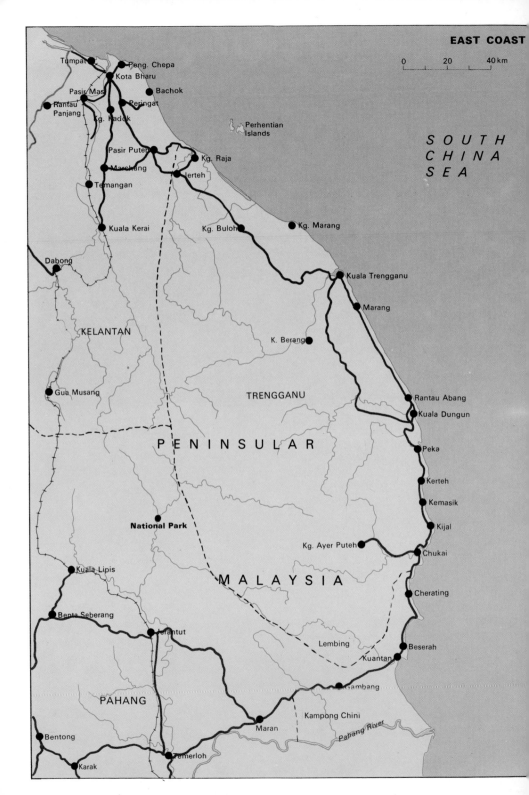

0   20   40 km

SOUTH
CHINA
SEA

Tumpat

Peng. Chepa

Kota Bharu

Pasir Mas   Bachok

Beringat

Rantau
Panjang

Kg. Kadok

Perhentian
Islands

Pasir Puteh   Kg. Raja

Marchang   Jerteh

Temangan

Kuala Kerai   Kg. Buloh   Kg. Marang

Dabong

Kuala Trengganu

KELANTAN   Marang

K. Berang

TRENGGANU   Rantau Abang

Kuala Dungun

P E N I N S U L A R   Peka

Kerteh

Gua Musang   Kemasik

Kijal

National Park

Kg. Ayer Puteh   Chukai

Kuala Lipis   M A L A Y S I A

Cherating

Benta Seberang

Jerantut   Lembing

Beserah

Kuantan

Gambang

PAHANG   Kampong Chini

Bentong   Maran   *Pahang River*

Karak   Temerloh

208

far from the madding crowd

To discover the soul of Malaysia, one should visit the East Coast. Bordered by Thailand on the north, isolated from the west by a chain of rugged mountains and separated from the south by swamps and rivers, the East Coast has retained her own identity through the ages. Her relaxed villages and *kampungs*, where leisure nurtured her arts, have survived more or less unchanged. The Sultan of Johore has a birthday celebration, and the dancers are imported from Kota Bharu. The University of Malaya puts on a cultural show and they recruit the *Mak Yong* actors from Kelantan. Foreign dignitaries are being entertained and the *Wayang Kulit* shadow play comes from Trengganu.

The East Coast's exquisite silver artisans, her cloth weavers and batik makers are renowned throughout the country. And where else but on the East Coast can you see seasoned farmers competing in top spinning and kite flying and watch $3\frac{1}{2}$-meter-long, 750-kilo turtles lay their eggs on a particular stretch of beach.

Peaceful, timeless fishing villages, palms bending out over a blue sea, colorfully painted fishing boats pulled up on the shore waiting for the tide to carry them to their fishing grounds, islands floating upon an unattainable horizon — these are the scenes on the quieter side of the Malay peninsula.

The East Coast is unsophisticated in the most natural sense of the word. Even the advent of the oil industry centered at Kuala Trengganu has done little to change the gentle, traditional atmosphere. Anyone looking for a highly-geared "tourist paradise" will be disappointed. Although all visitors are welcomed, they are still regarded as being slightly strange.

Not so many years ago the East Coast, which embraces the states of Kelantan, Trengganu, Pahang and

Elegant prahus, *their bows pointed high, await the fishing season on Peninsular Malaysia's East Coast (previous pages).*

Johore, was without road. Travel between ports was mainly by boat. Now a scenic road links Kota Bharu in the far north to Kuantan and Johore Bahru in the south — a distance of 733 km. Anyone who travels the road takes away memories of beauty.

It is advisable not to visit the East Coast during the monsoon season, from November to January. December is normally the wettest month. During this time rivers may overflow their banks, making the drive quite difficult.

Ordinarily, it is possible to leave Kuala Lumpur in the morning by taxi or private car and be in Kuantan for lunch. The road from Kuala Lumpur winds up and through Genting Pass and cuts across the peninsula to Kuantan. Visitors coming from Singapore and Johore Bahru travel the East Coast road via Mersing on the coast, occasionally catching glimpses of the blue sea and empty beaches.

Halfway between Kuala Lumpur and Kuantan is the town of **Temerloh**. It has several pleasant Chinese hotels and a Government Rest House. It is a good stopover for a meal or a night's lodging. Temerloh lies on the mighty Pahang River and on Sundays *kampung* folk from up- and downriver come to town to sell coconuts, bananas, yams, bamboo shoots and other produce. From Temerloh it is possible to take a river trip to Pekan, the royal capital of Pahang. The boat stops at villages established in ancient days when traders from China bartered for gold and tin. Enquire for details at the Temerloh Rest House.

For those who travel north up the coast and do not want to return by the same route, there is a scenic circle route through the National Park. From Kota Bharu in the extreme north, to the village of Kuala Krai. Here you can board a passenger train together with your car (if you have given several weeks' notice in advance) and make the rest of the journey by rail to Kuala Lipis or all points south as far as Johore Bahru.

Another highlight of the East Coast is a visit to any one of the many lonely offshore islands. Thirty-two km off Dungun lies lovely **Pulau Tenggol**. It has a lonely, white sand beach shaded by jungle trees. Good coral gazing can be had at **Pulau Kapas**, an hour's boat-ride from Kuala Trengganu; of all the islands up north, it is the nearest to the coast. The two most charming island groups are **Perhentian** and **Redang** which can be reached by launch from Kuala Besut or Kuala Trengganu. On each island there is a fishing village run by a headman. Fine coral reefs fringe the islands, and the beaches are long and empty except during the fishing and turtle seasons. Should you wish to linger, obtain permission from Jerteh District Office to stay at the Rest House on Pulau Perhentian.

On all these islands shells are numerous and interesting, the scorpion, the great tiger cowrie and the large turban shell being among the most attractive. No need to fear giant clams: they are highly sensitive to light and close up at the shadow of a finger above them. The large, black, prickly sea-urchins, which the Malays call *mata bulu* or "furry eyes," are to be avoided as their spines inflict painful wounds if broken off in one's foot. But it is easy to keep clear of them when equipped with goggles, as one always should be when exploring the reefs.

The East Coast is a place to explore. Do not hesitate to travel off the beaten track to a small fishing village. A friendly gesture will be the return of a smile, or perhaps an invitation to tour the village where the soothing rhythms of Malay life have endured

The more traditio relaxed atmosphe invites leaving the beaten path to explore back road

A small typical Malay village along the coast ne Kuantan.

210

for centuries. Only then, does one come to know the soul of Malaysia.

Islam, Royalty and Polo

Immediately before reaching **Pekan** the road north turns sharply left. The traveler is advised to ignore this and to drive straight ahead on the road which parallels the river. The Pahang River, the longest in Malaysia, is gentle and sylvan at this point and with its Chris-craft and houseboats reminds one of the Thames at Henley rather than the tropics of Southeast Asia.

Pekan was the original capital of Pahang and is still a royal town, being the residence of the Sultan of Pahang who is the present Yang di-Pertuan Agong (King) of Malaysia. (This position rotates among the nine sultans, with an election every five years.) In the town center, separated only by a new mausoleum, are two handsome, white marble mosques with a riot of golden domes. One of the mosques is newly built and attests to the vitality of Islam in this part of the country — and also to the population boom. Further on is the sultan's Istana (palace) and the enormous polo ground which when not being used for that sport provides what must be the world's flattest golf course.

Bustling, yet in a Trance

Forty-four km north of Pekan is **Kuantan**, the capital of Pahang and its commercial center. There is not much here to detain the visitor unless it be the handsome new stadium, a pleasant children's playground alongside the Kuantan River or the 1 km of river esplanade where

e East Coast has etches of bright m-tree-lined stline.

there are some good eating stalls serving Muslim food. However, there are lots to see and do around Kuantan.

All kinds of accommodation are available in Kuantan but most visitors will prefer to stay at the beach. Drive through town for 3 km and a crossroads is reached at the corner of which is a small villa belonging to the sultan. You may now drive straight on for a further 1 km to the splendid beach of **Telok Chempedak** where there is the very pleasant Merlin Hotel, the Kuantan Hyatt and other less expensive accommodations. Alternatively, turn right and after 1 km the Government Rest House is reached. This chengai and tiled building is one of Malaysia's finest Rest Houses and is a far cry from the days when travelers showered with a dipper in a Shanghai jar and kept cool with a ceiling punkah fan. It has hot tubs and showers, piped-in music and a beautiful beach that is sheltered by a sandbar and is ideal for children. Alongside it are the clubhouse of a sporting eighteen-hole golf course and a splendid 50 by 30 meter public swimming pool. About 200 metres away is an excellent children's playground.

The Tourist Bureau will make arrangements — although it may take two or three days — for performances of *Silat* (see page 78), *Wayang Kulit* (see page 83) and of two local dances — *Mak Yong* and *Rodat*. The latter is a traditional fishermen's dance in which hand movements feature prominently. *Mak Yong* is a remarkable trance dance in which one of the villagers clutches a bunch of betel nut flowers and is lulled into a trance by his fellows chanting a song, inviting the spirits of seven princesses to cast a spell upon the dancer. This forces him to dance the steps and movements of their choice. At the conclusion of the chanting the dancer collapses and so tightly does he clutch his bouquet that it takes half a dozen men to pull it from him.

Naturally, the best time to see

Silat (see page 78), Wayang Kulit (see page 83)

these happenings is during a festival. The alternative is to have the Tourist Bureau hire an entire village to stage a festival. The charges are moderate if divided among several patrons.

Kuantan and its surroundings are noted for authentic craftsmanship — wood carving, brocade, *batek* and weaving. Places where handicrafts are made or the arts performed are marked by a board with green, yellow and red circles and a ten-point red star. However, most of the signs are dilapidated and should not be taken too seriously. The **Brocade Weaving Center** at **Selamat** village (part of Kuantan town), where silk sarongs are handwoven with intricate designs in gold and silver, and one of the block printing shops on Jalan Selamat, which uses primitive methods in preparing designs, can readily be visited. There is also a **Batek Center** at **Beserah**, a few miles north of Kuantan.

Side Trips from Kuantan: A Second Loch Ness Monster?

Some excellent side trips can be made from Kuantan. One unusual journey is to **Lake Chini**, actually a conglomerate of twelve connecting bodies of water. The lake is large and, from June to September, is covered by a brilliant carpet of red and white lotuses which contrast sharply with the surrounding green hills. Legend tells of a sunken city beneath the lake and of a Loch Ness type monster inhabiting the deep. The Orang Asli, who live along the shores of the lake and who may be visited, believe in the latter and some British officials claim to have actually seen a mysterious beast swimming in the lake.

To reach the lake, travel along the Kuantan-Temerloh highway as far as the 56-km stone. Then, bear sharp left. The road soon deteriorates and becomes little more than a rough track, although it can still be driven over. It ends at the 27-km stone at Kampung Tasek Chini where you can hire a boatman and guide. The safari

Kuantan is well known as a cente of Malaysian handicrafts. The Tourist Bureau ca schedule performances of *Silat* and *Wayang Kulit*.

Nearby Kuantan Lake Chini reputedly contair monster; but it certainly hosts m fish.

starts by crossing the wide, placid Pahang River. The boatman expertly navigates his fragile wooden sampan past rocks and fallen trees, beneath a canopy of 30-meter-high plants covered with moss and vines. Your companions will be many of Malaysia's 900 species of butterflies and the occasional kingfisher. Gradually, the river widens and you are in the lake. If fortune shines, there will be sea-eagles overhead and baboons on the shore.

The entire trip can readily be done in one day but for those who wish to linger and enjoy the superb fishing — 5-kilo bites are but nothing — camping equipment and food should be taken along.

Another interesting side trip is northwest in the direction of Sungei Lembing. At about the 24-km stone a dirt track points to the north, through dusky rubber estates and lush green oil palm plantations.

A cliff of limestone rises up without warning: it is just there. When you step out from your car and look upwards, there seems to be no top, but far above is a ledge and a railing. Chances are a monk has heard you coming. He will be leaning over the railing, pointing to a rickety stairway. You will not expect to find what you do.

With effort you reach the ledge. The monk, a Thai, introduces himself — Than Acharn Sakatapunya. Ten years ago he came to Pahang and saw the mountain. He scaled the cliffs and discovered a huge cavern deep within. He petitioned the sultan and received permission to build a Buddhist shrine in the cavern now known as the Charah Cave. For many years he labored, carrying supplies and building

stretch of sandy ach near Pekan.

materials up the steep cliff. If you wish to see the shrine he will guide you up another set of rail stairs to the cave's entrance. It is like a spook show with Oriental overtones. The path leads downward. It is slippery; walking leads downward. It is slippery; walking is difficult. It takes a while for your eyes to adjust to the darkness. Suddenly the monk stops and points upward. Unbelievable! It is not a cave but a cathedral. Thin shafts of light filter down through cracks hundreds of meters above. In the half light distances are deceptive. Water drips somewhere in the darkness. Bats flutter away. The monk starts a generator for lights and leads you to a second cave, almost as big as the first. Here is his life's work, a giant statue of the Sleeping Buddha, measuring 9 meters long. There are more caves, more exploring to do. If you wish, the monk will arrange for a guide. He also accepts donations from visitors.

If you continue driving on the same road to Sungei Lembing, and if you have made prior arrangements with the Manager of Pahang Consolidated Ltd, you can tour the world's second largest and deepest tin mine. Tin mines, however, can be dangerous and most supervisors are hesitant to allow visitors on the premises and will certainly not allow them underground. Travelers must obtain special permission in advance before they are allowed a closeup view of Malaysia's third most valuable export.

The Road North: Seaside Chalets and Working Monkeys

For 50 Malaysian cents a young boy will scamper up a coconut tree

In a vaulted cave near Kuantan, a Thai monk has dedicated his life building a sanctu with a giant carvi of a sleeping Buddha.

Cave near Kemas. on the East Coast which once may h been a pirate's lai

e route
ntinuing north
ong the East Coast
sses pleasant
aches, offshore
ands, and
mfortable
commodations.

and bring down fresh coconuts, special delivery. For about ten times that sum, his father will command a long-tailed monkey to scamper up the same tree and, according to the instructions it is given, throw down small or large, green or ripe coconuts. In either case the drink is cool and refreshing. All along the road are desolate beaches inviting picnics and swims in the South China Sea. For those inclined to linger, accommodation is available in three motels, all situated on the beach.

The **Twin Island Motel** at the 37-km stone has twelve pleasant rooms in the main building and ten chalets. Four km north is the **Titik Inn**, a welcome retreat, owned and operated by a bearded Englishman who is married to a lovely Malay princess, Tunku Zarah. Here are sixteen chalets spread out among 25 hectares of trees, green lawns and a profusion of flowers. Music is provided by the myriad birds. Last year, the Titik Inn opened twenty minichalets, a communal kitchen and a barbecue range for the budget traveler. It is most pleasant to spend the evening discussing Malay life with Brian, who came to the country more than twenty years ago and is a storehouse about Malaysia.

A mere 800 meters offshore and readily reached from both the Twin Island Motel and the Titik Inn is the delightful, uninhabited tropical islet of **Pulau Ular** which is ideal for an afternoon picnic. The name means Snake Island but have no fear — there are no snakes on Pulau Ular.

At the 46-km stone is the large **Chendor Motel** which offers a wide variety of air-conditioned and non-air-conditioned chalets and dormitory accommodation. It is a favorite spot for turtle watchers (see page 216).

Immediately before Chendor Motel is **Cherating** village whose inhabitants are accustomed to having travelers stay with them, so here is your opportunity to live like a Malay. At the other extreme, Club Med-

iterrane, an international chain of holiday villages famed for its beautiful and out-of-the-way locations, has chosen Cherating for the site of its new hotel. On occasion, 2 to 3 meter-long crocodiles are seen in the nearby Cherating River.

Crossing the border into Trengganu, the road continues north through the fishing village of Kemasik and follows the sea to Kampung Paka. There is little traffic. Waves break along the sandy beaches. Inland there are rice fields where imaginative farmers have animated the landscape with lifelike scarecrows, some dressed in regal splendor. At Paka, the road leads over a bridge, offering a striking view of the village nestled on the bank of the Paka River. The road now turns inward for the last few kilometers to Dungun.

Kuala Dungun, a dreamy little seaside town and port, was once an outlet for the state's great ore mining industry at Bukit Besi. But most of the mines have closed down and once again the town has reverted to its ancient trade of fishing. Three miles north of Dungun is the new government-developed **Tanjong Jara Beach Hotel**. Initial planning includes first-class accommodation and cuisine, a natural swimming lagoon and facilities for water sports.

From Tanjong Jara the road follows the sea along a 65-km stretch of exquisite shoreline. It is dotted with houses and willowy casuarina trees, which the Malays say grow only near the sound of the surf. During the months of good weather the houses are on the east side of the road near the beach, since the folk are fishermen. However, during monsoons the fishermen carry their houses farther inland. Pulled high up the beach are the elegantly designed *prahu*s with their bows pointing upward to form a peak. Fishing nets hang to dry on trees. Swimming is excellent and one can stop almost any place en route and take a plunge.

Turtle Watching:
A Controversial Subject

A popular entertainment on the East Coast is turtle watching. On a stretch of beach 35 to 50 km north of Kuantan, all seven known species of turtles struggle ashore, lay their eggs in the sand and then depart, never to see their young. If the eggs survive the attacks of predators, they will hatch after six to eight weeks, depending on the species.

There can be no doubt that the star of this attraction is the giant leatherback turtle and, like any great performer — it may be the largest reptile in the world — it is determined not to be upstaged. Although on occasion they do put in an appearance at Chendor Beach, leatherbacks are best seen at the turtle watchers' Mecca. At **Rantau Abang**, 160 km north of Kuantan and 56 km south of Trengganu, giant leatherbacks return to lay their eggs year after year, along the same 32-km stretch of desolate beach. Seldom do other species use Rantau Abang for their accouchement. There is a new **Visitors' Center** at Rantau Abang where you may rent self-contained wooden chalets and visit the turtle museum.

The leatherback grows, it is claimed, to a length of three and a half meters and may weigh up to 750 kilos. Like the other species, it lays its eggs from May through September, the last two weeks of August being the peak of the laying season. During these months visitors come from the world over to await the turtles. The best time to see them is at night, especially at high tide. All that is needed is a flash lamp and patience. Industrious village folk at

Although their eggs are coveted as a delicacy, leatherback turtles are not yet an endangered species, because of preservation measures taken by the Department of Fisheries.

Turtles come ashore at Rantau Abang, near Dungun, to lay their eggs before returning to the life-waters of the s

216

Rantau Abang have built shelters along the beach in which travelers can pass the night dozing on a simple bed or drinking coffee. Youngsters with flash lamps search the sands and at the first sighting of a turtle give the signal.

The subject of turtle watching is controversial. Observers are often appalled by the way local people gather up the eggs, ride on the backs of the already straining turtles, flash lights in their eyes and even molest them. It might appear that the magnificent leatherbacks are on the road to extinction, since turtle eggs bring good prices at the marketplace. But a short walk down the beach during daylight would prove otherwise. Here members of the Department of Fisheries keep close tabs on turtles and record their habits and migrations across the seas. Even more

important is their systematic collection of eggs.

A great leatherback usually lays about a hundred eggs in a large hole it digs in the sand with its rear flippers. The gestation period for the eggs is fifty-four days. Danger to unprotected eggs during gestation comes not so much from man as from certain predators, such as crabs and various insects. Even more critical is the period after the eggs are hatched when young turtles must make their way to the sea, usually across several hundred meters of open, hostile beach. Many fall prey to the flocks of birds circling overhead. When the young turtles hatch, they crawl to the surface. Each morning before dawn inspectors collect and release them in the sea. Only after some 40,000 young have returned to the sea each year are people allowed to collect the eggs.

ahus at a fishing
¹lage near Kuala
¹ngun.

Leatherbacks have been sighted in waters as far from Malaysia as the Atlantic Ocean, yet the huge turtles return to lay their egg only on this one stretch of beach. To watch their laborious and brief sojourn on land is reason enough to visit the East Coast.

Setting Its Own Pace

Time seems to have slipped past **Kuala Trengganu**. There are no historical sites or modernistic "wonders," but the city does have certain charms that set it apart from contemporary worries. It is a relaxed town, no place for people in a hurry, typified by the fact that there are no town taxis - only trishaws. Near the beach, just outside town, is the nine-hole **Batu Burok Golf Course,** Malaysia's oldest golf course which is free.

The pulse of Kuala Trengganu is felt in the **Central Market** alongside the river in the early morning when fishermen bring in their catch. They come directly to the market with their boats and soon the scene is alive with heated haggling over prices. The market is a modern concrete building with fresh food stalls downstairs in the courtyard and general merchandise shops on the first floor.

The main thoroughfare through town is **Jalan Bandar,** a narrow, congested, crescent-shaped street. The architecture of some buildings dates back ten generations when Trengganu was an independent sultanate. Shopping is good and inexpensive. Foreigners seldom stop to buy and you may find your presence a local novelty. "From where do you come?" you are asked time and time again. The MARA Center in town will assist travelers who want to see any

The market at Kuala Trengganu.

uala Trengganu is
quiet town
thout taxis; but it
asts Malaysia's
dest golf course.

of the cottage industries at work. Good buys in batik from the Trengganu area can be had at the center, which has on display many of the state's arts and crafts.

Around the corner from the Central Market is the **Istana Mazia**, a little Malay *kampung* which looks as if it had been lifted out of the 19th century—intact. Indeed, the *kampung*, in which some members of the royal family reside, is from that period. It is a cluster of wooden pavilions with high, tapering roofs and hand-carved windows. Each window is a wood carving, some with ornately entwining patterns which form Koranic inscriptions, others with swirling, free-flowing designs which make the shadows dance. One building has been carefully dismantled and rebuilt board by board on the outskirts of the town—4 km before entering Trengganu from the south —opposite the sultan's new palace.

For those who wish to go out and do things there are a number of interesting side trips from Trengganu. For M$10 an hour you can hire a boat to cruise along the island-studded estuary of the Trengganu River and get a close look at typical Malay villages. Arrangements can be made with the boatmen near the out-station taxi-stand. **Pulau Duyung**, immediately opposite the boat-landing, is the largest island in the estuary. It is renowned for its shipbuilding. Those interested in boats will be fascinated by the old techniques still in use. The *Bedor*, a unique junk with fore- and main-mast and bowsprit, was built here. Further upriver the fishing is excellent and 10-kilo bites are not uncommon.

Boats can also be rented to the offshore islands of Kapas and Redang. Both are a sheer delight for the skin-diver, sun worshiper, coral collector and fisherman. It is a voyage of a little over one hour to **Pulau Kapas** which, however, can be reached more easily by driving south to the interesting, bustling, large fishing village of Marang. From here, it

e Central Market
d the MARA
ek center are
cellent places to
y locally made
oths.

is a mere thirty-minute voyage to the island. Three pleasant hours are necessary to reach **Pulau Redang.** If you are a solitary traveler and cannot afford the luxury of renting a boat, Thursdays and Fridays are the best time to make this trip. Then you are sure to find locals returning to the island after having spent the week in the office or at school in town. Thursdays and Fridays? Yes! In the states of Trengganu and Kelantan to the north it is Friday and not Sunday which is the Lord's Day. In both states, everything, banks included, shut down at midday on Thursday, not to re-open until the following Saturday morning.

The adventurous traveler may want to visit the picturesque **Sekayu Waterfall** near Kuala Brang, 56 km west of Trengganu. To reach the falls entails a 3-km hike from the end of the road at Kampung Ipoh. A refreshing swim is the reward. For those, especially the photographer, who are looking for a view of the Trengganu coast and the South China Sea, there is the drive or hike up Bukit Besar on the outskirts of the town. It is only 1 km, but very steep.

Impromptu Festivals: A Lively Get-Together

Though village life in Trengganu and Kelantan has changed, many of the traditional arts it fostered are as lively as ever. Seasonal fishing and farming brought village folk leisure and from leisure came time to devote to their arts. Folk dances, shadow plays and traditional games such as kite flying and top spinning were celebrated during festivals after a harvest. Many processions and rituals were related to the spirit of the rice, a carry-over from ancient animistic beliefs. Today village festivals are rarer occasions, since farmers are busy planting rice twice a year instead of once, and the Islam doctrine discourages customs connected with spirit worship. Yet the fun-loving Trengganu Malays have not forgotten the good old times and all the song and laughter that went with them.

Patrons may now arrange a festival through the Department of Youth, Culture and Sports in Kuala Trengganu or Kota Bharu. It is rewarding to patronize native dances because the entire village uses the occasion to enjoy themselves. Visitors never have the feeling of watching a staged performance but rather of experiencing village life, and since the ceremonies initiated by foreign guests continue all night, visitors always depart in the middle of an impromptu carnival.

The dances most usually performed are the *Mak Yong* and the *Menora*. Both are more correctly theatrical plays or dance dramas. Both dances are similar in that they tell magical tales of old about beautiful and divine princesses and the princely adventures of their suitors. In Mak Yong all but three of the roles are performed by women whilst Menora has an all male cast.

A festival is sure to include some other traditional dances. The *Ronggeng* with its catchy rhythm is the most typical of Malay dances and has many variations. Probably the most popular is the *Changgong*, a lively courtship dance in which no physical contact is allowed whilst the dancers sing impromptu verses in praise of their partners. *Tari Piring* is a graceful dance symbolizing the offering of gifts to the gods, usually in the form of food served in small *piring* or plates. Another version of this, found in Negri Sembilan, is performed with lighted candles. Two dances of Arabic origin are the *Hadrah*, a slow, graceful dance in praise of the Almighty and the more dignified *Zapin*. Following

Wooden pavilion with ornately carve windows is a relic Kuala Trengganu' royal past.

Arabic custom, both dances are performed only by men.

A comparatively new form of
entertainment often staged at festivals, particularly in Kelantan, is
Berdikir Barat, a verbal art form
developed after the Second World
War. Villagers of poetic inclination
form teams who meet in friendly
competition to match their verbal
ability and poetic wit in an impromptu
rhyme-verse exchange of badinage
and repartee.

A festival often begins with unseen gongs and drums approaching
an open field in the fast tempo of an
excited heartbeat. From the coconut
trees in the distance emerges an ebullient procession of merrymakers led
by lovely Malay girls bearing offerings of food which are later enjoyed
as a feast. No sooner have the drums
died down, than farmers take out

*elaborately
igned bird kite is
ut to take flight
ing a festival at
la Trengganu.*

their tops, smooth out a small circle
in the earth, and begin hurling spinning objects with the precision of a
major league pitcher.

As tops twirl, kites climb the
skies under the command of some
skillful maneuvering at the far side of
the field. East Coast kites are beautiful creations — Moon Kites, Bird
Kites, Cat Kites — all completely
covered with minuscule designs cut
out of thin, translucent colored paper.
Some have a bow-like device fixed to
their neck so that they hum in the sky.
When the weather is good and the
moon full, they are often left flying all
night so that the pleasant humming
sound will lull their owners to sleep.
Those copied after birds are so realis-
tic in flight that their strings mar the
effect.

According to Malay annals, kite
flying as a sport dates back to the

reign of Sultan Mahmud of Malacca during the 15th century, but probably kites were introduced from China a century earlier, along with paper umbrellas and dragon masks. Competitions nowadays are keen. The kite which attains the greatest height is the winner. Formerly, there was also a prize for the most belligerent but this resulted in so many disputes that it was forbidden by the Government.

Weavers and Silversmiths: As Quickly as the Fingers Can Move

A day in the life of a Trengganu village woman may include sending the children off to school, cooking the midday meal, putting the house in order, feeding the baby, weaving a meter of sapphire blue silk spun with silver, serving dinner, doing the dishes and sending the children to bed. In

Kampung Tanjong, a suburb on the seaward side of Kuala Trengganu, and on the north bank of the Trengganu River, nearly every home has a loom or two. It usually is set up around the stilts supporting the house so that the housewife can weave luxuriant silks and watch if the laundry is dry at the same time. All the East Coast's cottage industries fit into a pattern of life that has endured for centuries. Only the small road signs saying "Basket Weaving Here" in uneven letters are new. Selling household items to world travelers is a 20th-century phenomenon, but in most cases it still remains a family affair.

Of all the cloths woven on the Malay peninsula, Trengganu's *kain songket* — deep blue, forest green, maroon or purple silks studded with silver and gold thread — is the most highly prized. One piece of cloth can

Around Kuala Trengganu cottage industries centuries old still thrive.

A woman spins thread which will woven into kain songket, *in Kampung Tanjong, near Kuala Trengganu.*

require the talents of five different weavers, each specialized in a certain pattern interwoven in the overall design. Malay women cultivate a hierarchy of weavers, the most experienced arranging the warp threads on the loom and the least experienced flicking the shuttle. Young girls do most of the manual labor, gradually learning simple patterns and later intricate designs from their mothers and grandmothers. The body of the cloth is usually plain with an ornate border of stylized floral and geometric motifs. In olden days, the entire *kain* was a melody of silver thread on silk and the finest of all were sent for inspection at the sultan's palace.

Weaving mats from screw-pine or pandanus leaves is a more down-to-earth craft, which is practiced from Mauritius in the Indian Ocean down to East Timor. In little huts by the roadside, small girls sit on the floor plaiting dried, shredded leaves as quickly as their fingers can move them. They begin at the center of the floor mat and move outward, using dyes to produce simple crisscross patterns. Their more professional mothers fashion hexagonal boxes out of pandanus or nipa palm leaves.

A typical roadside shop in Trengganu has enough floor mats stacked in the corner to cover a basketball court. Usually, the lady of the house does the selling, shyly inviting her foreign guests to look around. Her collection may feature hats, fans, bags, baskets and dish covers. Her prices include little or no overhead since her children are her mat-makers and her house is 6 meters away. As things go on the East Coast, hospitality is worth more than a sales pitch.

Though all craftsmen on the East

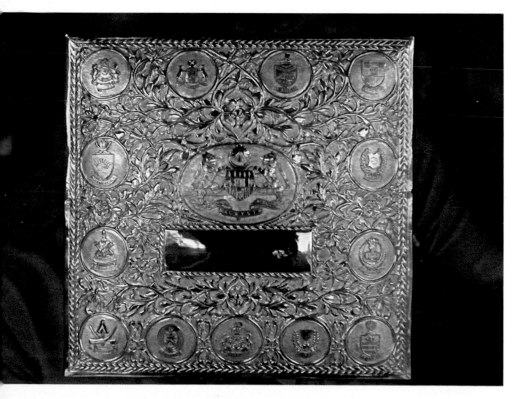

Coast share a common heritage, Kelantan State to the north of Trengganu has certain distinctions which link its name to silver and *batek*. *Batek* means wax painting in the Javanese language, but Egyptians were using the same technique 2,000 years ago. Today, there are far easier ways to print cotton, but none of them is in such popular demand as *batek* is in Malaysia. *Batek* hangs on Kelantan clotheslines and boutique mannequins in Kuala Lumpur. Malaysian ambassadors' wives wear *batek* as part of their national dress, while gamblers in *batek* shirts are granted entrance to local casinos without having to wear a tie.

The best Malaysian *batek* is created by hand in Kelantan where artisans use metal stencils to stamp cotton with wax designs. The cloth is then dipped in a dye bath, stamped again and dipped again until the absence of colors caused by the wax combine in a dazzling print. Malaysians favor more modern motifs than their Javanese neighbors, though these are interspersed with stylized birds, flowers and plants that were printed on *batek* centuries ago. Now visitors, if they wish, can fill a room with waxed patterns: *batek* table cloths, place mats, serviettes, bedspreads, pillow cases, seat covers and even wall paper.

At **Kampung Sireh**, a suburb of Kota Bharu, a dozen men bend over tiny, wobbly desks hammering lotus blossoms onto silver plates. Each silversmith is engaged in his own creation, whether it be a filigree butterfly or a repousse (ornamental metal work hammered into relief from the reverse side) cosmetic case. Apprentices begin with simpler objects like souvenir spoons and work their way up to exquisite tea sets for banquet tables. There is no division of labor. Each man finishes what he begins and keeps his own time schedule.

Aside from the individuality of each piece, Kelantan silver is distinguished by its cosmopolitan flavor. Some patterns of the *bunga raya* (hibiscus flower) are found on Javanese Majapahit jewelry 600 years old. Others inspired by shadow play figures show Siamese influence, while the conventional lotus blossom is Indian in origin. In days past, the finest silversmith in the land was summoned to work in the sultan's palace where all his needs were supplied. Now Kelantan silver lies behind velvet showcases in all big jewelry shops between Bangkok and Singapore. Only the precision of the hand is unchanged.

Remote and Unspoiled

From Kuala Trengganu the road runs north for a distance of 171 km to Kota Bharu and soon loses sight of the sea. About midway at Pasir

A sunny day for several of the prettier residents of traditional Kampung Sireh.

Puteh there is a turnoff that leads to **Kuala Besut**, a remote and unspoiled fishing village on the coast. Twice daily, at dawn and at dusk, fishing boats make a dramatic show as they arrive from across the sea and unload their catches at the jetty, where some tough bargaining takes place between fishermen and merchants. Visitors go completely unnoticed, and photographers can snap away without anyone paying attention. For those who want to stay over, there is a simple Rest House at **Ayer Tawar**, with a double room costing M$8. Kuala Besut is also a jumping off place for the idyllic **Perhentian Islands**, only 21 km distant. Weather permitting, local fishermen willingly ferry passengers across the waters. They will spend the day waiting for passengers while they picnic and explore, or arrangements can be made for them to return in a day or two. Camping on the islands is excellent and there is a primitive, three-room Rest House. The entire house may be rented by groups if reservations are made in advance at the Jerteh District Office. Twenty km north of Kuala Besut is **Bisikan Bayu Beach,** which means "Whispering Breeze." It is isolated and offers fine swimming and, as the name says, is cooled by the "whispering breeze" blowing from the South China Sea.

South of the Thai Border

Kota Bharu, the capital of Kelantan, is the northernmost town on the East Coast, only a few kilometers from the Thai border. It has one of the best-known market squares in Malaysia, and certainly one of the most interesting. In the early morning, fishing folk arrive with their catches and farmers bring in their produce from the countryside. The market is also a good shopping place for East Coast arts and crafts, particularly *batek* and silverwork for which the state is famous. Intricately designed

beach mats are a good bargain and craftsmen can work up your own design in a day or two.

Another early morning pastime is the training of *burong ketitir,* the merbok, a jungle bird greatly prized for his sweet song. The merbok enthusiast takes immense pains to train his birds for the dawn competitions. But the highlight of the year is the great bird-singing competition held in Kota Bharu in June. Contending merboks are hoisted aloft on thirty foot poles whilst an entourage of judges determine the champion on the basis of loudness, pitch and the melody of its song.

Just beyond the market is **Padang Merdeka** (Liberty Square) on one side of which is the state mosque and on another the old Istana. The mosque exhibits a syncretism of architectural styles and looks, at a first glance when approached from certain directions, more like a house of Christian worship than one of Muslim prayer. But there are few in Kelantan who are not Muslim and even many Chinese have accepted the word of the Prophet.

The old Istana, which was built within a fort, is called **Istana Balai Besar** (Palace with the Large Audience Hall). It was built in 1844 by order of Sultan Mohamed II and at the first ceremony ever held there the Sultan received a letter from the King of Siam recognizing him as ruler. The building, which is open to the public, contains the Throne Room, the State Legislative Assembly Hall and the enormous, multi-columned Hall of Audience. On entering this hall, look to your right. Here is the magnificent Royal Barge with a figurehead of a legendary bird whose head and tail are gold-covered. The barge, named *Pertala Indera Seri Kelantan* (Flower of the Gods — the Splendor of Kelantan), was used once only — by Sultan Mohamed IV for a pleasure cruise on the Kelantan River in 1900.

Ten km south of Kota Bharu, on the road to Kuala Krai, is **Kampung Nilam Puri** where Malaysia's oldest mosque is located. It was built entirely from chengai wood without the use of nails. During the monsoon season (usually from November to January) the region between the bus terminal and the river is flooded and *sampans* are the only mode of transport. Then there is a festive spirit about the town; conviviality fills the air and young girls carry a brilliant rainbow of colored umbrellas.

Kota Bharu has also a 20th-century claim to fame. **Pantai Dasar Saba**, 13 km north of the town, is a pleasant, wide, casuarina-shaded beach which is popular with the locals. It was here, at 4:55 p.m. on 7 December 1941 (Greenwich Mean Time), that the Japanese started World War II in the East and began their march southward to Singapore. (The attack on Pearl Harbor was not to take place until ninety-five minutes later.)

There are many other beautiful beaches in Kelantan among them **Pantai Dalam Rhu** near the fishing village of Semerak to the south of Kota Bharu and **Pantai Irama** near Bachok.

Inland adventurers will find beautiful waterfalls feeding natural swimming pools in the midst of tropical jungle in the region of **Pasir Puteh.** Jeram Pasu, also known as Air Terjun, is frequented most by little local residents during school holidays and can be reached by a five-mile jungle path. Other waterfalls are at Jeram Tapeh and Jeram Lenang.

Despite its contacts with the Thais and Japanese, life in Kota Bharu follows the gentle rhythms of the Malay countryside, with the muezzin's call to prayer from the minaret sounding from morning to evening. The town is well served by a number

The Japanese lan at Kota Bharu, launching their involvement in World War II, ju prior to their atta on Pearl Harbor.

A mosque in Kota Bharu.

avelers may cross
Thai border and
ard a train
ding north to
ngkok.

of hotels. Kota Bharu is also the terminus for the East Coast railway. Only a few kilometers away, across the border, begins the line that connects to Bangkok.

Beach of Passionate Love: Poetry in Motion

White sands, a blue sea that shimmers beneath the tropical sun, a surf that gently unrolls along the beach, palm trees nipping at the blue of the sky, a breeze that brings the fragrance of the land...the place— *Pantai Chinta Berahi* or "The Beach of Passionate Love."

The road that leads to the beach is lined with coconut palms and banana trees, with green tropical growth up to the very edge of the pavement. At times it crosses streams and passes through quaint villages.

beach of
sionate Love near
a Bharu.

Along the road are a number of small, *songket*-weaving "factories" which are open to the public. Kelantan's weaving factories often consist of nothing more elaborate than a spare room in a private home. Young Malay girls, some in their early teens, sit behind huge looms, turning fine balls of silk and cotton into finished fabric. Visitors can purchase cloth and handicrafts from display counters at very reasonable prices. *Batek* purses, table cloths and napkins, and bedspreads are a good buy.

At the end of the road is the big, empty beach with the romantic name. Perhaps its most attractive features are its remoteness and its allusions to secret rendezvous on moonlit nights. One company has capitalized on the romance by building a hotel facing the beach. It has a swimming pool and sixteen chalets.

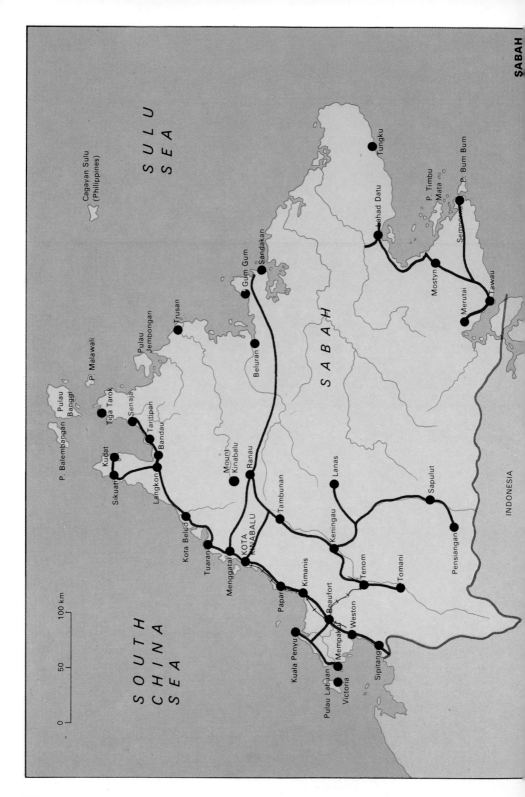

SOUTH
CHINA
SEA

SULU
SEA

Cagayan Sulu
(Philippines)

P. Balembangan

Pulau
Banggi

P. Malawali

Pulau
Jembongan

Trusan

Senaja

Tiga Tarok

Kudat

Tartipan

Sikuati

Bandau

Langkon

Beluran

Gum Gum

Sandakan

Mount
Kinabalu

Ranau

Kota Belud

Tuaran

Tambunan

Lanas

SABAH

Mengatal

KOTA
KINABALU

Kimanis

Keningau

Sapulut

Papar

Beaufort

Tenom

Tomani

Pensiangan

Kuala Penyu

Mempakul

Weston

Pulau Labuan

Victoria

Sipitang

INDONESIA

Lahad Datu

Tungku

P. Timbu
Mata

P. Bum Bum

Mostyn

Semporna

Merutai

Tawau

0   50   100 km

230

in an island of legends

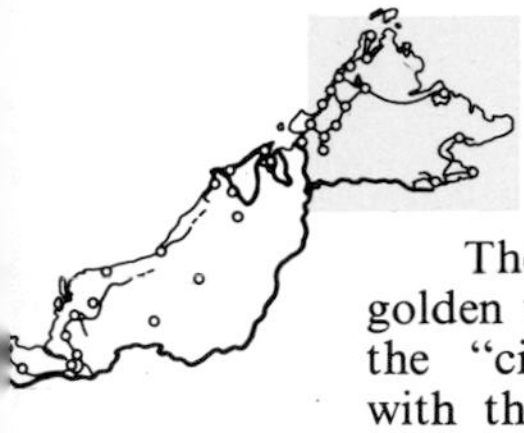

The mystery of Borneo spun a golden thread through the history of the "civilized" world. It glittered with those unrealities on which all rumors thrive. For centuries, no one knew its shape or size, other than the vague irony of a boundless island. Buckles of "Golden Jade" adorned the imperial belts of the Son of Heaven, yet none of the audacious Chinese merchants who bartered Sung Porcelain for Golden Jade had ever seen the sacred hornbill from which it came. The merchants discreetly resigned that privilege to the jungle dwellers, who disappeared back into sunless forests. At the turn of the century, the world was still stupefied. Western outsiders had populated the coasts in scattered settlements, claiming to govern vast tracts of land they had never seen. Impressionable British officials wrote strange stories in which the hero was held captive by head-hunting savages and published them in leading magazines back home. Their tales were half-truth and half-fiction, just as Borneo had always been.

Out of this eerie heritage emerged the state of Sabah in 1963, the year British officialdom ended and north and northwest Borneo became part of the Federation of Malaysia. Sabah covers the northern tip of the world's third largest island with Sarawak to the south. Together they bridge 1,000 km of sea to join the Malay peninsula as a nation. Though Sabah and Sarawak occupy only the north and northwest coast of Borneo, together, they are larger than Peninsular Malaysia, and on an island with footprints dating from the Ice Age, their nationhood is newer. Sabah and Sarawak were formerly known as East Malaysia.

Modern Sabah seems as if it is just beginning, awakened to a bright future that few foresee in concrete

Kadazan woman arrives at Mt. Kinabalu National Park where she works as a porter (previous pages).

form, yet everyone recognizes with such gusto that when TV Malaysia Sabah started broadcasting in December 1971 it took only three months before Saturday nights and the Bob Cummings Show became synonymous. Kota Kinabalu, the state capital on the northwest coast, has the cumbersome and orderly grace of the 1950s, except perhaps for Kampung Ayer, a neighborhood standing 6 meters above water on stilts. Yet even some of Kampung Ayer's sea-worthy sidewalks have come tumbling down in the rapid wake of progress. Sabah's capital city changes swiftly. Not far from Bajau boat people, who raise a family of five right on deck, loom the Secretariat and 6-meter-high Silver Kris, symbols of national unity. The state mosque stands nearby, draped in scaffolding that climbs a little higher each day. New government buildings gracefully introduce onion-shaped domes and windows to Kota Kinabalu's contemporary scene.

Outside the city, in an eternal landscape, freshly cut roads crisscross the Crocker Range to the far side of Mount Kinabalu. All the gravel is new but the asphalt has still to arrive. Landrovers with strange names painted on their doors, such as "The Tamparuli Express," and noisy Caterpillars make up the limited traffic, leaving long trails of billowing dust as they go. Along the wayside, hardy Kadazan market women unload their omnipresent *burong* baskets and set up spontaneous fresh-fruit stalls. True to Sabah's traditions they sometimes leave the fruit behind with a money bag and trust to their customers' honesty.

The native people of Sabah have ancestors who practiced the most diverse trades. The Kadazans were farmers, the Muruts were blowpipe hunters, the Bajaus were sea gypsies and the Illanuns were pirates. Sabah's Brunei Malays belonged to a sultanate that once ruled all Borneo and then sold most of it piecemeal to ambitious and adventurous Euro-

[margin text, left side:]
1963 a new state ...erged taking ...pe in an island of ...ndary jungles ...1 tribal peoples.

peans. Its Chinese have ancestors who sailed over in quest of kingfisher's feathers and bezoar stones before the days of Kublai Khan. Now, the off-spring of all these people are the citizens of the state. On big occasions —Queen Elizabeth's visit, National Day, or travel agent conventions — they don the ceremonial dress of their forefathers and parade their traditions. In daily life, they toil the rice fields, build the roads, man the factories and control the trade—timber, palm oil, copra, prawns and cocoa —on which Sabah's economy depends.

To visitors, Sabah's people are congenial, informal and polite, treating each foreigner as a stranger and guest simultaneously. When requested, they seldom hesitate to help ease a traveler's mind — give directions, explain a price list, or even book you a room at the local rest house if they are able to telephone. The word "Tourist" with a capital "T" has not filtered down through the ranks to the point where he wears a dollar sign on his lapel. This is not to say Sabah is inexpensive — in fact, hotels are quite the opposite. Most merchandise is imported, and hotel and transport prices are higher than they are on the peninsula. But accommodation is easily found at small Chinese hotels or government rest houses found in almost all of Sabah's small towns. Travelers are a novelty and curiosity is mutual.

The small tourist trade works on a personal level. Exploring Sabah with a flexible itinerary leaves visitors open to unexpected "tips for travelers" which local citizens may volunteer in a coffee shop, a mountain retreat, a riverboat or a hotel lobby. The "tips" go on, offering new directions and old memories of Sabah. They can take you to the little island of Labuan, diamond and sapphire center and a free port over many centuries; to a pearl station in the timeless town of Semporna set down on a picturesque peninsula in a sea strewn with

enchanting islands; or to the furthest southeast corner where Tawau lazes away each peaceful tropic day. They can lead way up north to Kudat town, near where the Illanun and Rungus tribes meet at the Sunday fair and where the beautiful Bak Bak beach spreads wide and desolate. Or they can lead deep into the interior, past the Murut settlement of Pensiangan, where the legends of Borneo still sleep in the trees.

"Where the Eye Lingers"

Judging by the bold letters designating Sabah's capital city, map gazers might expect a fanfare of taxi horns and business bustle. Yet **Kota Kinabalu,** home of 60,000, is still a gentle, unimposing town with an elevated water village on one side, unpretentious bank buildings on the other, and Chinese shop houses crowded together in the "modern" midtown in between. "KK" is possibly the narrowest city in Asia. Streets parallel to the shore run on for kilometers but turn any corner and in less than five minutes you are climbing a hill or wading in water. Luxury apartments and European prewar bungalows grace the green mountains which serve as a backdrop. A seaside sprinkled with islets and a harbor lie at the city's front door.

This cluster of real-life Robinson Crusoe islands, just a few minutes from "KK" by boat, make up the Tun Abdul Razak National Park, where swimming and skin-diving are among the finest in the world. Visitors can view breathtaking corals from the safety of a glass bottomed boat and soon sunworshipers will be able to stay overnight in chalets built on the most beautiful beach of all on Gaya Island.

Come afternoon, schoolchildren are all over the place, running, playing soccer or kicking the *sepak raga* ball. On the traditional *padang,* husky collegiates enthusiastically wield hockey sticks, mindless of the tropic heat.

Sabah and its sis
state of Sarawak
together larger t
Peninsular Mala
which is 1,000 k
away across the

Kota Kinabalu,
Sabah's unimpos
capital city, nest
between its harb
and green
mountains behin

Meanwhile, young Malays stroll around the city's small seaside park gazing silently at the sunset or at any young girls who happen by. Chinese hawkers at the adjacent seaside marketplace pack up their vegetables and dismantle their makeshift stalls. At night, few things are more spectacular than the local cinema house whose sample programs may include "The Great Battle" or "The Singing Sword." One sensual and sleazy billboard provocatively promises: "The intimate secrets of Sex! Men would fall at her feet to win her favor . . . the kind they knew would bring them untold pleasure!" The film is "Madame Bovary."

KK "After Dark" has none of the epicurean diversions of its airline-linked neighbors: Hong Kong and Singapore. It is, rather, a pleasant place to take an evening walk. You meet the corner gang, literally clustered at the corner curb outside a noisy coffee shop, engrossed in some fascinating topic of conversation in Cantonese. Young Kadazan swingers, cruise on motorcycles or meet old friends out on the town. Nightclubs call themselves simply "Night Club" and that is enough. As the name foretells, their interior is darker than a moonless midnight and is lit only by glowing cigarette butts, a red spot on the local band, and a waiter's flashlight guiding new arrivals to their chairs.

Yet KK has much about it that a metropolis would be too busy to preserve. In **Kampung Ayer**, which is Malay for "Water Village," Chinese housewives burn joss papers to keep everything lucky on the rickety catwalks that bind houses like latticework over still water. Here, in

Chinese housewife
rns joss papers in
mpung Ayer, Kota
nabalu.

attractive, modern clapboard homes perched on stilts, or even in the family boat itself, live the local fishermen and their kin. Children wearing clothes delightfully free from all logical sizes scurry from shore to fishing boat with their tiny torsos bent at a 45-degree angle under the weight of a tin of gasoline fetched for their father. Kampung Ayer was here before KK's city pavements entered the concrete mixer. It remembers a long tradition of Bajau water villagers who earned their keep on pirates' booty. But the modern age has shrunk its size.

Kota Kinabalu has a phoenix in its history. It was demolished several times, only to rise again. It entered the map under the name of *Api Api*, "Fire! Fire!," thanks to North Borneo pirates who threaded their warboats through the coral-grit islets and burned the settlement down. The Chartered Company, following a penchant British colonialism had for offshore islands, set up shop on Gaya Island out in the bay. But the famous rebel Mat (Mohammed) Salleh destroyed the place during the greatest surprise attack of his career in 1897. Thereafter, the Chartered Company cautiously reassembled its town on the shore, naming it after Sir Charles Jessel, the vice-chairman of their Board of Directors. As a trading port Jesselton grew important enough to be bombed to ruins in 1945, and thus Sabah's modern capital began once again.

In 1968, Sabah now a new state with a new city in the independent Federation of Malaysia, the government shed the old name of Jesselton, passed up the romantic Malay name for the pleasant town — *Singgah Mata*, "Where the Eye Lingers" —

Kota Kinabalu has had a phoenix-like history, having been razed by pirates, rebels, and the Japanese in 1945.

Tanjong Aru Beach 10 km south of Kota Kinabalu.

234

and settled upon Kota Kinabalu in honor of the great mountain that symbolizes the unity of the land. But where the eye still lingers is 7 km south of the city at **Tanjong Aru**, a long, ivory-toned, lazy beach where gentle waves caress the shore, and the horizon is broken only by island silhouettes and a fiery red sun. It lingers on the third floor of Nosmal Court across the street from the old post office where rich Bajau prayer mats and Borneo conical hats hang in the Sabah Museum. And it lingers among the palm-thatched villages of **Penampang**, 13 km away, where Kadazan women tend sago palm gardens and bend over rice fields flooded by the monsoonal rains.

dazan women act
porters for the
nb up Mount
nabalu, Southeast
ia's highest
untain.

Southeast Asia's Highest Mountain

Everyone in Sabah knows about the otherworldliness of **Mount Kinabalu**. The closer one journeys toward its famous jagged profile with clouds as white whiskers, the more one wonders if the Kadazan people who dwelt in the summit's shadow were not right, after all. Long ago, they named the mountain *Akin Nabalu*— "home of the spirits of the departed." To them, an ethereal life among those still peaks was what one had to look forward to after one died. They held the mountain to be sacred and it was audacious for anyone to intrude upon their ancestral abode. The Kadazans only journeyed there on very rare occasions to offer sacrifices of thanksgiving to the spirits of their kin.

However, a young British officer named Hugh Low started a whole new trend in 1851 when he boldly wandered up the mountain, accompanied by a Kadazan chief, and

placed a bottle with a note in it to prove that he had reached the top of Southeast Asia's highest mountain. His name is immortalized by the highest peak between New Guinea and the Himalayas — and the deepest gully. Typical of the English understatement, "Low's Gully" happens to plunge 1,800 meters straight down with terrifying vertical exactitude. Nonetheless, hundreds of botanists, mountaineers and adventurers have been following Low's trail ever since.

Latter-day intrepid conquerors, of course, travel in different circles. Instead of beckoning a native chieftain over a cup of rice wine, climbers today jet into Kota Kinabalu on a Boeing 737 and take the nearest taxi straight to the Kinabalu National Park office downtown. There, a friendly secretary writes down their names in the park's diary and books

them a cabin at the "base camp" and another cabin the next night several hundred meters higher. The climb has commenced.

Three days is the golden mean for exploring Kinabalu, but before even journeying to the park headquarters 1,700 meters up, climbers should stock up on canned food, sweets and a bottle of kerosene for cooking. The park rents out sleeping bags and kitchen utensils, but it leaves the menus to its guests. Accommodation at the base camp is varied but uniformly pleasant. For the impecunious there is a dormitory accommodation (sheets and blankets may be rented) and for the wealthy — although prices are very reasonable — there are three- and four-bedroom bungalows complete even with dishcloths. The "club-house" has a restaurant serving Chinese food and

Kinabalu's Natio Park extends fro an elevation of 2 meters to the top Mount Kinabalu 4,040 meters abo sea level.

Above 3,000 mete mist enshrouds th stunted trees grasping at Kinabalu's slopes

ch morning a bus
ves Kota
nabalu for the
tional Park, some
km to the north.

a shop where you may buy the provisions you forgot to stock up in KK.

The trip from Sabah's capital city begins at seven o'clock in the morning at the municipal bus station where awaits "The Kinabalu Express," a big, gray Landrover which potential climbers share with Kadazan farmers, Chinese schoolgirls and Bajau clerks. The Landrover rolls along paved roads at a modest speed until it reaches **Tamparuli**, 47 km north of Kota Kinabalu, where the driver stops for his cup of morning coffee. So far the trip has been a mellow voyage through green Asiatic landscapes studded with small farm houses and grazing water buffaloes. But less than 1 km past Tamparuli, the level ground says goodbye, the asphalt disappears, the driver shifts into first gear, and the mountain takes over.

Sabah's interior roads have the aura of intruding upon a vast nature, as if the people who so industriously built them were Lilliputians on the stomach of Gulliver. With dirt tracks delicately entwining the ridges of a rising mountain range and with tropical deluges splashing down from the afternoon skies, passengers on "The Kinabalu Express" may find themselves enjoying a literally "groovy" ride.

Kinabalu commands the entire country from an immobile and majestic stance that earned it a place of honor on the Sabah flag. The National Park surrounding its regal dome is a sanctuary for rare wildlife, and when climbers arrive at the alpine cottages clustered around the park's headquarters, it takes little time to recover from the Landrover giggles and begin an affair with the ozone.

The park headquarters, or the "base camp" as the Rangers call it, is where people climbing up and down meet to tell their stories. The park has a good library of magazine articles on the mountain climb to occupy enthusiasts until the next morning. Though to Sherpas down from the Himalayas and other members of the moun-

taineering elite, climbing Kinabalu is a breeze, not all pedestrians come off the mountain trail so lightly. As one out-of-breath vacationer suggested: "To get in practice, try running up and down the emergency exit of a skyscraper for a couple of days."

In fact, climbing 1,500 meters in one day—from the power station above the base camp to Panar Laban Hut—does take inordinate reserves of zest for folks who have just flown in from their desks in the office. But this is when the mountain is approached as a "rush job" for uphill racers, which it need not be. A modicum of competition sometimes crops up around the fireplaces in the base camp. Stories circulate about the local chapter of the hunt-and-hike group known as the "Hash House Harriers" who bet a bottle of Scotch that two of its members could not leave the base camp in the morning, climb to the summit and return to the camp within twelve hours—and lost. Botanists seem to have the best alibi for eluding such grueling precedents. One of the park's experienced wardens fondly remembers a climb to the summit when a member of his party would stop every half-hour and ask in a winded voice: "Could you tell me the name of that plant?"

One of the pleasures of climbing Mount Kinabalu is the native company; explorers are never alone. Awok, a Kadazan woman barely 1.5 meters tall who chews betel nut, rolls her own cigarettes and presides over no less than fifteen grandchildren, is a familiar personality among the guides and Rangers. One of her employers was a vivacious American wife determined to climb up and down the summit in one-and-a-half days. She awoke at dawn all set for the climb, spotted Awok leisurely smoking one of her hand-rolled cigarettes at the base camp and ran to tell her husband to come quickly and photograph this charming market woman standing against the mountain's morning silhouette. Her husband returned saying, "You won't believe it, but that's our porter" — a fact which knocked considerable wind out of the young lady's liberationist bag.

Meanwhile, Awok stuffed a heavy knapsack, twelve cans of food, camera equipment and her own belongings into her woven *burong* basket which Sabah's village women carry everywhere and proceeded with steadfast stamina to climb the mountain. As a porter, Awok earns M$5 each way, though she climbs only to Panar Laban Hut where she unloads, builds a fire and waits while her zealous employers trudge up the summit. The park requires all climbers to be accompanied by a guide who is paid M$15 to M$20 a day, depending on the size of the group. He is also in charge of the porter and brings his scale along to weigh the luggage in case it is over the normal limit of 10 kilos and requires an extra fee. The extra fee is usually well worth paying, for unless the climber goes hiking every other weekend he will probably not be fit enough to carry anything heavier than a National Park brochure.

The scenery on Kinabalu is too vivid for burdens. It shifts its character as the climb proceeds. At first, a staircase made from tree branches winds up through the green shade of the montane forest. It is hot and humid. Bunches of *Epiphytes* — most of the park's 1,000 species of orchids and mosses — cling to tree trunks and tumbling vines. The forest canopy drips from heavy rains and cloud mists that saturate the muddy sandstone bottom of the Crocker Range which the mountain dominates. To most beginners this is the steepest, most arduous part of the climb, so the

Porters are availa to help you carry your gear and gru up to the hut at Panang Laban, 3,500 meters high and just 500 mete from the summit.

Toward the top of Mount Kinabalu, hard slabs of gran create vertiginous footing along the climb.

Rangers have carefully spaced the stairs to invite an easy, steady stride.

A couple of thousand steps later, the montane forest opens onto Carson's Cabin, the first stopover where climbers may spend the night. But since the cabin has no cooking facilities and a limited view, it is best to stop here only for a good rest, a hot cup of coffee (water can be obtained from the stream nearby) and some light refreshments — chocolate, nuts or dried fruit. Climbers can amuse themselves without exerting much by peeping into the insect-ensnarling cup of the famous pitcher plant that grows behind the rocks near Carson's Cabin. Hapless flies that take the wrong turn and land in the liquid-containing cup of the pitcher plant have nothing to look forward to other than being slowly digested.

Pitcher plants stand out in the wild beauty of the "cloud forest" which lends the second stage of the climb a silvery hue. Twisting iron-wood, bleached silver by moist clouds at the high altitudes, extend from 2,900 meters to Kinabalu's granite dome. Curvilinear, stunted trees swerve with Baroque exuberance under the influence of a wind storm. Vermilion tube-shaped blossoms of the *Rhododendron ericoides*, wild orchids and white *Leptospermum* flowers sprinkle the forest with brilliant colors that jump out of a silvery monotone. The steps are there no more and the path begins to weave over a maze of gnarled roots which cling to the red rock bed. Hard slabs of granite start breaking through the sandstone as clouds enwrap the green sides of Kinabalu sloping below.

From the silvery forest, climbers emerge at the front door of an alumi-

ting on top of ount Kinabalu's nite dome, a peak 40 meters above e world below.

num cabin with clear mountain streams trickling across the scenery. **Panar Laban Hut**, the nicest and best equipped hideaway on the mountain, lies at the foot of a gargantuan slope of granite. It is 3,500 meters above the sea and the weather cools down considerably. Finicky clouds whisk past the barren dome in a big hurry— smothering it, surrounding it, or leaving it alone. Here Kinabalu takes on the other worldliness huge mountains cherish.

Before the next dawn, the guide shifts his weight forward and begins to tread the concrete stone steps that are carved out of the giant dome. The undulating tree-belt below bows out as if in reverence to the fabulously stark and spacious freedom above. The path disintegrates. Solitary stone markers lead up a wide valley of smooth rock bordered by lofty pin-nacles and spires that jab the ice-blue skyline. The last stage of the mountain climb is the secret of its beginning— the perpetual desire of mankind to escape human dimensions. Some do and some do not. When climbers finally attain the highest boulder on Low's Peak, 4,040 meters above sea level, they find a visitors' book with comments scrawled inside. Some say, "Heavenly!" Other say, "Once is enough."

"Finicky clouds whisk past Kinabalu's barren dome, smothering it."

Ranau and Hot Springs

Picture yourself sitting in a typical coffee shop in downtown **Ranau**, Sabah. On the signboard outside is the simple invitation: *Johan's Kedai Makan dan Minum*, which means "Johan's Eat and Drink Shop." It contains one dog, two Kadazan sisters doing the serving,

After climbing Kinabalu the hot springs at Poring will soothe tired muscles.

and a rice farmer enjoying a Guinness stout. The walls are plastered with glossy advertisements.

One wall of the eat and drink shop is completely covered by shelves which contain stacks of cabbages, cans of sweetened cream corn, packages of two-minute noodles with chicken flavor, 352 Bubble Up bottles, candy and peanut jars and Sunkist! signs. The waitress is wearing rubber sandals and a T-shirt with a saucy slogan stenciled across her bosom. The radio is broadcasting news in Malay, seductively read by a young woman newscaster who sounds like a Brylcreem commercial. One weary German traveler is sipping the inevitable cup of milky tea and saying, "I guess you could sit here for the rest of your life."

Ranau is an uncomplicated small town with neat houses dotting the foothills of Mount Kinabalu as if they had been sprinkled from the sky. Suburbia is less than 200 meters from the commercial center — one street of weathered clapboard shops stuck together like glue. Not surprisingly, the Chinese pervade this commercial oasis. Fried noodles or hot vegetable soup will be served up less than three minutes after the traveler sits down.

Life in Ranau flows as smoothly as the river that runs through the center of town. Miniature blue and white uniforms color the roadsides as children return home from *sekolah* (school). Young men in Landrovers drive these prized possessions down to the riverbank for a daily wash. Every house, whether that of a government official or a farmer, has chickens rushing about pecking the lawn. Water buffaloes graze in front yards.

e rock-strewn
nau River flowing
rough the foothills
Kinabalu.

For the young Sabah citizen who has settled with his family in Ranau the future is bright indeed. Ranau lies directly on the East-West Highway with the result that the town has blossomed into a busy waystation between Sandakan harbor on the east coast and Kota Kinabalu on the west. The comfortable Government Rest House is frequently booked solid with Public Works engineers en route to construction sites on the East-West trail. But the best road from Ranau, from a sybaritic point of view, is the wide dirt track that leads to the hot springs at Poring, 19 km away.

The supreme climax for the outdoor man or woman who has climbed Mount Kinabalu is a long, soothing sulfur bath in the hot springs of **Poring**. The Kadazans named the place *poring* (bamboo), after the towering forests where bamboo shoots are as thick as elephants' legs. But it took the refined traditions of Japan to tap the potential of a hot spring. During the Second World War, jungle-weary Japanese officers would come here, shed their fatigues, bathe and relax. Now, the old wooden tub has been dismantled and seven new baths built in its place. They sit in a well-trimmed garden populated with swallowtail butterflies and shaded by tropical rainforest. To the wobbly-legged ex-Kinabalu climber, the serene nature of Poring provides a bath to remember. "They even have adjustable hot and cold faucets" boasted a 13-year-old tourist who had tested her favorite combination of hot spring and cold stream for a full three hours.

However, there are other ways to spend one's time in Poring: looking for Orang Utans, for instance. Kinabalu's nature reserve is one of the few places in the world where Orang Utans still swing in the wild. However, it is very difficult to see the "man of the forest," which is the English translation of his name. He is, with good cause, acutely shy: native hunters and poachers with a zoo in mind

have dwindled his ranks to near extinction. Poring's park Ranger recommends that visitors in search of Orang Utans should spend several days camping in the jungle. The park will arrange for porters and guides if advised in advance. Even if the "man of the forest" eludes you, the trip should prove worthwhile. Poring's rainforests also harbor mouse-deer, barking deer, bearded pigs, gray monkeys, hornbills, mynah birds and honey buzzards — more than 200 species of fowl in the area alone, reported one totally satisfied bird-watcher.

In addition, Poring has several lush and lonely forest paths that wander up and down knolls to far-out bat caves and tumbling waterfalls. They pass by nature's largest flower — the *Rafflesia*, which yields an orange blossom up to 1 meter wide when in bloom and looks like a withered cabbage made of rubber when not. With family cabins and well-equipped camp-grounds and a bathtub out in the garden, Poring belongs in an escapist's notebook. A hanging bridge over a bubbling stream leads to the springs. There the Ranger has put up a small sign saying: "Please: Take nothing but — photographs. Leave nothing but — footprints."

Kota Belud: a Betel Nut Sales Counter with a Water Buffalo Parking Lot

---

On Sunday mornings, from seven to noon, the mossy banks of Tempasuk River vanish beneath an avalanche of bare feet and upcountry merchandise. Bajau market women, their faces crinkled by harsh weather and hours of laughter, their stained teeth welded onto the ever-present betel nut, and their heads draped casually with floppy cloths, squat beside tobacco wrappers and sugar doughnuts for hours on end. Lovely Malay teenage girls, wearing the loose tunic-like *baju kurong*, sweep past big piles of anchovy and kicking crabs.

The future looks bright for Ranau located on the east-west highway Sabah's main thoroughfare.

The world's large flower, the *Raffles* can be seen near Poring, along wit the orangutan and other wildlife.

There is always more on sale at the *tamu* than mundane necessities, even if these include everything from breakfast food to cattle and ponies. A Pakistani medicine man, with a prize-winning, 15-cm white moustache, strikes up his one-man band accompanied by a histrionic sales pitch in four languages, while his assistant officiously sorts out pink bottles filled with sticky liquid. Three stalls down, an enterprising Chinese boy draws crowds with a supermarket-like demonstration on how to manipulate two steaming waffle irons at the same time.

Of course, an entire row of market displays is devoted to the art of nut chewing, which every saleswoman unconsciously and continually demonstrates. Lengthy conversations touching upon such universal topics as "Who's who at the marketplace?"

provide the best entertainment among the distaff side at the *tamu*.

Tamus are Sabah's open-air weekly markets, Sunday being the favored day. They were fostered in prewar British Chartered Company times, when district officers would encourage villagers from kilometers around to visit the towns and trade among themselves. It was also a convenient opportunity for the government to meet with the headmen of the *kampung*s to exchange business matters and advice. For the common *kampung* folks, *tamu*s were the big chance to catch up on gossip with old friends from different villages. The word *tamu* means "a meeting place" and even today it is as much a picnic as a sales counter. All the taste treats are on sale and there is the familiar patrol of market dogs to clean up the scraps.

rket day at Kota ud, a riverine n 77 km north of a Kinabalu.

Kota Belud, a river town backed by the blue peaks of Mount Kinabalu 77 km north of the capital city, stages the biggest *tamu*. It is one of the few thriving markets today which have a water buffalo parking lot. Vendors, young and old, arrive with the long shafts of morning light. They bring their buffaloes in the easiest manner imaginable — by riding them along with the rest of the family, unless the lady of the household prefers to make her entrance alone as she often does. The parking lot and water buffalo auction is clearly for men only. Each owner proudly leads his big beast by the nose and weighs it on a scale almost strong enough to support a tank. Buffaloes are big money in upcountry Sabah and *songkok*-capped villagers scrutinize the animals for hours before a bargain is sealed. Meanwhile, with impeccably good manners in domesticity, the huge beasts simply stand around swishing flies off their backs and wait until the show is over.

The other all-men corner of the *tamu* is the cockfighting arena where a fallen feather can cause spectators to howl for victory. Crumpled dollar bills change hands in an uproar a full five minutes before a fight begins. Bets on the better cock can take a half hour to win since in Sabah, unlike Indonesia, the sport does not include the lethal spurs which can end a battle within seconds. The cock that tires first or that gets "chicken" and runs away from its opponent is the loser. So dollars and hollers fill the air most of the morning.

Kota Belud is Bajau country. The Bajaus, a Muslim people originally from the southern Philippines, are reputed to be great lovers of the tall tale, the best "cowboys" in Borneo, excellent fishermen and, until a few decades ago, the most dauntless and most successful water buffalo stealers around. The Bajaus themselves claim to be descended from Johore Malays in a rather haphazard manner. Folklore says the Sultan of Johore sent a

powerful escort of war boats to deliver his beautiful daughter to a Sulu prince. But she was captured by the dashing, young Sultan of Brunei and her escort, too scared to return, became wandering sea-gypsies who founded the Bajau tribe.

They also became notorious pirates and were belligerent enough in times past to push the unassuming Kadazan people back from the coast to the foothills of Kinabalu. For centuries, relations between these two tribes were cool at best. The Bajaus condescendingly thought of the Kadazans as country bumpkins, and the Kadazans retaliated with legends like: "When the Almighty created mankind, two people got away. One escaped downriver to the coast and became a Bajau; the other scrambled into the deep forest and became a monkey."

No feud today could penetrate the serenity that pervades the farmlands enwrapping the great mountain. Kadazans and Bajaus have bargained over bananas and betel for years at the *tamu* of Kota Belud. Now tourists who have made the two-hour drive by Landrover from Kota Kinabalu (price: M$12 per person for a return trip) can focus their cameras in the water buffalo parking lot free of charge.

Round Trip to Tenom: Zipping Along in a Railcar

Along the south coast from Kota Kinabalu runs a small and romantic railway — the only one in Borneo. A funny little railcar shaped like a three-dimensional trapezoid zips along a diminishing track, stringing small towns together in a changing yet changeless countryside where one-room schools are still in session and motors are rare. Neighborhoods and towns combine in miniature clusters of wooden houses with rice fields as gardens. Occasionally, the swishing trees part to reveal a calm bay on the

At Kota Belud y⟨ get a feeling of th old Borneo, as tr groups come dov to market to bar⟨ and haggle.

Borneo's only railway runs alon⟨ the south coast, cutting through t⟨ heart of the jung⟨ past dizzying rap⟨ and inclines.

244

South China Sea, its beaches fringed with feathery casuarina trees and its waters as placid as a still life. All along the track to Beaufort lie the continuities of Asia: the perpetual cycle of the rice harvest, the tenacity of small towns struggling to grow.

But after Beaufort, the trapezoidal railcar turns a sharp corner and zips into the rugged hills of the Crocker Range. Passengers snap out of the mesmerizing landscape and begin to put great trust in the little railcar, as it cuts through stone tunnels and skirts the awesomely uninviting rapids of the Padus River. This is what England's armchair travelers knew a hundred years ago as the dark side of Borneo, "The Interior." And, in those days, when one had to either hack his way through jungle or negotiate the tumultuous rapids to get there, it is no wonder that the *Orang*

Puteh (White Man) was very scarce. Of the first few Europeans who trudged through, several became missing persons.

The Muruts, "men of the hills," as the Bajaus named them, have always lived there. A Murut was less likely to call himself a Murut than a Tagal or a Timogun or a Bukan or a Semandu. Forever accompanied by his *parang*, or working knife, the Murut today is the grandson and great-grandson of a warrior and hunter who shared a virile life with his tribe, and who also, as was the ancient custom, married only after he had taken at least one human head in battle.

"Life in the jungle with the Muruts," wrote one author, "is like camping out, with all its advantages and disadvantages". Young men, renowned for their skill with blowpipe

and poisoned darts, scoured the jungles with their hunting dogs in search of deer, python, wild buffalo or boar — anything edible. Tribes cultivated rice and tapioca on the mountains and, believing that the earth spirit set a time limit on these disturbances, would shift to a new site every seven years. They also warred with one another. Should warriors return victorious, longhouses rocked with feasting and dancing all night.

When Western civilization finally trickled into the interior, the life of centuries changed overnight for the Muruts. They were forced to abandon customs ingrained in their existence longer than anyone could remember. Their population dropped, and it is only quite recently that the Muruts have begun to settle on the outskirts of towns and develop a sedentary economy. Many prefer the exhilaration of a "camp out" life in a familiar jungle. Others come down from the hills for hard work, such as tending the forested tracts which border Borneo's one and only railroad.

From the hilly inland town of Tenom, where the railway stops, you can travel by Landrover through Keningau and Tambunan, completing a round trip from Kota Kinabalu. The Government Rest House at Keningau is a popular stopover for excursions to Murut country. In **Tambunan**, an old stone on a grassy plain marks Mat Salleh's last fort. The tall and striking rebel built the fort completely underground in the middle of the jungle, supplying his dugout with water through a sophisticated, split bamboo system which ran from a river 6 km away. He might have survived longer than 1900 had not a villager betrayed his location to

The Borneo nob who resisted the British made his stand in a jungle redoubt at Tambunan.

The railway from Kota Kinabalu to Tenom slices thr Sabah's wildernе

British Chartered Company forces which promptly cut off Mat Salleh's water supply, surrounded the fort and waited. The rebel and his thirsty followers were all shot down when they emerged, and the rebellion launched by a native lord who refused to pay tax to foreigners ended.

The Other Side of the Mountain

In **Sandakan**, Sabah's big, busy, boom town, people call the huge logs bobbing in the Sulu Sea "floating money." They float down the wide rivers from timber forests surrounding the harbor, pass through the hands of Chinese entrepreneurs, and are lifted onto massive freighters bound for Japan. So Sandakan prospers, like a mini Hong Kong, with the clatter of *mahjong* tiles and the wail of Chinese opera.

Once the capital of North Borneo, Sandakan was burned to its pavements during the bombings of World War II and completely rebuilt later with some new trimmings: the rare and pampered foliage in Orchid House, wildlife realities at the Forestry Exhibition. Sandakan has the world's largest Orang Utan suburb —**Sepilok Sanctuary**, 24 km from town — and three offshore islands are populated almost entirely with green turtles. Thirty-two km across the bay are the hallowed **Gomantang Caves** which are rich in birds' nests used to make birds' nest soup. MAS (Malaysian Airline System) offers forty-five-minute flights from Kota Kinabalu to Sandakan every day. You can also travel overland on the East-West Highway. Consult the Landrover drivers at the bus stations in KK and Sandakan.

epilok Sanctuary, 4 km from andakan, houses e world's largest angutan suburb.

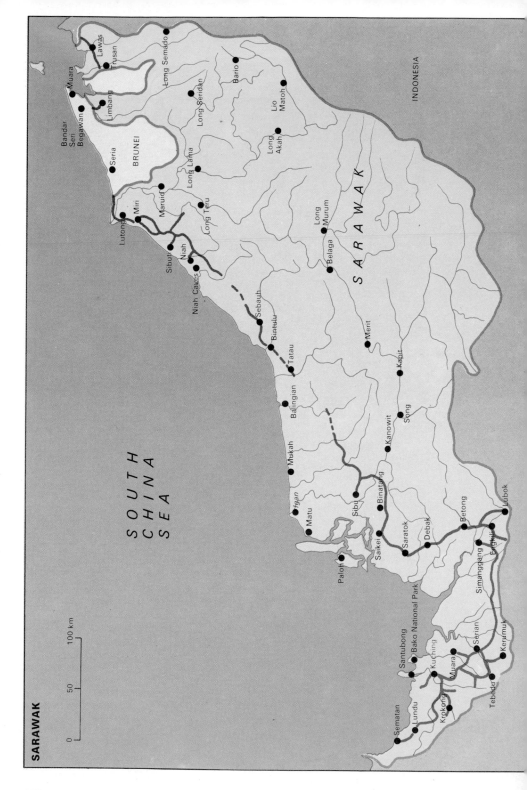

SARAWAK

SOUTH
CHINA
SEA

0   50   100 km

INDONESIA

S A R A W A K

BRUNEI

Lawas
Trusan
Long Semado
Bario
Muara
Bandar
Seri
Begawan
Limbang
Long Seridan
Lio
Matoh
Seria
Long
Akah
Long Lama
Miri
Maruid
Long Teru
Long
Murum
Lutong
Niah
Belaga
Sibuti
Niah Caves
Sebauh
Bintulu
Tatau
Merit
Balingian
Kapit
Mukah
Song
Iyan
Kanowit
Matu
Paloh
Sibu
Binatang
Betong
Lubok
Saikei
Saratok
Debak
Engkili
Santubong
Simanggang
Bako National Park
Kuching
Skrian
Kerumuk
Sematan
Lundu
Krokong
Muara
Tebedu

250

tales from the longhouse

Sarawak is still a name that evokes more romance than reality. White Rajahs and Borneo headhunters ring more bells than 125,000 square km of hills, jungle and swampland just north of the equator. Sarawak is a land of abundant rainfall and innumerable rivers that weave over one-third of the Borneo isle. Borneo is now divided into Indonesia's Kalimantan, Malaysia's Sabah and Sarawak states, and the tiny sultanate of Brunei which once ruled them all.

Actually Sarawak is a Kelabit agricultural center, a Malay fishing village, an Iban longhouse, a Punan jungle camp, a Malanau sago factory and a Land Dyak rice field all at once. The Brooke dynasty created Sarawak's borders, suppressed headhunting, established peace, and safeguarded the economy against land-hungry entrepreneurs. For a hundred years, from 1841 to 1946, Sarawak was a contented Raj governed by a handful of dedicated European officials. They allowed each Borneo tribe the individuality of its inherited customs and promised a future with few abrupt changes from the past. Though the white Rajahs' rule ended more than three decades ago with a dignified resignation to the British crown, it left a legacy that characterizes Sarawak today — the idyllic royal residence which graces the well-trimmed gardens across the Sarawak River, the old fashioned portraits of the Rajahs enshrined on a longhouse wall, the Sarawak flag which bewildered local chroniclers who tried to determine whether James Brooke wanted St. George's cross deep blue or purple. On wide, silent rivers lined with mangrove forests one can still envision Rajah Charles Brooke under a plumed sun-helmet, standing knock-

The legacy of Sarawak—Iban wedding ceremonies, family gatherings and Rajah Charles Brooke — remains enshrined in faded snapshots framed on a longhouse wall (previous pages).

kneed on the bow of a longboat en route upriver to sign a peace treaty.

Yet the Rajahs' days have inexorably passed. Since 1963 Sarawak has been a member of the independent Federation of Malaysia, struggling against all traces of colonialism to develop a modern state. Some of the old serenity is gone, with the advent of the oil industry and as government ministries launch five-year development plans with an emphatic push. Communist influence has grown among some Chinese and inland people. But compared with many countries in Asia, Sarawak is an oasis of calm, particularly for foreigners.

Sarawak's long tradition of open hospitality is what makes city or jungle travel so genuine. A traveler can strike up a conversation with a Chinese salesgirl over a fresh-fruit stand in Kuching, or chat with an Iban longhouse chief over a glass of the heady, home-brewed *tuak,* the ubiquitous palm wine of Sarawak.

An assortment of travel agents contacted through the tourist association will streamline the local scenery for a couple of days by arranging a longhouse visit or a riverboat tour. But the real challenge of Sarawak is an expedition upriver to visit the Kayans, Kenyahs, Muruts, Kelabits and Punan people who have made the hinterland their home for nearly forty millennia. Most who have made the trip rightly claim that explorers should spend a couple of weeks, take their own provisions and enough money to hire river transport. Arrangements are best made right on the spot by contacting district officers who man the outstations. The tourist association is the best source of information. For details, write the Sarawak Tourist Association, Kuching, Malaysia.

A new road has recently been opened linking Kuching to Sibu. MAS flies from Kuching to all major towns in Sarawak, offering excellent short cuts for inland river expeditions. It also links Sarawak directly to

Singapore, Brunei and Sabah. For a slow sea cruise from Singapore to Kuching, contact the Straits Steamship Company for your bookings.

Sampans in Midtown

Kuching is a riverine town with contrasting sides, new and old, busy and serene, fluctuating and timeless. All the noisy, tightly packed one-way streets and concrete multi-story buildings are on the left side of the Sarawak River. In the late afternoon enough citizens quit work to slow the city down. Elderly laborers in baggy shorts relax at a tiny park on the riverbank, which has a painted dragon fountain and old stone balustrades. They find a bench as the river's sheen reddens with the sunset, and gaze across the water to the noble residence and rolling lawns cultivated by the white Rajahs. They would have seen the same scene a century ago.

The young, debonaire James Brooke, whose admiration for Sir Stamford Raffles lured him to the little known East, chatted with the ladies on the Singapore cocktail circuit in 1838, promising he would keep in touch after his voyage to Borneo. Aside from a brief stint in the Indian Army, James held no titles among the British foreign legion, but he came across as a cultured Englishman who was the embodiment of romantic adventure, and what he lacked in rank he made up for in publicity. He was also a diplomat and a strategist, assets which, aside from his awe-inspiring appearance, earned him almost by accident sole rule of Sarawak.

When James Brooke's ship *The Royalist* wound its way upriver to

Rajah James Brooke conceived of Sarawak as an Asian state benevolently guided by Europeans.

Kuching huddles beside and lives on the Sarawak River.

Kuching in 1839, Sarawak was suffering. Brutal extortions demanded by the Brunei overlords had reached such extremes that the inland Dyaks, assisted by some indigenous Malays and Chinese, had rebelled. The Brunei aristocracy ruling these lands urged James to stay on as their protector. To the amazement of all he managed to talk both sides into agreeing upon a truce, but even more flabbergasting to the Brunei overlords was his insistence that the lives of the rebels be spared and that they be allowed to return to their villages. Thus, James befriended the Dyaks, Malays and Chinese. He had quelled the rebellion for the Brunei overlords and in return was promised their lands as Rajah of Sarawak. And he had introduced a novelty which became the essence of the white Rajahs' rule: justice without favoritism.

If the peculiar genius of James Brooke conceived Sarawak as a state where a handful of Europeans should guide numerous Eastern races to a life of harmonious peace, it was his nephew Charles Brooke, second white Rajah, who sealed its reality and bestowed on it an unmistakable aura that the town of Kuching still possesses. Unlike James, who lived in a nimbus of international glamor, Charles was reserved in manner, difficult to approach. He had accustomed himself to months of loneliness as a district officer in the jungle where he lived among Dyak friends. Throughout his reign he cultivated a betel nut plantation in the back of the Astana (palace) which provided gifts when he entertained Dyak chieftains. He was often more relaxed in their presence than during the stiffly formal tea parties he staged each Tuesday —

ort Margherita is ɔw a police museum ɔsplaying weapons the warlike tribes.

with a Sarawak Ranger fanning the guests with a palm leaf—for his European officials.

Typical of his taciturn nature, Charles Brooke proposed marriage to the young Margaret de Windt by handing her a note while she was playing the piano. It read:

"With a humble demean
 If the King were to pray
That You'd be his Queen,
 Would you *not* say *Nay*?"

Margaret, twenty years his junior, laughed at first and then said "Yes," and much to the dismay of her snobbish family, left Europe to live in Kuching. The Ranee Margaret soon grew to love Sarawak. She wrote several books about her life there and accompanied her husband on journeys upriver where her gentle kindness to her native hosts did much to create an atmosphere of goodwill. She found that life with the Rajah demanded more understanding than affirmative replies. Though she was an exceedingly accomplished pianist, no one would ever request her to display her musical skill on the battered old Erard piano. The Rajah's vocal renditions of Victorian ballads, however, were much admired by everyone except his wife. The Rajah went to great pains trying unsuccessfully to change Margaret's spendthrift ways, but his deep respect for her never wavered and when the fort was built he named it after her.

Fort Margherita has been converted into a police museum housing a multitude of lethal weapons and interesting exhibits. Many objects survive from the Rajahs' days. There is the one and only cannon ever cast in Sarawak which was hauled up Sandok Mountain by 500 Dyaks in 1861 to defeat the famous rebel chief named Rentap. It did its job. One tower of the fort is called *Bilek Antu Pala*, "Chamber of the Laughing Skulls." The original owner of the skulls, a Sea Dyak who claimed they

were 200 years old, sold them to the police because, as he explained, the skulls sometimes emitted sounds like "human laughters."

The Execution Kris recalls one of Sarawak's most colorful personalities—a tremendously strong and tall Malay named Subu who held the titles of State Executioner and Royal Umbrella Carrier until 1873. Subu was an expert at the kris and would tell the condemned man to kneel down as if he was sitting by his bedside. The man never knew when Subu would approach him from behind and send him to eternity with one swift blow. Once when Subu was sick his son took over and plunged the kris into the wrong side. Undismayed, he withdrew it, said "I'm sorry," and plunged it in again without a murmur from the condemned man.

For many years Fort Margherita was the first glimpse all newcomers had of Kuching. It protected the town from attack by commanding the long stretch of river at its entrance. During the Rajah's rule sentries would pace the ramparts calling out "All's well" every hour on the hour throughout the night. Their cries carried a long way, certainly long enough to reach the Astana. Not that the Rajah wanted to know the time, but he did want to know that the sentries were not asleep.

Charles Brooke was a benevolent despot who insisted his fingers be in every pie in Sarawak. He personally selected which marble slabs were to be used for the fish stalls in the Kuching Market. He commissioned the design of all public buildings, supervised the construction of the Astana, chose the paint color for Fort Margherita and the uniforms for the Sarawak Rangers. He sailed to the Philippines to personally select a conductor for the Municipal Band and determined all its music. He created a virtual "hot line" in memoranda to his district officers in the outback insisting, among many other things, that they should never be

The second white rajah, Charles Brooke, built Kuching into a modern town.

caught sitting in an easy chair.

Until his last years, he would rise with the five o'clock gun, dress in white trousers and blue serge coat with a fresh sprig of honeysuckle in his buttonhole and ceremoniously proceed to the court house across the river, where he had the last word. He also spent some time in the Treasury, and though the accountants quivered beneath his sharp eye, Sarawak had never been so prosperous. Nor was it ever so peaceful for so long.

At 86, Rajah Charles Brooke still ruled his country in the morning and took 3 km walks in the afternoon. When he died in 1917, a significant era of white Rajah rule ended. Several years later, his eldest son — the third Rajah Charles Vyner Brooke — some European officials, Malay aristocrats, Dyak chieftains and Chinese merchants congregated outside the old court house to honor the man who had devoted sixty-five years of his life to Sarawak — forty-nine years as Rajah. As the Iban chief Penghulu Biju unveiled the obelisk memorial, the first airplane ever sighted in Sarawak appeared. Some guests were sure that the spirit of the old Rajah had risen.

The other side of Kuching is another world entirely. The past in which the white Rajahs dwelt is taken at face value — done and gone. The splendid isolation which nurtured rolling lawns and municipal bands has vanished. Most people are profit-oriented or development-oriented, or both. If vendors cannot squeeze their wares into the walk-in sundry stores crowded together on a shop-house row, they set up their sales pitch on the sidewalk. With jewelers, cobblers and barbers competing for the pave-

e market at ching briskly des in fresh fish ught in from the rounding waters.

ment, many shoppers resign themselves to the pedestrian confusion and stroll on the streets — or across the street to the riverside fish market where breathing space is even more elusive.

Kuching is an Asian rendezvous. James Brooke found only a couple hundred Malays and a dozen Chinese. Ten years later 5,000 people had come to his town. Malay nobles, whose families had ruled the Borneo coasts since the 15th century, moved down from upriver. Land Dyaks living in nearby longhouses came to don proudly the uniform of a Sarawak Ranger. Indian Muslims arrived under the auspices of the East India Company to work as sepoys or domestic servants. Now Kuching, with a population of around 130,000, has a lively night bazaar on India Street, congregational prayers at the Malay mosque, and a Dyak Minister of Culture in the state cabinet.

Above all others in numbers came the Chinese to seek their fortunes in a land their countrymen had recorded at the dawn of the Christian era. They came from Dutch-controlled Indonesian Borneo, from Singapore and from China to work the gold mines in the interior. Immigration was often a nightmare. Junks tossed about like corks in rough seas with passengers packed so tightly on deck that they could hardly move, much less eat their daily rations of a bowl of rice and three teaspoons of water. Understandably one of the first duties of the immigrant was to build a shrine to offer thanksgiving to the gods for a safe delivery. Most dreamed of returning home from the "land of promise" as rich men — a dream which sustained them

The days of the white rajahs long gone, Sarawak today strives to establish a moder Malaysian identit

Indian as well as Chinese merchant trade at Kuching'. market.

256

during grueling labors in malaria-infested jungles. Many successful merchants found their wish had come true and settled in Sarawak. Downtown Kuching is a splash of bold, red Chinese calligraphy and brightly painted temples filled with burning incense. Business hours are filled with the sound of Chinese pop tunes.

The Brooke dynasty surfaces to the present only on contemporary reflection. A Sarawak-born Governor now resides in the Astana. When he travels to the other side of the river, he does so behind the sirens of motorcade escort and inside a polished, white Rolls Royce with the Sarawak flag flapping above the bonnet.

Images Charged with Intensity

Sarawak Museum not only contains laughing skulls, Chinese shrines and old Islamic graveyards, but it links the present with the past. Its conception probably took place over a cup of tea in the Astana, for among the second Rajah's innumerable pre-occupations was the Sarawak Museum which was designed by his French valet after a town house in Normandy. The Rajah built it in 1888 largely under the influence of his friend Alfred Russell Wallace, co-founder of the evolutionary theory. Wallace spent two years in Sarawak and compiled not far from Kuching his first paper on natural selection. Now, every student considers the Orang Utan mankind's first cousin, and Kuching's only Normandy town house has become an exotic showpiece for a rare decorative art.

The museum's facade may have its origins in France, but its interior is dedicated to the soul of Borneo.

*e skull of a slain
?my taken by
1d-hunting Ibans,
display at the
rawak Museum.*

The Brookes were steadfast in their sense of justice. They suppressed crime and established peace. But they wisely refrained from imposing any "civilized" *vs* "primitive" comparisons upon the native cultures. The Rajahs personally insisted upon capable curators, whose Western expertise was to serve only to illuminate the ethnological richness of Borneo and the vivid expressions of the societies it nourished.

The museum is jammed with exotic fineries of the inland tribes. One display case is devoted to the bead-conscious Kelabits who have names for sixty varieties of ancient glass beads, each one with a special price. Another case houses figurines carved 2,000 years ago by the now-extinct Sru Dyaks. An entire corner of the museum has been transformed into an Iban longhouse, with simu-

lated fires burning, genuine skulls hanging from the rafters, and a warrior's headdress and finely sharpened weaponry resting near his bedside as if he were about to walk in and sound the battle cry. The Sarawak people's deep love for adornment is reflected by the high walls painted with free-flowing designs. A museum employee found one end of a Kenyah longhouse in Long Nawang completely covered with a mural celebrating "The Tree of Life" and commissioned the painter to reproduce it.

Past rituals that lent a somewhat brutal aspect to tribal societies remain on record. Giant, hand-carved burial poles with the ashes of the dead enshrined in lofty niches have been carried from upriver graveyards and propped up on the museum lawn. In olden days, slaves were sometimes sacrificed by being crushed to death

The Sarawak Museum, built at the prompting of Alfred Russell Wallace, is a treasure trove of native artifacts and nature displays.

A native Kenyah artist decorated the interior wall of the Sarawak Museum with "The Tree of Life," a motif originally found in a longhouse in Long Nawang.

at the foot of the pole, if a family was in dire need to appease the spirit of the deceased. An isolated loft in the longhouse display recreates the tradition of *Anak Umbong* (Secluded Daughter), whereby a Dyak chief refused to allow anyone to catch sight of his daughter until a heroic warrior claimed her as his bride.

The museum has a fanciful eclectic character that recalls a succession of spirited curators, as well as the marvelous diversity of Sarawak. There is a human dental plate on display that was found in the stomach of a 6-meter crocodile. A rhinoceros-horn cup that can detect poison is another item. The drink bubbled up if it was contaminated and since Chinese princes were always trying to poison each other, rhinoceros horn was in high demand during the days of the dynasties. Over in the Invertebrate gallery, visitors can find out that Damsel flies have been on earth for 300 million years, that the Long-Horned Beetle was Wallace's favorite insect, and that the flea is the world's strongest jumper, leaping as much as 200 times the length of its body, which is roughly equivalent to a midget jumping 300 meters, the write-up explains. The museum even has a piece of red, white and blue ribbon salvaged from the opening ceremony of the first American Consulate.

If the museum is the storehouse of an odd but wealthy heritage, it is also a living museum. Throughout the week, schoolchildren breeze past exhibits during their Cultural Hour, pausing only long enough to jot down facts in their note pads. Young office workers may spend a half-hour looking at the "Where Oil Comes From" display. On Sundays, large families mill through the exhibition galleries, making a museum visit the social occasion of the week. Outside are peanut and candy stands, an open-air aquarium in the museum's gardens, which double as a public park, and a handicraft shop. Patrons are invited to help support the native arts

by buying those items on sale as souvenirs. The handicraft shop is a non-profit-making organization run by the government to help encourage local craftsmen. Though the items are new, they retain the unmistakable entwining patterns that mirror the intensity of a jungle environment and the perception of those who live there.

Yet the museum in essence reflects a change in Borneo life. As Sarawak moves into the eighties, museum pieces move back from reality. What was preserved differs from the goals of progress and modernization, and the luxuries they promise. The white Rajahs have been safely canonized. They are a regal if strange page in the history of Sarawak, but today's horizons are much wider than the Rajah's social elite in Kuching.

Temples and Side-Trips

Like many other Malay towns, Kuching has its share of ornate and interesting temples. The Tua Pek Kong Temple is Kuching's oldest temple built in 1876 on a small hillock at the junction of Thomson and Padungan Roads. Fishermen pray for good catches and a safe return from the sea at the temple of Tien Hou, Goddess of Seamen, in Padungan. If you have a special request visit the Hong San Temple on the corner of Ewe Hai and Wayang Streets. This temple is dedicated to the thousand year-old Hokkien god, Kuek Seng Ong, who is reputed always to reward those who pray to him.

If you have more time in Kuching there are several interesting side trips which can be made in less than a day. Sunworshipers will enjoy the hour's express boat ride to **Santubong**, Kuching's most popular seaside resort and fishing village. Santubong's history dates back to the Tun and Sung dynasties (between the 7th and 13th century AD) when it was an important trading center. Ancient Hindu and Buddhist-influenced rock carvings have been discovered around the river delta.

Longhouses are a unique feature of life in Sarawak and although the more interesting ones are to be found up-river in the remote areas of the State, there is a longhouse just 35 km from Kuching at **Segu Benuk** which is accessible by road.

An hour's trip by speedboat, or two by motor launch and fishing boat, brings you to **Bako National Park**, situated on a peninsula at the mouth of the Sarawak river. Bako's relatively small area - 10 square miles of primary rain forest bounded on one side by a picturesque coastline of sandy beaches and steep cliffs - nevertheless has much flora and fauna to interest the nature lover. There is good, safe bathing on the beaches whose rocky coves provide safe haven and fine hunting grounds for kingfishers, sunbirds and reef egrets.

The rain forest is home to beautiful, albeit deadly to the unwary insect, carnivorous flowers and plants and to small animals such as the long nosed monkey, pigs and sambar deer which often may be seen on the beaches even in daylight. Within the park there is a system of well-marked paths. The Lintang trail leads to a salt lick and a small observation hide where, if you are enormously patient, you may see animals come to drink.

Bako National Park is an easy day trip from Kuching, but should you wish to stay in the Park there is accommodation at the Rest House at Telok Assam. Reservations may be made by telephone or writing to the Forest Warden, Bako National Park, Post Office, Forest Department, Jalan Badrudin, Kuching. Telephone 24479. Bako is accessible only by boat and during the monsoon months from November to February when the sea is often rough, it may not be possible to reach or leave Telok Assam, so it is advisable to check first with the Forest Warden.

Journey up the Rajang River

Beyond Kuching, cosmopolitan city life fades and the innumerable rivers that mark Sarawak's green interior reclaim their high status. **Sibu**, capital of Sarawak's third and largest division, is an easy-going, predominantly Chinese town where trishaws are still in service and where fish markets overflow with gigantic freshwater carp. A forty-minute flight from Kuching leads to the gateway of the great Rajang River delta where most of Sarawak's inland people dwell. To journey there is to experience their life.

From Sibu a big, bulky speed-boat, aptly called "The Kapit Express," roars upriver past rural Chinese settlements to the last out-station on the Rajang. The bottom of the boat is reinforced with steel plate. It has a definite purpose. The Rajang River, Sarawak's longest water highway, is Route 66 to the local timber industry. Rafts with as many as 200 logs float downstream, and should one break off and become water-logged, it could mean farewell to an outboard engine. But to the steel-plated Kapit Express it merely means a thunderous crash and a skip in the ride.

Passengers on the Kapit Express may include a Malay district officer, a Chinese merchant, a Eurasian clergyman or an Iban farmer with a neck tattoo showing above his shirt collar. The boat skims past long-houses half hidden by jungle, and past longboats so crowded with people and goods that only a centimeter of free board remains above water. It passes **Kanowit** where the second Rajah built a fort to suppress head-hunting, and **Song** where Japanese troops spread tidings of the new Asia Co-Prosperity Sphere. By the time it reaches **Kapit** — a five-hour ride from Sibu — coffee shops are serving fried noodle luncheons and workmen are taking their afternoon nap. Kapit has 8 km of road, ten automobiles and traffic

A trip upriver ventures into the hidden jungle, to riverine villages, a to Dyak longhous

problems. But to people who live far up the Rajang, Kapit is London — the town with bright lights, variety of shops, Western imports and two cinemas. Not that the bulletins advertising the night's show coincide with the film on screen, but when you live upriver in a TV-less longhouse, nobody really minds.

Kapit lies in the heart of Iban country — Sarawak's largest indigenous population. Ibans were once the belligerent headhunters who romanticized Borneo into the fantasies of the world. Warriors set out in huge longboats, fearlessly chasing trading ships out to the high seas, when piracy was at its zenith. Thus, Ibans earned the incongruous appellation of "Sea Dyaks" — "Dyak" basically defining the non-Malay tribes — even though their habitat was the hinterland where they cultivated hill rice on mountain sides and hunted food in the surrounding tropical rain forest.

Ibans are a proud and democratic people, sharing a communal way of life in longhouses, honoring the supernatural forces recognized by their religion, and remaining loyal to their heritage and to their heroes. One early leader was the warrior Rentap, whose name in Iban means "one who makes the world shake." Tribal wars were common in Rentap's days when natives competed for favorable soils in which to plant their rice. Sarawak is basically an infertile land where top soil erodes quickly. For many years, longhouse dwellers were continually forced to resettle, even if it meant destroying another longhouse to do so.

Rentap, being a powerful and dauntless Iban chief, did not want James Brooke or any other foreigner to rule over his people. He fought so

n Iban warrior in aditional dress.

fiercely against the Rajah's foot soldiers that it took five years and a 4.4-kilo cannon to defeat the chief. Rentap eventually surrendered, but not before letting the Rajah know that Ibans could not be pushed around.

After Rentap's battle cries had died down, Ibans grew to respect the Brookes even though their new-fangled ideas conflicted with the traditions of head-hunting and piracy. The second Iban to rise to the heroic limelight mirrored the change. His name was Penghulu Koh and every joint of his fingers was covered with tattoos signifying that he had taken heads in battle.

Penghulu Koh reformed to become one of Rajah Brooke's staunchest supporters. As an influential Iban chief, he was present at every truce the Rajah made with the Borneo peoples. He became Sarawak's Master of Peace Ceremonies and for his service was awarded the honor of Penghulu Temenggong Koh, paramount chief of all Ibans. His loyalty to the British administration never wavered. One of Koh's best friends, whom he later adopted as his son, was Malcolm MacDonald, British Commissioner-General in Southeast Asia after the Second World War. When MacDonald's critics wrote letters to the newspapers denouncing his "pronative" social mixing as being beyond the bounds of protocol, Temenggong Koh approached his adopted son and enquired: "Can we go and take the writers' heads?"

The spirit of Temenggong Koh still lingers in many Iban longhouses. Faded photographs of the Rajah Brookes and Queen Elizabeth in her twenties reverently hang from longhouse walls, along with contemporary magazine clippings immortalizing Asian beauty queens, racing cars or Mr. and Mrs. Elvis Presley pictured cutting their wedding cake.

Iban life is in transition. Much about a longhouse today differs from the impeccably kept replica in the Sarawak Museum. The "secluded daughter" tradition has lapsed. Many longhouse heirlooms — beautiful antique swords and silver dollar belts — have been sold to Chinese jewelers in big towns. Children who once enjoyed carefree play days around the longhouse are now in school studying English and Bahasa Malaysia. The virile and difficult dance of the warrior, and the chants and the gongs that accompanied it, are a traditional revival rather than the contemporary norm. Even tattoos are being forsaken by many young Ibans.

Yet much of Iban life continues as it always has. In the Sarawak Museum, one never hears the rumble of split-bamboo floors as people scurry from a rain shower. Or old farmers after a workday in the rice fields comparing their fighting cocks. Or the *tuai rumah*, headman of the longhouse, requesting his wife to bring hot coffee for his foreign guests. Iban hospitality is as strong as ever. Visitors are received by the *tuai rumah* as house guests in his home. It is polite to bring one's own food — canned provisions bought in Sibu or Kapit — and a small gift for the *tuai rumah* — candy or cigarettes.

Secrets from the Stone Age

Niah Caves may not look impressive from the outside, but the Great Cave alone has a floor space of 11 hectares and is high enough to shame a jungle tree. In the 1870s, animal collector and adventurer, A. Hart Everett, came across the caves — already well-known and protected by the local people — only to dismiss them as rather dull. Everybody believed him for the next sixty years. It was not until the 1950s that the Sarawak Museum heard of the potential archeologist's goldmine. Sure enough, when the curator dug down 5 meters he found the skull of a young *Homo sapiens* who had lived in the caves 40,000 years ago. The "deep skull" was what remained of the earliest

Though tribal life continues much as once did, the future is uncertain. TV wi come to the longhouses and modernization is inevitable.

A Kenyah Dyak woman has traditional ornamental elongate ears, but also sports a batik T-shirt.

known modern man in the East. It disproved any haughty theories which insisted that mankind's true ancestors dwelled on the west side of the Middle East and wandered over later. As the museum delicately probed the layers of soft deposit, it unearthed the evolution of a human culture. Many agreed it was the greatest discovery since the Java Man.

Forty millennia ago, the Niahian had primitive stone tools and little else. But by 10000 B.C. he was working with sophisticated instruments made from bone and shell, and by 4000 B.C. he was carving burial boats with polished adzes and using scarlet haematite to paint the symbolic death ships on the cave walls. When the Iron Age reached Borneo in A.D. 700, the Niahians were trading hornbill ivory and edible birds' nests for Chinese porcelain and beads. They

decorated enormous earthenware urns and placed them beside the graves of special men. Then in 1400 they seem to have entered a tropical Dark Age which forced them to desert the caves. They then vanished from history.

The Niahians were probably the forefathers of the nomadic Punans whose elders still maintain beliefs and rituals that allude to those in the prehistoric graveyards of the Great Caves. The Punans rediscovered the caves in the 19th century and found them to be unbelievably rich in edible birds' nests. Millions of tiny swiftlets inhabit the bowels of Niah Caves. Their glutinous saliva with which they build their nests remains the most expensive food in Borneo. For good reason. A man in the birds' nest collecting business has no hope of collecting life insurance as well. A

Borneo's history goes back to the Stone Age, but many of the Dyak peoples are probab fairly recent settler

In the longhouses o Borneo the entire community is house under one roof, sharing a common veranda. Each family has a private compartment.

264

typical day's work entails scurrying up 60 meters on a slender bamboo pole, scraping nests off rock ceilings, and keeping balance where any fall could be fatal.

Nevertheless, nest collectors guard their trade jealously and pass their inherited territory only to their sons. The hundreds of chambers, chimneys, and subcaves where the swiftlets nest are divided into sectors, each privately owned. Some yield but a few hundred nests, others many thousands. The "cave-owners" live in nearby villages or longhouses and during birds' nest season — two or three times a year — they may bring the entire family along to help gather up the riches.

The Niah Caves are not exactly around the corner. Travelers must fly or sail to Miri, Sarawak's oil town near the Brunei border; drive for two hours to Batu Niah where there is a hotel; hop on a longboat for forty-five minutes to Pangkalan Loban and there take an hour's plank-walk to the awesome western caverns of the Great Cave, which excavators named "Hell." The walk, which weaves through noisy, dense, triple-canopied jungle, is a journey *extraordinaire*. Within the cave the floor is covered with guano — oily, stinking, excellent fertilizer. The ancient "writing on the wall" is hidden in the dark and people who wish to see it must make prior arrangements with either the Sarawak or the Brunei Museum. Yet, there is no other place where one can watch five million bats and swiftlets pour out of the darkness; suffer with laborers who lug 100 kilos of guano on their back; and stand on the same spot that a *Homo sapiens* stood 40,000 years ago. Borneo is still Borneo.

southeast asia's oil sultanate

Brunei is a goldleaf, dome-dominated realm — Islamic and gentle. Though locked into the geography of Sabah and Sarawak like a strong link in a chain, Brunei remains an autonomous sultanate, connected to its neighbor through history, culture and faith, yet separated by a long tradition of independent rule. Both Malaysia and Brunei share the classical fineries of their Malay heritage. They speak a common national language and hark back to a common race. Yet Brunei today has a singular distinction: the Sultan rules. Gold minarets command the national skyline. Arabic script tops the signboards on Chinese shop houses. The muezzin's lofty call to prayer is the municipal timepiece, awakening **Bandar Seri Begawan**, Brunei's capital city, at dawn and lulling it back to sleep in the evening.

A certain smugness surrounds Brunei, a combination of wealth, dignity, leisure and wistfulness.

The government provides an extensive pension scheme for the needy. Nobody pays income tax. Coffee shops and barber shops are packed with morning customers until well after ten.

Brunei has its own color television station and TVs sell like hot cakes. The government provides longhouses with a TV and generator, treating jungle-dwellers to mind-boggling encounters with the 20th century. After Queen Elizabeth's 1972 visit was telecast, the country bubbled with excitement. Brunei is a tiny nation of 5,765 square km, split in two by the Limbang river basin of Sarawak. It is also a British Protectorate where the portrait of the Sultan hangs side by side with that of the Queen of England. "The Rajah Brookes were just about to gobble up Brunei entirely," said one candid resident, "until the British discovered oil."

Gold minaret glistens above the famous water village which is part of Brunei's capital city (previous pages).

The friendly relations that were struck up between the Empire and the Sultanate when oil was found in Brunei have continued to this day.

Aside from the modern touch — the muezzin taking the lift to the minaret — **Omar Ali Saifuddin Mosque** conjures up all the stark and somber elegance that surrounds Muslim worship. Its interior hues are as subdued as a forest in autumn, and the silence therein is powerful enough to arch the dome. The mosque's construction demanded a world-wide search. The land was reclaimed from the Brunei River, the granite was imported from Hong Kong, the bronze Koranic inscriptions sent from England, the marble and masons from Italy. Above all, the mosque reflects the wishes of its namesake who designed it. Sultan Sir Omar Ali Saifuddin, the ruler who guided Brunei to its modern age and then abdicated in

1968 in favor of his son, desired that his country's material wealth contribute to the strengthening of its faith. In this wish, he is preceded by twenty-seven sultans.

Brunei entered the ancient world in A.D. 600 but it was not until the illustrious reign of Bolkiah, fifth sultan of Brunei, that the Brunei Malays could wander over the entire island of Borneo and the southern Philippines beyond without leaving their land. That was in the 15th century when Sultan Bolkiah, known

Oil rich Brunei is a intriguing amalgar of the traditional and the modern.

The Churchill Museum houses o of the best collections of Churchill memorabilia.

among his people as "The Singing Admiral," was fond of journeying to his territories and scattering one speck of pepper at every place he visited until he had used up a full gallon. When Magellan's fleet sailed past the Brunei River after it had lost its captain in a battle at Cebu in the Philippines, great note was taken of the sultan's palace — his elephants, horses and unusual cannons.

The first plank at **Kampung Ayer**, Brunei's famous water village, was probably nailed into place in the middle of the 16th century by fugitives escaping from Spanish warships downriver. Inadvertently, they had hit upon an ideal spot: a sharp bend in the river with hills rising on either side. With these foundations laid and with international commerce thriving, Brunei settled down to a long period of prosperity as a pirate lair. Flotillas of longboats, forty armed men to each, would swoop down on unexpecting traders who dared to linger at the mouth of the river. The pirates would return with copra, nutmeg and pepper, and occasionally a prisoner, if she was pretty. All went well until James Brooke and Admiral Sir Henry Keppel wiped out the pirates from the Borneo coast. Then Brunei began to decline, ceding its territory north and south, until the 1929 oil strike when the economy took a sharp upward turn. It has not looked back since.

* * *

In **Seria**, the oil city in the southwest, on a highway, everyone seems to smoke imported cigarettes, drink good whisky and speak with a Texan accent, or with a British Texan accent. English and Dutch engineers help hold up the umbrella of Shell Company that safeguards Brunei's economy, while American experts at offshore drilling rigs disappear for two weeks at a stretch.

Yet because Brunei is so internationally unpretentious it makes a good place to visit. Three miles outside Bandar Seri Begawan, where the Sultan's palace once caught the eye of Magellan's men there now stands the sparkling new and rich **Brunei Museum.** Here are to be seen, if you can focus your attention on the collections rather than on the magnificent vista of the Brunei River, ornate bronzes, Chinese porcelains, dioramas of natural life and artifacts of the tribes which populate not only Brunei, but all Borneo. In the center of Bandar Seri Begawan is the **Churchill Museum** which is devoted to Churchill's life and times and which houses a collection of his memorabilia. The only reason for this museum is that Sultan Sir Omar Ali Saifuddin is a great admirer of "Winnie." Next to this museum is the **Aquarium** which, although small, is unusually absorbing simply because one attendant took pains to display each local fish individually and then write about it.

The majestic Omar Ali Saifuddin Mosque, in Bandar Seri Begawan.

erfect blend of modern technology and the watch maker's art.

OMEGA

A proud Malaysian tradition

 ention Malaysian handicraft, and along with images of bright, bold batik emerges the satin glow of Selangor Pewter. The most reknowned pewter in this part of the world, Selangor Pewter has earned itself a name as the hallmark of this highly specialised craft.

What is now a multi-million dollar industry started out very humbly. In 1885, a young pewtersmith from Swatow, China, came to Kuala Lumpur. He started out by making traditional joss-stick holders and incense burners used mainly for ancestral worship.

Today, with 500 craftsmen producing over 100,000 pieces of pewter a month, Selangor Pewter still maintains a proud tradition of painstaking care and craftsmanship. Craftsman continue to hand-finish every single piece of Selangor Pewter.

Soldering by a skilled pewtersmith

It takes three weeks from ingot stage to finished product. There are two methods used in pewter making — spinning and casting. In spinning, a lathe is used to fashion the metal into the desired form.

Selangor Pewter is mostly cast. Weight for weight, cast pewter is stronger. In casting, a molten alloy containing tin, some antimony and copper, is poured into the design mould Selangor Pewter uses a formula of 97% Straits Refined Tin, 3% antimony and copper.

Once the pewter cools, it is first polished with very fine steel wool. and then a 'stone leaf' is used. This leaf finer than the finest sandpaper, is the gentlest possible abrasive for this stage of careful polishing. The final stage is hand polishing with a felt cloth. And this is what brings the satin glow of the pewter to immaculate perfection

As useful it is beautiful

As beautiful, as it is, Selangor Pewter is extremely useful. Whether it is only a goblet or a coffee service, Selangor Pewter has proven to be the choice of discerning people everywhere. But that isn't all. Selangor Pewter has acquired a reputation wherever fine quality momentos, gifts and trophies are required.

Selangor Pewter is more than just a name. Today, it is the name for quality pewter. Pewter that is known by its soft sheen, its lustre and its quiet elegance.

We fly the world the way the world wants to fly.

Everyday, Pan Am flies you to San Francisco and New York with convenient same-day connections to all major U.S. cities. And, five times a week, we take travellers from Singapore for the best bargains in Hong Kong. In fact, we fly more people to the United States than any other airline — with the fastest one-stop hop from Singapore to the West Coast. All on the world's largest fleet of 747s and 747SPs.

And because we have a whole world to fly, we have a good idea what the world wants from an airline.

See your Travel Agent and ask for Pan Am.

TWIN PEARLS

The Rasa Sayang and its younger twin, the Golden Sands offer you a priceless experience of a holiday in Penang. Set on the same stretch of golden beach, they give you precious encounters of the sea, the sunshine, an indescribable feeling of la dolce vita with Malaysian hospitality. When you next visit Penang, come to the Rasa Sayang or the Golden Sands. They are for epicureans of beach resorts.

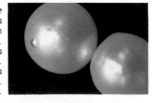

 **Rasa Sayang Hotel**

P.O. BOX 735, BATU FERINGGI BEACH, PENANG, MALAYSIA.
CABLE: "RASAYANG" PENANG. TELEX: RASTEL MA 40065. TEL: 04-811811.

 Golden Sands HOTEL PENANG

P.O. Box 222, BATU FERINGGI BEACH, PENANG, MALAYSIA.
CABLE: "GOLDSANDS" PENANG. TELEX: GOSAND MA 40627. TEL: 04-811111.

For reservations, please contact:
SINGAPORE: RASA SAYANG HOTEL/GOLDEN SANDS HOTEL SALES OFFICE, 13-15 Carpenter Street, Singapore 1. Tel: 912711. Telex: RS21295 KUOKS. Cable: KUOKBROLIN Singapore. **KUALA LUMPUR:** RASA SAYANG HOTEL/GOLDEN SANDS HOTEL SALES OFFICE, 8th Floor, Wisma MISC, Jalan Conlay, Kuala Lumpur, Malaysia. Tel: 424077. Telex: MA 30322 FEDMIL. Cable: FEDERAMIL Kuala Lumpur.

A Vacation Well Spent

JBL Bayview Beach Hotel

Batu Ferringhi, Penang, Malaysia.
Tel: 811311, Cable: BAYBEACH, PENANG.

For reservation and enquiries, please contact
your Travel Agent or the General Manager.

3. traveler's guide in brief

Coming to Malaysia   274
  by air
  overseas
  overland
Exchanging Formalities   274
  immigration
  customs
  currency
  changing money
  traveler's checks and credit cards
  business hours
Getting Acquainted   275
  climate
  what to wear
  packing your bag
  health
  finding your tongue
  electricity
  places of worship
Mixing with the Media   277
  television
  radio
  the press
  photography
  museums
  art galleries
  cinemas
  nightclubbing
Airlines   279
Banks   280
Embassies   281
Hotels   281
Celebrations   288
Speaking Malay   295
Reading On   297
Index-Glossary   299

coming to malaysia

By Air

Few first sights in Malaysia can compete with the elegant M$52 million international airport that greets air passengers at Kuala Lumpur. Its bold design came as such a novelty to the sleepy landscape of Subang, 22 km from the city center, that several myopic citizens ran into trouble. "The first victim," reported a newspaper several days after the official opening in 1965, "was an airport porter who walked right into a glass pane at the north arrival hall. He injured his nose but did not break the pane which is quite strong and thick."

Kuala Lumpur's glassy airport serves about twenty international airlines linking key cities of the world to Malaysia and providing the country with more than 90 percent of her visitors. Nearest international connections are with Singapore, a pleasant 35-minute flight away, and with Bangkok, an hour and 20 minutes away. Malaysia's capital is also accessible by air from Sabah and Sarawak or Penang Island to the north. Departing passengers are advised to keep some Malaysian dollars handy for the airport tax—at present, M$2 for domestic flights, M$5 for flights to Singapore and M$7 for international flights. Request on-the-spot information at the counter just below the airport's sculpturesque world time clock. The 35-minute ride into town by taxi costs around M$15.

Overseas

Sailors first glimpse Malaysia from bustling Port Klang (previously called Port Swettenham), 42 km west of Kuala Lumpur or from the historic port of Penang, ancient sanctuary for those once escaping the wrath of mainland lords. A number of cargo-cum-passenger ships and cruise liners call regularly at one or both ports.

Overland

Train tracks have a legacy in Malaysian lore. An inscription along the railway 5 km from Telok Anson reads: "There is buried here a wild elephant who in defense of his herd charged and derailed a train on the 17th day of September 1894." Though elephants have ceased being so chivalrous, smooth tracks still cut through the jungles roamed by wildlife, making train travel a chance to peek into the forested hinterland without having to slow down.

Bangkok to Kuala Lumpur is a two-day train ride costing M$140 first class and M$51.50 second class. The Malayan Railway links Singapore to Kuala Lumpur every morning on the Magic Arrow and every evening on the Southern Cross Express. Rates range from M$36 for first class (beds, berths and air-conditioning entail extra charges) down to M$19.90 for an ordinary seat. The Rapid Train leaves Singapore at 8:00 a.m. and arrives in Kuala Lumpur at 2:30 p.m. The fare all the way to Penang in air-conditioned comfort is M$45.

The more casual traveler can pick up a "shared" taxi at Johore Bahru, just across the causeway from Singapore, and settle down to a six-hour drive to Kuala Lumpur, without spending more than M$20. The secret of the bargain is that four or five passengers share one taxi. Bus fares are more reasonable on the air-conditioned express to Kuala Lumpur departing Singapore daily from the New Bridge Road fringe car park at 9:00 a.m. for the eight-hour ride.

exchanging formalities

Immigration

Valid passports and a health certificate of vaccination against yellow fever, if traveling from an infected area. Citizens of countries enjoying diplomatic relations with Malaysia do not need a visa for a fourteen-day stay, which may be extended up to a three months' visit. However, this courtesy does not apply to citizens of communist countries, Israel, or South Africa, who must have visas to enter Malaysia. An extension of a visitor's pass can be obtained at the Immigration Department, Jalan Tugu, Kuala Lumpur (tel.03-299151) open weekdays from 8:15 to 12:45 p.m. and from 2:00 p.m. to 4:15 p.m. except Fridays when the office is closed from 12 noon to 2:30 p.m., and on Saturdays from 8:00 a.m. to 12:45 p.m. A visitor's pass generally comes up for renewal every two weeks.

To expedite formalities, dress respectably and bring along airline tickets and money as proof of solvency.

Customs

Import duties seldom affect the average traveler, who may bring in 250 grams of tobacco or cigars, or 200 cigarettes and one quart bottle of liquor duty free. Used portable articles are normally exempted from import tax. However, should the latter include such items as opulent jewels, expensive cameras, a gold watch, a typewriter, a deposit may be required, which will be repaid to the visitor if he or she leaves Malaysia within three months and re-exports the articles. Narcotics, pornography, daggers, and walkie-talkies are strictly prohibited; firearms are subject to licensing.

Currency

The Malaysian dollar is a sound currency which has been in circulation since 1957, and is now valued at around US$0.45. Singapore and Brunei dollars are approximately of the same value, but no longer circulate freely in Malaysia. The importation of traveler's checks and letters of credit is unlimited. Visitors may import up to M$10,000 in Malaysian currency and export up to M$5,000. It is much easier to take out cash if it has been declared upon arrival. Malaysians call their dollar the *ringgit*.

Changing Money

Large hotels change money for a fee: five to ten Malaysian cents on each US dollar, amounting to a service charge of 2 to 4 percent. Banks offer better rates, and so do the money changers with offices in downtown shop houses. If you are not in a rush, avoid changing money in the arcades of luxury hotels, since many of these shops levy a service charge by offering lower exchange rates. Deal directly with a bank or a licensed money changer and have plenty of local currency on hand when traveling to small towns and in rural areas. Banking hours are Monday through Friday, 10:00 a.m. to 3:00 p.m., and on Saturday 9:30 to 11:30 a.m.

Traveler's Checks and Credit Cards

In the more flashy, chic quarters of the larger towns—in department stores, shops, first-class restaurants and hotels—traveler's checks change hands easily. Bring your passport along when cashing traveler's checks: a formality which must be done before heading off the beaten track where such checks are unacceptable. Established credit cards—Diner's Club, American Express, Carte Blanche—are honored in the major cities. Several hotel chains maintain their own credit card system. But when travelling through Malaysia, nothing could be better than the coin of the realm.

Business Hours

In an Islamic nation with a British colonial history, weekly holidays vary. In the former Federated States which were united under the British—Selangor, Malacca, Penang, Perak, Pahang, and Negri Sembilan—there is a half-day holiday on Saturday and a full-day holiday on Sunday. The former Unfederated States, which remained semiautonomous under British rule—Johore, Kedah, Perlis, Trengganu, and Kelantan—retain the traditional half-day holiday on Thursday and full-day holiday on Friday. Saturday and Sunday are treated as weekdays.

In all government institutions, the workday begins at 8:15 a.m. and ends at 4:15 p.m., with time off on Fridays from 12:00 to 2:30 p.m. for communal Jumaah prayers at the mosques. Most private business stick to the 9:00 to 5:00 routine. Shops start to close at 6:00 p.m. Large department stores, like Weld Supermarket and Selangor Emporium in Kuala Lumpur, keep their cash registers ringing past 9:00 p.m.

getting acquainted

Climate

A tropical sun and clouds laden with the makings of a sudden downpour compete for the skies of Malaysia, with the odds on the sun. Malaysia's seasons follow the monsoon winds, which splash rains inland from September to December on the West Coast of Peninsular Malaysia, only to be overtaken by sunshine within the hour. Rains arrive later on the East Coast of Peninsular Malaysia and in Sabah and Sarawak, where umbrellas sell well from October to February. Malaysia's weather, however, is generally warm, humid, and sunny all the year round, with temperatures wavering between 20° to 30°C. The highlands, both during the day and at night, and the lowlands in the evening are comfortably cooler, which may explain why Malaysia's nightlife is liveliest outdoors.

What To Wear

Light, cool, comfortable clothes, for both men and women, fare well in Malaysia where informal styles prevail throughout the year. Batek cotton fashions, on sale everywhere, are an easy "in" to local color. Well-worn airy shoes or sandals are a favor to the feet. For some formal occasions, men may be requested to dine in suits and ties; but sport shirts are otherwise the ubiquitous Malaysian style for anything from cocktails to floor shows. Ladies are at liberty to take any hint from Vogue's summer pages, though when visiting mosques and outlying Malay villages, women should dress modestly. Shorts, tiny T-shirts and miniskirts have yet to win acceptance in Asian towns and villages.

Packing Your Bag

Several everyday items are useful during trips through the Malaysian countryside. If you do not fancy a shave at the local barber shop, take along a safety razor, because you cannot rely on having an electrical outlet. The quality of toilets and washrooms varies widely, making it advisable to carry a small packet of tissues and some sort of ingenious instant freshener, like Wash 'n' Dry. In the highlands during the evening (and even during the day in the cool season) temperatures drop to sweater weather, so pack handy warm clothing. A waxed-paper umbrella, made locally and selling for a couple of Malaysian dollars at the nearest sundry shop house, is a practical buy as a shield against the showers or as a sun shade. Inexpensive straw hats are a perpetual solution to keeping cool in the tropics, though Malaysians seldom wear them.

Health

Travelers have few worries in a country the health standards of which are ranked among the highest in Asia. Water is generally safe for drinking, but it is safest to drink boiled water, tea, coffee, or bottled beverages. Coffee shops in small towns sell fresh fruits and bottled drinks. Fresh hot food, cooked on the spot, has made *nasi goreng* (fried rice) and *mee goreng* (fried noodles) the local equivalents of hot dogs and meat pie. One seasoned traveler who has zoomed in and out of Malaysia over the past twenty years insists that there is only one secret ingredient to shiny eyes and a healthy mind in the Orient: The siesta after the national lunch of noodle soup.

Finding Your Tongue

In Kuala Lumpur, chances are that the taxi-cab driver knows a smattering of four languages. Among Malaysia's urban population, people shift tongues with neighborhoods. Malay is the national language, used officially in all government departments. English is widely spoken by people from all walks of life, along with the clicking sounds of Tamil, brought from South India, and a half dozen Chinese dialects—Cantonese and Hokkien predominating in the towns. A traveler can step into the most unlikely small town coffee shop and encounter a shopkeeper with a Senior Cambridge Certificate. Almost every village, however small, harbors a linguist. One way to find out who he or she is is to enter the nearest snack bar, order a soft drink and wait for the word to get around that a *turis* or *tamu* (guest) is in town. Eventually, the local translator will appear.

Electricity

Do not expect to plug an American electric razor into the communal circuit of a clap-board coconut palm-shaded *kampung*. Malaysian current is 220 volts, 50 cycles, though most first-class hotels can supply an adaptor for 110-volt, 60-cycle appliances.

Places of Worship

Minarets, spires, domes and steeples adorning the skyline of Kuala Lumpur reflect a rich diversity of faiths within Malaysia. Below is a small selection of places of worship close to the city center. Hotels and travel agents provide the times of services and can help arrange transportation. In mosques, Hindu and Buddhist shrines, it is customary to remove your shoes before entering and to refrain from smoking. Small Chinese temples have no such requirements, though it is always a polite gesture to ask the temple caretaker if you may look around and to leave a small donation in the charity box before departing. Unfortunately, some tourists who were not properly informed have been known to climb on temple statues in order to pose for a snapshot. Incidents like this have caused some monks to request that visitors refrain from taking photographs in their monasteries. This request, however, is rare.

Evangelical Lutheran Church
  21 Jalan Abdul Samad, KL
Kuala Lumpur Baptist Church
  70 Jalan Hicks, KL
Mar Thoma Church (Syrian)
  Jalan Ipoh, KL
National Mosque
  Jalan Sultan Hishamuddin, KL
See Yeoh Temple (Taoist)
  14A Leboh Pudu, KL

Seventh Day Adventist Mission
166 Jalan Bukit Bintang, KL
Sikh Temple, Jalan Bandar
Sri Maha Mariamman Temple
(Hindu) 163 Jalan Bandar
St. Andrew's Presbyterian
Church
31 Jalan Raja Chulan, KL
St. Francis Xavier Church
(Jesuit)
Jalan Gasing, Petaling Jaya
St. John's Cathedral
(Roman Catholic) Bukit Nanas
St. Mary's Church (Anglican)
Jalan Raja, KL
Wesley Methodist Church
Jalan Wesley, KL

mixing with the media

Television

Possibly the most cosmopolitan tube this side of Suez, TV Malaysia treats its viewers to programs such as: Royal Banquets at Istana Negara (National Palace). "Charlie's Angels", "Peristiwa", "The Glacial Age of Tokyo" and Mandarin and Arabic movies. Ringside entertainers and national football teams reign over prime times with roaring support from their fans. When British Wrestling and the Ed Sullivan Show were screened at the same hour, it stirred up a teeny flutter in newsprint.

"Any sportsman who knows his onions," insisted one tenacious viewer, "knows that wrestling is a good show. The old and the young and even Grandma love to hiss at the villain and, if given the chance, would love to stick her hairpin in him."

Radio

Tunes that blare out of Malaysia's streetsides carry wild assortments in sound. A flick of the dial turns to Indonesian pop, Malay rock, Indian classical, Chinese theatrical, "I Don't Know How To Love Him" from *Jesus Christ Superstar* or the latest hit from the Rolling Stones. Soap operas and programe of daily events happening throughout Malaysia add local color to news. Just listen in.

The Press

True to its reading public, Malaysia churns out daily newspapers in Malay, Chinese, English and Tamil which go to press in key towns from Kota Kinabalu, Sabah, to George Town, Penang. *The New Straits Times*, venerable breadwinner of the English press, arrives every morning crammed with national and world news, occasional eye-opening letters to the editor—and "Peanuts." *The Malay Mail*, less formal and more chatty, entertains its readers by focusing more on local entertainment. Features also appear on newsmaking tourists—like the two young Yorkshiremen who bicycled 14 000 km in seven months and only once (in India) were suspected of being spies (from Pakistan).

Photography

Professionals working in the tropics have one big suggestion for good results in color: beware of the heat. Hot sun causes changes in the chemical emulsions of the film, which may detract from natural color. Whenever possible, store camera and film in a cool place, if not in an air-conditioned room, at least in the shade. Experienced photographers also recommend buying film in the cities rather than the countryside where proper storage facilities for color films are not guaranteed.

Humidity can be another tropical handicap, particularly with jungle photography. The solution here is to carry equipment and film in a closed camera bag that contains Silica Gel, a chemical that absorbs the moisture. For subtle tones and rich color, the best times to photograph are before 10:30 a.m. or after 3 p.m. Few films take noontime sunlight well. Pictures often lose subtle gradations in color because the light is too strong. In the early morning or late afternoon, sidelights give softer contrasts and deeper color density. You perspire less as well.

Most Malaysians are more than amiable about having their pictures taken. It usually takes a gang of schoolchildren less than fifteen seconds before they begin merrily jabbing peace signs in front of your 20 mm lens. Mosques and temples are rightly more reserved about photographers posing their subjects in front of altars. It is polite to always ask permission when photographing within a place of worship, and to keep a respectful distance during religious ceremonies.

Film processing in Kuala Lumpur is offered by Ruby Photo on Jalan Tuanku Abdul Rahman and Eastern Photo on Jalan Mountbatten. Komal, in Petaling Jaya, develop Kodak colorfilm only. Black and white is normally a 24-hour service. Kodakcolor and Ektachrome take a few days, Kodakchrome one week.

Museums

On Sundays, the *Muzium Negara* (National Museum) in Kuala Lumpur draws curious crowds like a roving band of medicine men draws onlookers. A stately building adorned with the handiwork of Malaysian artists, the museum during holidays is as popular as a park bench in the shade. Schoolchildren, newly-weds, housewives and uncles drop in to take a second look at their culture—revealed in everything from sultans' headdresses to moon kites. A salesman and his sweetheart linger before an opulent display of jeweled krisses—the ancient weapon reputed to have magical powers that can stop fires from burning or cure snake bites. Exhibits show off the refineries of Malaysian life and art in such an inviting manner that Muzium Negara is among the liveliest in Asia. Open hours: daily 9:00 a.m. to 7:00 p.m. Closed on Fridays from 12 to 2:30 p.m.

Malaysia has more than one museum. Most intriguing and most talked about is Sarawak's museum, founded in 1888 by the second white Rajah, Sir Charles Brooke, and the great evolutionist, Alfred Russell Wallace. Their foresight resulted in the finest collection of Borneo artistry yet amassed, and what was once "a true flower of the early Brooke imagination" has since blossomed into the pride of Borneo peoples, who visit their museum at the rate of 90 000 a year.

Malacca's museum, set in a centuries-old Dutch house facing the waterfront, recalls Malay sultans and Portuguese, Dutch and English colonialists who made Malacca the great sea town of antiquity. Seremban's small and distinctive museum was transported intact out of a royal Malay palace built in the 19th century. Within its handcarved wooden walls glisten the weapons and coat of arms glorifying the state of Negri Sembilan, settled largely by Sumatrans, called "Minangkabau," from across the straits.

The friendly, hilly town of Taiping, 320 km north of Kuala Lumpur, houses the Perak museum, largely dedicated to the ingenuity of jungle tribes who dwell deep in the interior. Alor Star's museum in Kedah displays fragments from the ruins of a Hindu civilization that thrived on nearby plains 1 000 years ago. Gigantic Chinese "birthday tapestries"—gold embroidered on vermilion silk—hang from the halls in Penang's museum. One room retraces the island's history in lithographs of bygone scenes. Another is an old Chinese bridal chamber so luxuriant in detail that modern hotel honeymoon suites pale in comparison.

Malaysia's museums invite you to travel upriver, beyond the coasts, or through time. Most are modest enough to get to know quickly, and all are free to the public.

Art Galleries

Batek painting, an ancient waxing and dyeing craft which is flexible enough for avantgarde themes, united painters in a common medium unique to Malaysia and Indonesia. Of course, today's galleries contain much more: watercolors, oils, pastels, graphics, aluminum reliefs, acrylics and sculpture. In many ways modern Malaysian art is still in its adolescence, drawing freely from Western technique and style, yet still searching for a singularity that can only be its own.

Gallery walls mirror the Malaysian scene, the harmony of traditional life and the bold grasp of the future. Frequent exhibitions, ranging from aboriginal mask carving to abstract expressionism, are patronized by a discerning and dedicated art circle. Its nexus is the National Art Gallery on Jalan Ampang in Kuala Lumpur—an outlet for Malaysia's immediate imagination. Galaxy Gallery, 43 Jalan Hicks, KL, makes it a point of discovering new talent among Malaysian painters. The bright, delightful exhibition of children's art held annually at the Muzium Negara should not be missed. While in Penang visit the Yahong Gallery and home of the renowned batek painter, "Teng" on Batu Ferringhi. The Galerie de Mai on Burma Road is also worth a visit.

There are several more art galleries in Kuala Lumpur, Penang and smaller towns. Often they tell more about Malaysia than meets the eye.

Cinemas

Subtle drama never stays on the flashy, action-packed billboards long. Most Asians buy tickets for wild, noisy entertainment and the more for the money the better. A moderate, homemade-looking movie called *Big Boss* jammed the box offices for weeks, with a plot that included bloody fist fights, mass murder, dope smuggling, opium smoking, prostitution, kidnapping and lastly, police sirens. But *Big Boss* had an undeniable hero: the charismatic fighter for justice. Fans flock to see vengeance take its toll in the expert hands of sword fighters, war heroes, gang leaders, tough detectives and sharpshooting cowboys. "Everybody wants CATLOW murdered, mangled and massacred," wails a long-standing billboard.

"His only hope is a Marshall, who wants him hanged."

The Asian cinema, if you can take the gore, is an unabashedly explosive time-consumer. Vampires and dinosaurs shriek across the screen nearly every week. There are, of course, soft moments that linger on young love and filial comedy brought to you by Walt Disney or Run Run Shaw. There are tales of "uncontrollable passion" whose advertisers make more promises than the censors can keep. An odd and unpredictable selection of Western films are always on show, but few can compete with *Big Boss* for big business.

Nightclubbing

Floodlights focused on long legs in mesh stockings seem a bit too bright for the mild Malaysian evening. Occasionally, a headline will shout "Censor Puts Clamp on No-Bra Shows" and striptease will fall back into perspective. Malaysia does not have the show-biz abandon of neighboring Bangkok. Nor does it have the ostentatious flash that sprang out of the hotel boom in Singapore. What it has are dance hostesses who must be in by midnight, bar girls who never touch liquor, and a modest but marvelous assortment of floor shows.

At the moment, floodlights and sequined bikinis confine themselves to tall hotels and a few established nightclubs. But interest in the jazzy nightlife is rapidly growing.

Tourist Development Corporation

The TDC offices in the various regions of Malaysia have a wealth of useful information for the tourist. Friendly receptionists are on hand to answer enquiries on places of tourist interest, transport facilities, accommodation and so on. The TDC publications are also available at these offices.

The TDC have overseas information centers in Sydney, Australia; Bangkok, Thailand; London, England; San Francisco, U.S.A.; Tokyo, Japan; Frankfurt, Germany; Singapore and Hong Kong. Addresses and telephone numbers can be found in the local telephone directory.

Here is a list of TDC Regional Offices in Malaysia:

Kuala Lumpur/ Malacca	17th Floor, Wisma MPI, Jalan Raja Chulan, P.O. Box 328, Kuala Lumpur.	Tel: 03–423033
Penang/ Langkawi	10, Jalan Tun Syed Sheikh Barakbah, Penang.	Tel: 04–20066/7
East Coast	2243, Ground Floor, Wisma MCIS Jalan Sultan Zainal Abidin, Kuala Trengganu, Trengganu.	Tel: 096–21433 096–21893
	Lot 1 and 2, 2nd Floor Tun Abdul Razak Complex, Jalan Ah Fook, Johor Bahru, Johore.	Tel: 01–23590/1
Sabah	Block L, Lot 4, Bangunan Sinsuran, Kota Kinabalu, Mail Bag 136, Sabah.	Tel: Kota Kinabalu 58732
Sarawak	Room 403, 4th Floor, Bangunan Bank Negara Malaysia, Jalan Satok, Kuching, Sarawak.	Tel: Kuching 56775

airlines

Aeroflot Soviet Airlines Yayasan Selangor Building Jalan Bukit Bintang Kuala Lumpur	03–42321
Air France Hotel Equatorial Kuala Lumpur	03–427620
Air India Bangunan Angkasa Raya Jalan Ampang Kuala Lumpur	03–420166
Alitalia Airlines Chartered Bank Bldg. 2 Jln Ampang Kuala Lumpur	03–204266
Biman Airlines (Bangladesh) Bangunan Angkasa Raya Jalan Ampang Kuala Lumpur	03–483765
British Airways Merlin Hotel Kuala Lumpur	03–425847
Cathay Pacific Airways Oriental Plaza Jalan Parry Kuala Lumpur	03–486166

China Airlines
  64 Jln Bt Bintang
  Ku..a Lumpur   03–427344
Czechoslovak Airlines
  68 Jln Ampang
  Kuala Lumpur   03–80176
Flying Tiger Line (freight)
  Wisma M.P.I.
  Jalan Rajah Chulan
  Kuala Lumpur   03–21501
Garuda Indonesian Airways
  Bangunan Angkasa Raya
  Jalan Ampang   03–483542
Japan Air Lines Co.
  Bangunan AIA
  Jln Ampang
  Kuala Lumpur   03–25102
KLM-Royal Dutch Airlines
  Komplex Antarabangsa
  Jalan Sultan Ismail
  Kuala Lumpur   03–427011
Korean Air Lines
  Wisma M.P.I.
  Jalan Rajah Chulan
  Kuala Lumpur   03–428460
Lufthansa German Airlines
  Hotel Merlin
  Kuala Lumpur   03–425555
Malaysian Airline System (MAS)
  Bangunan UMBC
  Jalan Sulaiman
  Kuala Lumpur   03–206633
  Jln T Ibrahim
  Alor Star   04–721186
  1A Jln Sultan Iskandar
  Ipoh   05–514155
  Bangunan Azizah
  off Jln Ah Fook
  Johore Bahru   01–55342
  Hotel Kesina
  Kota Bahru   097–22718
  Wisma Maju
  Kuala Trengganu   096–22266
  Bangunan LKNP
  Kuantan   095–21218
  Bangunan AIA
  Jln Munshi Abdullah
  Malacca   06–2647
  Komplex Tun Abdul Razak
  Jalan Pinang
  Penang   04–21403
  1 Chester Street
  Kota Kinabalu   K.K. S 1455
  Electro House
  Power Street
  Kuching   Kuching 24331
North West Orient Airlines
  27 Jalan Bukit Bintang
  Kuala Lumpur   03–429868
Pakistan International Airlines
  Angkasa Raya Building
  Jalan Ampang
  Kuala Lumpur   03–420564

Pan American World Airways
  Bangunan AIA
  Kuala Lumpur   03–420564
Pan American World Airways
  Hotel Equatorial
  Kuala Lumpur   03–425044
Philippine Airlines
  Wisma Stephens
  Jalan Rajah Chulan
  Kuala Lumpur   03–425444
Qantas Airways
  Bangunan AIA
  Kuala Lumpur   03–26161
Sabena Airlines
  Hotel Equatorial
  Kuala Lumpur   03–425820
Saudi Arabian Airlines
  7 Jalan Rajah Abdullah
  Kuala Lumpur   03–84521
Scandinavian Airlines System
  84 Jln Ampang
  Kuala Lumpur   03–80361
Singapore Airlines (SIA)
  2 Jln Campbell
  Kuala Lumpur   03–987033
Swissair
  Hotel Merlin
  Kuala Lumpur   03–426744
Thai Airways International Ltd.
  Denmark House
  Jalan Ampang
  Kuala Lumpur   03–80361
UTA French Airlines
  Hotel Equatorial
  Kuala Lumpur   03–427620
Domestic Service
  Malaysian Air Charter
  Subang Airport
  Kuala Lumpur   03–769822
  Wira Kris Udara
  Subang Airport
  Kuala Lumpur   03–762158

banks

Arab-Malaysia Development Bank, Bangunan Datuk Zainal, Jalan Melaka, tel. 03–920329. **Bank Negara** (Central Bank of Malaysia), Jalan Swettenham, tel. 03–988044. **Algemene Bank Netherland NV,** Wisma Sachdev, 16–2, Jalan Raja Laut, tel. 03–989155. **Bank of America,** Kompleks Antarabangsa, Jalan Sultan Ismail, tel. 03–422755. **Bank of Tokyo,** 22, Medan Pasar, tel. 03–89174. **Bangkok Bank,** 105, Jalan Bandar, tel. 03–24551. **Banque de L'Indochine, Et de Suez** 13, Jalan Rajah Chulan, tel. 03–201322. **Bank Bumiputra,** 21, Jalan Melaka, tel. 03–205655. **Chartered Bank,** 2, Jalan Ampang, tel. 03–26551. **Citibank,** AIA Building, Jalan Ampang, tel. 03–25334. **Development and Commercial Bank (Ltd) Berhad,** 18, Jalan Silang, tel. 03–22111. **Chase**

Manhattan Bank NA, Wisma Stephens, Jalan Rajah Chulan, tel. 03–482011. **European Asian Bank,** Bangunan Yee Seng, 15, Jalan Raja Chulan, tel. 03–299453. **Habib Bank,** 11, Leboh Ampang, tel. 03–27375. **Hock Hua Bank,** 17, Jalan Klyne, tel. 03–81114. **Hong Kong & Shanghai Banking Corp,** 2, Leboh Ampang, tel. 03–200744. **Kwong Lee Bank,** 41, Jalan Klyne, tel. 03–23225. **Kwong Yik Bank,** 75, Jalan Bandar, tel. 03–25632. **Lee Wah Bank,** Medan Pasar tel. 03–88351. **Malayan Banking Berhad,** 92, Jalan Bandar, tel. 03–207522. **Overseas Chinese Banking Corp.,** Jalan Tun Perak, tel. 299571. **Overseas Union Bank,** Jalan Tun Perak, tel. 03–920344. **Pacific Bank Berhad,** 145, Jalan Bandar, tel. 03–205033. **Public Bank Berhad,** Wisma Hangsam, Jalan Cecil, tel. 03–209055. **United Asian Bank,** 4, Jalan Tun Perak, tel. 03–983022. **United Malayan Banking Corp.,** 42, Jalan Tun Perak, tel. 23671.

embassies

Australia: Australian High Commission, 6, Jalan Yap Kwan Seng, tel. 423122. **Austria:** The Austrian Embassy, 7th Floor, Oriental Plaza Building, Jalan Parry, tel. 03–27288. **Bangladesh:** High Commission of the People's Republic of Bangladesh, 204–1, Jalan Ampang, tel. 03–487940. **Belgium:** Embassy of Belgium, Wisma Bunga Raya, Jalan Ampang, tel. 03–485733. **Bolivia:** Embassy of Bolivia, 4th Floor, Komplex Antarabangsa, Jalan Sultan Ismail, tel. 03–425146/03–425139. **Britain:** British High Commission, Wisma Damansara, 5, Jalan Semantan, tel. 03–941533. Passport Office, 186, Jalan Ampang, tel. 03–487122. **Bulgaria:** Embassy of the People's Republic of Bulgaria, 6, Jalan Taman U Thant, tel. 03–424391. **Burma:** Embassy of the Socialist Republic of the Union of Burma, 7, Jalan Taman U Thant, tel. 03–423863. **Canada:** Canadian High Commission, AIA Building, 5th Floor, Jalan Ampang, tel. 03–89722. **China:** Embassy of the People's Republic of China, 229, Jalan Ampang tel. 03–428495. **Czechoslovakia:** Embassy of the Czechoslovak Socialist Republic, 32, Jalan Mesra, (off Jalan Ampang), tel. 03–427185. **Denmark:** Royal Danish Embassy, 86, Jalan Ampang, Denmark House, 3rd Floor, tel. 03–25357. **Egypt:** Embassy of the Arab Republic of Egypt, 28, Lingkungan U Thant, tel. 03–468184. **France:** Embassy of the Republic of France, 210, Jalan Bukit Bintang, tel. 03–484122. **Germany (West):** Embassy of the German Democratic Republic, 2A, Pesiaran Gurney, tel. 03–88779. **Germany (East):** Embassy of the Federal Republic of Germany, 3, Jalan U Thant, tel. 03–429666. **India:** High Commission of India, United Asian Bank Berhad Bldg, 19, Jalan Melaka, tel. 03–21728. Consular and visa section, 2nd Floor, Oriental Building, 32, Jalan Tun Perak, tel. 03–80429. **Indonesia:** Embassy of the Republic of Indonesia, 233, Jalan Pekeliling, tel. 03–421011. **Iraq:** Embassy of the Republic of Iraq. 2, Langgak Golf, tel. 03–480555. **Italy:** Embassy of the Republic of Italy, 8th Floor, Chartered Bank Building, 2, Jalan Ampang, tel. 03–26671. **Japan:** Embassy of Japan, 6th Floor, AIA Building, Jalan Ampang, tel. 03–21531. **Korea:** Embassy of the Republic of South Korea, 422, Jalan Pekeliling, tel. 03–21651. **Libya:** Embassy of the Socialist People's Libyan Arab Jamahiriya, No. 7, Jalan Ampang Hilir, tel. 03–464655/464646. **Netherlands:** Royal Netherlands Embassy, Denmark House, 3rd Floor, 86, Jalan Ampang, tel. 03–80387. **New Zealand:** New Zealand High Commission, 193, Jalan Pekeliling, tel. 03–486422. **Pakistan:** Embassy of Pakistan, 132, Jalan Ampang, tel. 03–483822. **Philippines:** Embassy of the Republic of the Philippines, 1, Changkat Kia Peng, tel. 03–484233. **Poland:** Embassy of the Polish People's Republic, 4, Jalan Madge, tel. 03–22816. Office: 8B, Jalan Ampang Hilir, tel. 460940. **Saudi Arabia:** Royal Embassy of Saudi Arabia, 251, Jalan Pekeliling, tel. 03–21387. **Singapore:** High Commission of the Republic of Singapore, Straits Trading Building, 5th Floor, Leboh Pasar Besar, tel. 03–25435. **Sri Lanka:** High Commission of the Republic of Sri Lanka, 29, Jalan Yap Kwan Seng, tel. 03–423094. **Sweden:** Royal Swedish Embassy, Wisma Angkasa Raya, Jalan Ampang, tel. 03–485981. **Switzerland:** Embassy of Switzerland, 16, Pesiaran Madge, tel. 03–480622. **Thailand:** Royal Thai Embassy, 206, Jalan Ampang, tel. 03–488222. **Turkey:** Embassy of the Republic of Turkey, 30, Jalan Inai, tel. 03–429832. **U.S.S.R:** Embassy of the Union of Soviet Socialist Republics, 263, Jalan Ampang, tel. 03–460009. **United States of America:** Embassy of the United States of America, AIA Building, Jalan Ampang, tel. 03–26321. **Vietnam:** Embassy of the Socialist Republic of Vietnam, "Vietnam House," 4, Pesiaran Stonor, tel. 03–484036. **Yugoslavia:** Embassy of Socialist Federal Republic of Yugoslavia, 353, Jalan Ampang, tel. 03–464561.

hotels

One may sleep in Malaysia in numerous styles— enamored by the old-fashioned elegance of a colonial lodge; tucked in a sleeping bag in an alpine mountain hut; soothed by Chinese singsong in a tiny hotel in midtown; or serenaded by the crickets outside the family guestroom of a Dayak long-house in Sarawak.

Accommodations leave themselves wide open to personal preference. Most Malaysian small towns do not offer the cosmopolitan facilities of a worldwide hotel chain, but they do provide the personal touch, simplicity, and cleanliness of a wayside inn. Nearly every prominent city in the country has a comfortable Government Rest House offering convenient accommodation to visitors traveling through rural Malaysia. A typical urban street is dotted with small budget hotels renting simply furnished rooms for around M$10 to M$20.

Below is a list of the better-known places available

for your overnight stay. Hotels combining casino and pleasure resort feature in discussions on Malaysia's future, but as of yet only the Genting Highlands Hotel has the roulette wheels spinning.

*Deluxe hotels with over 100 rooms, air conditioning, shopping arcade, and swimming pool are marked with an asterisk.

* * *

PENINSULAR MALAYSIA

Alor Star

Government Rest House, 75 Pumpong, tel 04–722 422; 15 rooms, some air conditioned.

Hotel Mahkota, Jalan Putera, tel. 04–721 344, Restaurant and bar.

Hotel Maha Wangsa, 449 Jalan Raja, tel. 04–721433, luxury air-conditioned rooms with telephone and bath, bar and restaurant.

Hotel Regent, 1536G Jalan Sultan Badlishah, tel. 04–721900, 04–721291, 15 min from airport, 5 min from railway terminal; 28 rooms, partially air conditioned with restaurants and shops.

Hotel Samila, 27 Jln Kanchut, tel. 04–722344; 52 rooms, restaurant, bar, nightclub.

Station Hotel, Jln Langgar, tel. 04–723855; 53 rooms.

Cameron Highlands

Brinchang Hotel, 36 Brinchang New Town, tel. 05–914744; 28 rooms.

Cameron Highlands Merlin, P.O. Box 4, Tanah Rata, Pahang, tel. 05–941222, 4 hours drive from Kuala Lumpur; 60 rooms, restaurant, bar, cocktail lounge, billiards room, children's recreation room, golf, conference facilities.

Cameron Highlands Rest House, Tanah Rata, Tel. 05–941254, 6 rooms.

Garden Hotel, Tanah Rata, Cameron Highlands, tel. 05–941254; 50 rooms, 7 chalets, restaurant, bar, coffee house, tennis courts, badminton courts, billiards, games room, conference room.

Town House Hotel, 41 Tanah Rata, Cameron Highlands, Pahang, 2 to 2½ hours from Ipoh airport; 12 rooms (6 without bath), air-conditioned, dining room, milk bar. Tel. 05–941666.

Ye Olde Smokehouse Hotel (formally Foster's Smokehouse Hotel), Tanah Rata, Jalan Pekeliling, Cameron Highlands, tel. CH–265, Tudor architecture with English country garden, 20 family suites, dining rooms, 2 bars, 18-hole golf course, jungle walks.

Foster's Lakehouse, 29/30th mile, Ringlet, Cameron Highlands, Pahang, tel. 05–941680. Tudor-style architecture, antique and reproduction furnishings, English country garden. Bar, restaurant, fishing, jungle walks.

Fraser's Hill

Fraser's Hill Development Corp. Bungalows, c/o Fraser's Hill Corp., Fraser's Hill, Pahang, tel.

071–60201 or 071–60248, 2½ hours from airport, 2 hours from rail terminal, 3 hours from seaport; 42 rooms, dining room, bar, tennis courts, 18-hole golf course, 11 shops, sauna, barber shop, squash courts, skating rink.

Fraser's Hill Merlin Hotel, Fraser's Hill, Pahang, tel. 071–60274; 109 rooms, restaurant, coffee house, games room, 9-hole golf course, horse riding, tennis court, squash.

Genting Highlands

*Genting Hotel, Genting Sempah Genting Highlands, Kuala Lumpur, tel. 03–353212; 51 km (1 hour) from Kuala Lumpur, 15-min helicopter flight from Kuala Lumpur or airport; tourist complex, mountain resort, 200 rooms, 3 restaurants serving Western, Malaysian, and Chinese cuisine, casino, coffee house, 2 bars, nightclub, bowling alley, golf course, heliport, flower nursery, sauna baths, beauty and barber shops, cable car, lake and boating.

*Hotel Genting Ria, Genting Highlands Hotel, Hotel Genting Pelangi, and *Sri Layang Hotel,* Genting Highlands, Kuala Lumpur, tel. 03–353244 (Hotel Genting Ria); 340 rooms, restaurant service, Malay, Chinese and Western cuisine, casino, nightclub, coffee house, cocktail lounge, grill, florist, shopping arcade, beauty salon, bank.

Ipoh

City Hotel, 79 Jln Chamberlain, tel. 05–73761; 67 rooms.

Caspian Hotel, 6 Jln Jubilee, tel. 05–72324; 29 rooms.

Embassy Hotel, 33 Jln Chamberlain, tel 05–2496; 15 rooms.

Hotel Eastern, 118 Jalan Sultan Idris Shah, tel. 05–73936, 20 min from airport, 5 min from railway terminal; 29 air-conditioned rooms, Maple Leaf Coffee court serving Western food, Fung Lum Restaurant serving Chinese food.

Hotel Mikado, 86 Jalan Yang Kalsom, tel. 05–515855, 3 km from airport, 1 km from downtown; 32 rooms, air conditioned, Chinese restaurant, coffee house, tour office, bank, beauty salon.

King's Hotel, 91 Jln Tambun, tel. 05–513211, 10 min from airport, in a residential area; 96 rooms, air conditioned, bar, cocktail lounge, restaurant, and nightclub.

Merlin Hotel, 92–98 Clare Street, tel. 05–71351; 35 air-conditioned rooms, dining room, bar.

Station Hotel, Jln Kelab, tel. 05–512588; 34 rooms.

Johore Bahru

Desaru Holiday Resort, Tanjong Penawar, P.O. Box 20, Kota Tinggi, Johore, tel. 01–22227. 35 beach chalets, swimming, boating, horse-riding, tennis, bar, restaurant.

Government Rest House, Jalan Sungei Chat, Sea Front, Johore Bahru, Johore, tel. 01–23676, 18 rooms with bath, air conditioned, dining room, Chinese restaurant with bar, barbecue hut, cocktail lounge, playground.

Government Rest House, 870 Jalan Tasek, Batu Pahat, Johore, tel. 072–711567.

Government Rest House, 490 Jalan Ismail, Mersing, tel. ME-791102. several air-conditioned rooms, dining room.

Senior Government Rest House, 40 Jalan A. Rahman, Muar, Johore, tel. 06–921373.

Grand Hotel, 80A Jalan Wong Ah Fook, tel. 01–355358; 31 rooms.

Johore Hotel, 69 Jln Ibrahim Sultan, Johore Bahru, tel. 01–24395/6, 1 hour to airport, 5 min from rail terminal; 38 rooms, dining room, bar, travel agent.

Ocean Hotel, 66 Jln. Wong Ah Fook, Johore Bahru, tel. 01–55231

Orchid Hotel, Bangunan Aziza, Johore Bahru, tel. 01–55932.

Pertama Emas Hotel, Tan Kim Chua Complex, Jalan Meldrum, Johore Bharu, Johore, tel. 01–25811. 115 rooms, coffee house, restaurant, nightclub, health center.

President Hotel, 29-11A Jln. Rahmat, Batu Pahat, Johore, tel. 072 –41455.

Straits View Hotel, Batu 2, Jalan Scudai, Johore Bahru tel. 01–24133, 01–24224, in suburban area, 20 min from airport, 10 min from railway terminal; 30 rooms, air conditioned, beach nearby, coffee house, garden terrace, discotheque.

Top Hotel, Jln Meldrum, Johore Bahru, tel. 01–55344/5; 37 rooms.

Kota Bahru

Bahru Hotel & Restaurant, Jalan Datuk Pati, Kota Bharu, tel. 097–21164.

Government Rest House, Kota Bharu, Kelantan, tel. 097–22409.

Hotel Irama, Jalan Sultan Ibrahim, Kota Bharu, tel. 097–22971; 31 rooms with air conditioning, dining room serving European, Chinese and Malay cuisine, bar, beauty and barber shop.

Hotel Kesina, Jln Pdg Garong, Kota Bharu, tel. 097–21455, 31 rooms, bar, restaurant, nightclub.

Hotel Murni, Jln Datuk Pati, Kota Bharu, tel. 079–22399, 15 min from airport, 30 min from railway station, 1 hr from seaport, in town center; 40 rooms, air conditioned, Chinese restaurant, steak house, coffee house, bar, nightclub, cultural dance performance on request.

Hotel Suria, 1870 A–C Jln Padang Garong, Kota Bharu, tel. 097–22188; 24 rooms.

Maryland Hotel, Jalan Tok Hitam, Kota Bharu, tel. 097–22811; 14 rooms, dining room, coffee shop.

Prince Hotel, Jalan Temenggong, Kota Bharu, Kelantan, tel. 097–22066, 20 min from airport, 10 min from railway terminal, 60 min from sea-port, located downtown on 2nd and 3rd floors of office building; 12 rooms, 8 air conditioned with bath, dining room serving European and Chinese cuisine, bar, nightclub, beauty and barber shop.

Resort Pantai Cinta Berahi (Beach of Passionate Love), P.O. Box 131, Kota Bharu, tel. 097–21307; 15 air-conditioned chalets, 19 air-cooled rooms, close to beach, 10 km from Kota Bharu, bar, dining room with Malay and Western cuisines, swimming pool, handicraft shops, local shows and tours to silverware and batik centers and to watch coconut-plucking monkeys.

Kuala Lumpur

Apollo Hotel, 106–110 Jalan Bukit Bintang, Kuala Lumpur, tel. 03–428133; 45 air-conditioned rooms. Chinese restaurant, travel agency.

City Hotel, 366 Jln Raja Laut, Kuala Lumpur, tel. 03–924466, centre of town, 30 min from rail terminal downtown; 90 rooms, air conditioned, grill room, coffee house, bar, reasonable rates.

Embassy Hotel, 205–211 Jln Imbi, Kuala Lumpur, tel. 03–481288; 35 rooms, all air conditioned with private bath.

*Federal Hotel, P.O. Box 896, Jalan Bukit Bintang, Kuala Lumpur, tel. 03–27701; 450 rooms, air conditioned, revolving lounge, 3 dining rooms serving Western and Chinese cuisine, 5 bars, 2 banquet halls, 6 international rooms, 2 supperclubs with international floor shows nightly, 24-hour coffee house, swimming pool, 18-lane bowling alley, 15 shop, sauna, massage, beauty and barber shops, air-conditioned limousine service.

*Holiday Inn, Jalan Pinang, P.O. Box 983, Kuala Lumpur, tel. 03–481066, 32 km from airport, 8 km from railway station, 48 km from seaport; 200 rooms all completely air conditioned, Malaysian restaurant, western grill, beauty and barber shops, 20 shops, car rental.

*Hotel Equatorial (Malaysia), Jalan Sultan Ismail, Kuala Lumpur, tel. 03–422022; 300 rooms completely air conditioned, 3 specialty restaurants, 2 bar lounges, 24-hour coffee house, swimming pool, shopping arcade, convention and conference facilities.

Hotel Jaya Puri, 2 Jln Barat, Petaling Jaya, tel. 03–774933; 371 air conditioned rooms.

Hotel Majestic, 1 Jalan Sultan Hishamuddin, Kuala Lumpur, tel. 03–84225, 30 min from airport, 40 km from seaport, opposite railway terminal; 51 rooms, completely air conditioned, dining room, bar, large garden.

Hotel Malaya, Jalan Cecil Bandar, Kuala Lumpur, tel. 03–27721; 250 air-conditioned rooms with private baths. Chinese dining room, nightclub, coffee lounge and bar.

Hotel Sentosa, 316 Jalan Raja Laut, Kuala Lumpur, tel. 03–925644, 30 min from airport, 10 min from railway terminal, located downtown; 42 rooms, air conditioned, dining room serving European and Cantonese cuisine, 2 cocktail lounges.

*Kuala Lumpur Hilton, P.O. Box 577, Jalan Sultan Ismail, Kuala Lumpur, tel. 03–422122/03–422222, 30 min from airport, 15 min from railway terminal, 45 min from seaport, 5 min from downtown; 584 rooms, air conditioned, Melaka Grill Room (Western and Malay food),

Planters Inn (24 hour), Chinese restaurant, the Paddock roof-top supperclub, Gazebo with nightly barbecue, movie theater, Tin Mine discotheque, 2 bars, swimming pool, squash courts, steam bath, sauna, massage, beauty and barber shops, 86 shops, travel and airline agencies, nightly Cultural Shows with Malay dinner.

*Kuala Lumpur Merlin, 2 Jln Sultan Ismail, Kuala Lumpur, tel. 03–480033, 32 km from airport, 10 min from railway terminal, 45 min from seaport, located in residential area, 5-min walk from commercial and shopping centers; 700 rooms, completely air conditioned, 5 restaurants, discotheque, 24 hour coffee house, 2 bars, cocktail lounge, 2 nightclubs, swimming pool, bowling alley, tennis and squash courts, massage, beauty and barber shops, shopping arcade including airline offices, travel agent, car rental.

Malaysia Hotel, 67–71 Jalan Bukit Bintang, Kuala Lumpur, tel. 03–428033; 30 min from airport, 10 min from railway terminal, centrally located; 60 rooms, completely air conditioned, steak house, Imperial Room serving Continental and Chinese cuisine, cocktail lounge.

Mimaland Recreational Complex, 11th mile Jalan Gombak, Kuala Lumpur, tel. 03–632133, 60 min from airport, 30 min from railway terminal, 1 hr from seaport, countryside location; 24 motel rooms, 10 bagans (native-style houses), 5 chalets (family size), all units air conditioned, Pelandak coffee house (Western Cuisine), Lakeside Restaurant (Malaysian food), Bagan Bar, Island Bar, Malaysian cultural shows upon request, swimming, boating, fishing, jungle trekking, children's playground, amusement center, flower garden, orchid farm.

Shah's Village Motel, 3 and 5 Lorong Sultan, Petaling Jaya, tel. 03–569322, 20 min from airport, 15 min from railway terminal, in suburban area; 44 rooms completely air conditioned, dining room, 2 bars, nightclub, bowling alley, sauna bath, swimming pool, conference and parking facilities.

*Southeast Asia Hotel, Jalan Haji Hussein, Kuala Lumpur, tel. 03–926027, 30 min from airport, 10 min from rail terminal, 45 min from seaport; 208 rooms airconditioned, Chinese and Muslim restaurants, bar, coffee shop, health center, movie theater, travel agent, shopping arcade.

*The Regent of Kuala Lumpur, Jalan Sultan Ismail, Kuala Lumpur, tel. 03–425588, 30 min from airports, 10 min from railway terminal, ½ hr from seaport, downtown; 400 rooms, completely air conditioned, Asian restaurant, Ranch grill, coffee shop, 'catch seafood' and Chinese restaurants, 3 bars, cocktail lounge, nightclub, swimming pool, shopping arcade, sauna and steam baths, massage, beauty and barber shops, medical and secretarial services.

Town House Hotel, 22 Jln Tong Shin, Kuala Lumpur, tel. 03–420233, 24 km from airport; 65 rooms completely air conditioned, 2 Chinese restaurants, 2 bars, nightclub, health center.

Wisma Belia, 40 Jln Syed Putra, Kuala Lumpur, tel.

03–26803–4, 30 min from airport, 5 min from rail terminal; 114 rooms, badminton court, shop, restaurant.

Kuala Trengganu

Government Rest House, Ayer Tawar, Besut, tel. 096–72224; restaurant.

Molek Inn, 210 Jalan Besar, Dungun, tel. 096–41270. Beach hotel with 6 rooms, 4 chalets and 1 bungalow. Restaurant and mini-bar.

Pantai Motel, Jalan Persinggahan, Kuala Trengganu, tel. 096–22100, beach resort, 74 twins, dining room, bar, swimming pool, sailing, fishing skiing, scuba diving, turtle watching tours.

Rantau Abang Village Resort, Dungun Village Center, tel. 096–41533. Beach location, 10 chalets, restaurant, bar, marine museum, observation deck, bazaar.

Tanjong Jara Beach Hotel, Tanjong Jara, Trengganu, tel. for reservations 03–428945. 100 rooms, sailing, water-skiing, fishing, tennis, golf park, squash.

Kuantan-Kemaman

Hotel Kuantan, Telok Chempedak Beach, Kuantan, Pahang, tel. 075–24755; 25 rooms with air conditioning, dining room serving Chinese and European cuisine.

Hotel Samudra Kuantan, Jalan Besar, Kuantan, Pahang, tel. 095–22688, 20 min from airport; 75 rooms, air conditioned, dining room, bar, car rental.

Hotel Merlin Kuantan, Telok Chempedak, Kuantan, tel. 095–22388. 75 rooms, swimming pool, golf, restaurant, discotheque.

Kuantan Hyatt, Telok Chempedak, Kuantan, tel. 095–25211. 185 rooms, squash, tennis, beauty parlor, health club, secretarial services, swimming pool, restaurant, bar, coffee house, discotheque.

Club Méditerraneé, Cherating, Kuantan, Pahang. Tel. 03–423033 for reservations or write to their head office at Place de la Bourse, 75083, Paris, Cedex 02. International Holiday village, sailing, boating, disco, swimming pool, tennis, badminton, yoga, 2 restaurants, 2 bars, boutiques.

Motel Kemaman, P.O. Box 7, Telok Mengkuang, Kemaman, Trengganu, tel. KMN-284; 16 rooms, 14 chalets, dining room, cocktail lounge, table tennis, fishing, 1 shop.

Titik Inn, Batu 25, Jln Kuantan, Kemaman, tel. 095–31329; 16 chalet rooms partially air conditioned, restaurant serving Malay, Chinese and Western food, bar, lounge, beach, turtle watching, fishing and jungle trips.

Kuala Kangsar

Government Rest House, tel. 05 851699; 16 rooms, some air conditioned.

Maxwell Hill

Government bungalows, contact Superintendent, Hill Gardens, Maxwell's Hill, Taiping, tel. Maxwell Hill 886241.

Mersing

Government Rest House, 490 Jalan Ismail, Mersing, tel. ME-791101, 18 rooms, air conditioned, seaside.

Mersing Hotel, 1, Jalan Datuk Timor, Mersing, Johore, tel. 791004. 20 rooms, seafood restaurant.

Langkawi Island

*Langkawi Country Club, Jalan Pantai Datuk, Pulau Langkawi, tel. 04-749209, on island off west coast of Malaysia, 65 nautical miles (119 km) north of Penang, boat and air service from Kuala Lumpur, Penang, Singapore; 100 rooms, air conditioned, Western and Asian restaurants, bars, swimming, boating, water-skiing, fishing, golfing, tennis, mountain climbing, conference facilities.

Sri Samudera Chalet, Pulau Langkawi, tel. 04-749215; 5 rooms.

Sang Bayu and *Sri Kenangan Chalets,* Pulau Langkawi; 6 rooms.

Government Rest House, Pulau Langkawi, tel. 04-7222088

Malacca

Government Bungalow, 8 m.s. Tanjung Keling, Malacca, tel. TKG-221.

Happy Land Hotel, 2435-C Klebang Kechil, Malacca, tel. 06-24523; 7 rooms.

Ng Fook Hotel, 154 H1 Jln Bunga Raya, Malacca, tel. 06-28055; 35 rooms.

Palace Hotel, 201 Jln Munshi Abdullah, Malacca, tel. 06-25355, 48 rooms completely air conditioned, dining room, bar, cocktail lounge.

Regal Hotel, 66 Jln Munshi Abdullah, Malacca, tel. 06-22595, 31 rooms, air conditioned, restaurant and bar.

Shah's Beach Resort, 6th mile Tanjong Keling, Malacca, tel. 06-26222, 30 min from airport and railway terminal; 50 chalets, completely air conditioned, dining room, bar, swimming pool, boutique, fishing boats, tennis court, golf.

Straits Travel Inn, 37A Jalan Bandar Hilir, Malacca, tel. 06-21101. 45 rooms, centralised air-conditioning, 24 hour coffee house, La Famosa Grill, Straits Club, discotheque, beer garden.

Pangkor Island

Government Rest House, Pasir Bogak, Pangkor Island. tel. Pangkor 236.

Hotel Pantai Puteri Dewi, (Princess Hotel) Golden Sands, Pangkor Island, Lumut, Perak, tel. PKR-291, 1½ hours by car from Ipoh to Lumut and 40 min from Lumut by ferry or hotel launch, resort hotel on beach; 55 rooms (chalets and Malay houses, some with shared bath), dining room serving European, Chinese, Malaysian food, bar, fishing boats, rowboats, motorboats, sailboats, fishing, drag-net demonstration, skin diving, ponies, archery, badminton, crabbing, tours.

Sea View Hotel, Pasir Bogak, Pangkor Island, tel. Pangkor 93 9256, 10 km by ferry from Lumut to Pangkor Island; 30 rooms and chalets, some air conditioned, bar, lounge, swimming, water-skiing, island boat trips, fishing.

Penang

Bayview Beach Hotel, Batu Ferringhi, Penang, tel. 04-811311. 75 rooms, kampong restaurant, coffee house, bar, swimming pool, sunken bar.

Holiday Inn Hotel, Batu Ferringhi, Penang, tel. 04-811601. 159 rooms, 24-hour coffee house, Baron's Table Restaurant, Bayan Bar, rock garden, games room, swimming pool.

Hotel Ambassador, 55 Jalan Penang, Penang, tel. 04-24101, located downtown; 75 rooms, air conditioned, steak room, Rajah Room, 24-hour coffee shop, cocktail lounge.

*Hotel Central, 404 Penang Road, Penang, tel. 04-21432, 20 min from airport, 10 min from railway terminal and seaport, free airport transfer service, centrally located; 116 rooms, completely air conditioned, restaurant serving Chinese cuisine, 24-hour coffee-house, lounge, bar, nightclub, conference rooms, bank, travel service, barber shop, health center.

Hotel Continental, 5 Jln Penang, Penang, tel. 04-26381; 120 rooms, air conditioned, dining room, bar, nightclub, coffee house, health center.

Hotel Malaysia 7 Jln Penang, Penang, tel. 04-23423; 117 rooms, nightclub, travel agency, discotheque, massage.

*Hotel Mandarin, 202-A Jln MacAlister, Penang, tel. 04-26131, 20 min from airport, 5 min from railway and seaport, downtown, 5 km from beach; 110 rooms, air conditioned, Peking Restaurant, coffee corner, nightclub, swimming pool, shopping arcade, beauty and barber shops, cinema, tours, car rentals.

Casuarina Beach Hotel, Batu Ferringhi, penang, tel. 04-811711; 160 rooms, all facing sea, boating tennis, water sports.

*E & O Hotel, 10/12 Farquhar Street, Penang, tel. 04-63543, 25 min from airport, 7 min from railway station and ocean terminals, set in 4½ acre tropical garden; 124 rooms, completely air conditioned bedrooms, two restaurants serving seafood and European cuisine, 24-hour coffee house, cocktail lounge, 3 bars and nightclub.

Golden Sands Hotel, 87 Batu Ferringhi Beach, Penang, tel. 04-811111, located in a suburban setting near the beach; 310 rooms, air conditioned, restaurant, bar, fishing excursions, water skiing, bicycle and car rentals, postal service.

Government Chalets, Jalan Jesselton, Penang, tel. 04-22393; 9 rooms, 3 chalets.

Government Rest House, 229 Jalan Kulim, Bukit Mertajam, tel. BM-0122.

Lone Pine Hotel, 10th mile, Batu Ferringhi, Penang, tel. 811511-2, 40 min from airport, 25 min from railway and ocean term... als, 16 km from George Town, directly on beach; 54 doubles (48 in separate annexe), dining room, cocktail lounge, sea swimming, fishing, tennis courts.

*Nang, tel. 896–291, ¾hour from airport, 30 min from railway terminal and seaport, resort directly on beach, 17 km from George Town; 160 rooms, completely air conditioned, dining room and coffee house, both serving Eastern and Western food.

*Oriental Hotel, 105 Jln Penang, Penang, tel. 04–23371, 25 min from airport, 5 min from railway terminal and seaport; 100 twin-bedded rooms, air conditioned, dining room serving Western and Chinese food, 2 bars, cocktail lounge, shopping arcade.

*Palm Beach Hotel, Batu Ferringhi, Penang, tel. 04–811621; 147 rooms, air conditioned, dining room, cocktail lounge, shop, bar and restaurant at beach-front garden, tennis court, swimming pool.

Paramount Hotel, 48F Jln Northam Road, Penang tel. 04–63772, 20 min from airport terminal and seaport, located in residential area near center of town; 24 rooms, air conditioned, dining room, bar, fishing, boating, and water-skiing.

Penang Hill Hotel, Penang Hill, Penang, tel. 892/256–7; on Penang Hill overlooking island, 12 twins, dining room, cocktail lounge.

*Penang Merlin Hotel, 25–A Farquhar St., George Town, Penang, tel. 04–23301, 20 min from airport, 10 min from railway terminal, 5 min from seaport, located downtwon, 144 rooms, air conditioned, revolving and other restaurants with European and Chinese cuisines, Chiengmai bar, swimming pool, discotheque, beauty shop, travel agent, 24-hour coffee shop.

*President Hotel, 171 Burmah Road, Penang, tel. 04–23456, centrally located; 100 rooms, air conditioned, dining room, nightclub, tour desk, travel agent, escort service.

*Rasa Sayang Hotel, 9½ m.s. Batu Ferringhi Beach, Penang tel. 04–811811, 40 min from airport, 45 min from railway terminal, 25 min from seaport, situated on Batu Ferringhi beach; 320 rooms, air conditioned, dining rooms serving Western, Chinese and Japanese cuisine, coffee shop, 4 bars, discotheque, swimming pool, tennis court, squash, croquet, putting green, waterskiing, fishing and sailing, 12 shops, gym, sauna and massage, beauty and barber shops, bicycle and car rental, travel office.

Town House Hotel, 70 Jln Penang, Penang, tel. 04–65133, 30 min from airport, 5 min from railway terminal, 5 min from ocean terminal, 5-min walk from shopping and entertainment areas; 50 rooms, air conditioned, 24-hour coffee house and restaurant, 1 bar, cocktail lounge, convention room, barber shop.

United Hotel, 101 Jln MacAlister, Penang, tel. 04–21361, 30 min from airport terminal and seaport; 118 rooms, air conditioned, restaurant, bar, 24-hour coffee house, health center, convention rooms.

Port Dickson

Federal Beach Hotel, 7½ mile Coast road, Telok Kemang, Port Dickson, Negri Sembilan, tel. 06–795244. 200 rooms, swimming pool, tennis court, discotheque, sea sports, golf.

*Si Rusa Inn, 7th mile Jalan Pantai, P.O. Box 31, Port Dickson, Negri Sembilan, tel. 06-795233, 1¼ hours from Subang International Airport, 64 km from Malacca Airport, 45 min from Seremban railway terninal, 11 km from Port Dickson, directly on beach; 170 doubles, air conditioned chalets, dining room, cocktail lounge, dance band Sat. evenings, Sunday luncheon music, deep sea and inshore fishing boats, sailboats, ski-boats, local golf club visiting arrangements, laundry service, babysitting.

Rawa Island

Rawa Island Holiday Resort, Tourist Center, Mersing, Johore, tel. ME – 791204, 16 bungalows and chalets.

Seremban

Carlton Hotel, 47 Jalan Tuan Sheikh, Seremban, Negri Sembilan, tel. 06–75336, 2 hours from airport, 10 min from railway terminal, 2½ hours from seaport, downtown; 38 rooms, air conditioned, dining room, bar, entertainment arranged on request, 1 shop.

Taiping

New Government Rest House, Taman Tasek, tel. 05-822044; 12 air-conditioned rooms.

Tioman Island

Merlin-Samudra Hotel, Pulau Tioman, P.O. Box 4, Mersing, Johore; Merlin-Samudra Reservation Centre (next to harbour), tel. Mersing 791771; 60 km off east coast of Peninsular Malaysia, boat or air transfer, 59 air-conditioned and 15 non-air-conditioned rooms, restaurant, beach bar, cocktail lounge, marine sports center, games room, tennis, volleyball, netball and badminton courts, football field.

SABAH

Kota Kinabalu

Ang's Hotel, 28 Jalan Bakau, Kota Kinabalu, Sabah, tel. 55433, 54466, 10 min from airport, in town center; 35 rooms, air conditioned, restaurant and bar.

Borneo Hotel, P.O. Box 567, Kota Kinabalu, tel. 55255 Sabah, near the airport, 20 min from railway terminal, 30 min from seaport; 6 km from down-town Kota Kinabalu, 100 meters from beach; 31 air-conditioned rooms, 10 chalets, dining room, bar.

Capital Hotel, P.O. Box 1223, 23 Jalan Haji Saman,

Kota Kinabalu, Sabah, tel. 53433, 20 min from airport, 5 min from railway, in residential area near center of town, 6 meters from ocean; 102 rooms, air conditioned, dining room serving Western and Chinese cuisine, cocktail lounge, nightclub, sailboats, outriggers, excursion boats, car rentals, tours of Kota Kinabalu and vicinity, beauty and barber shops.

Hotel Jesselton, P.O. Box 401, Gaya St., Kota Kinabalu, Sabah, tel. 55633, 5 km from airport, 1 km from railway, 2 min from seashore; 49 rooms, air conditioned, dining room serving European, Chinese and Malaysia cuisine, bar, cocktail lounge, golf, yachting, climbing tours of Mt. Kinabalu.

Hotel Shangri-La, P.O. Box 1718, Bandaran Berjaya, Kota Kinabalu, Sabah, tel. 56100, 10 min from airport and railway, 5 min from seaport; 150 rooms, air conditioned, dining room, 2 bars, swimming pool.

Hyatt Kinabalu, Jalan Datuk Salleh, Kota Kinabalu, Sabah, tel. 51777, 320 rooms, coffee house, restaurants, cultural shows, swimming pool, scuba diving, tennis, boutiques.

Kinabalu National Park, P.O. Box 626, Kota Kinabalu, Sabah, tel. 54452, 51595, 92 km by jeep from Kota Kinabalu, helipad at park headquarters; 6 chalets, cabins, youth hostel, electricity, piped water, log fires, refrigerator, gas/oil cookers, simply furnished, visitors expected to bring and cook their own food but simple food and bar available in clubhouse, hire of camping equipment, guides, and porters to climb Mt. Kinabalu.

Nam Hing Hotel, 32/34 Jalan Haji Saman, Kota Kinabalu; 1, tel. 51433, 34 rooms, airconditioned restaurant and bar.

Winner (Foh Yu) Hotel, 9 & 10 Prince Philip Dr., Kota Kinabalu, Sabah, on sea front; 55 Jalan Tun Mustapha, tel. 567/8/9 39 airconditioned rooms, bar, restaurant, nightclub.

Labuan

Victoria Hotel, Labuan, Sabah, centrally located; 39 airconditioned rooms, restaurant with Western and Chinese food, nightclub, saloon.

Hotel Imperial, 5 Jalan Merdeka, Lukas Kong Bldg., Labuan. 30 rooms, town area, partly-airconditioned.

Sandakan

Hotel Nak, Jalan Pelabohan, Sandakan, Sabah, tel. 2172, 12 km from airport, 100 meters from waterfront; 37 rooms, air conditioned, bar, restaurant, nightclub.

Sabah Hotel, P.O. Box 275, Sandakan, Sabah, tel. 3291, 20 min from airport, 5 min from seaport, 1 km from town; 28 air-conditioned rooms, dining room, bar, nightclub.

Tawau

Far East Hotel, Tawau. Jalan Masjid, tel. 73200 center of town, 22 rooms, nightclub.

Hotel Oriental, 10 Dunlop Street, Tawau, Sabah, tel. 71500 in center of town, 3 km from airport, 1 km from seaport; 28 rooms.

Hotel Emas, Jalan Utara, Tawau, tel. 73300. 100 rooms, center of town, fully airconditioned, nightclub and restaurant.

Tawau Hotel, 72-73 Chester St., Tawau Sabah, tel. 71100, 10 min from airport, 5 min from seaport, downtown; 34 rooms air conditioned bedrooms, dining room Chinese restaurant, bar, nightclub.

SARAWAK

Kuching

Aurora Hotel, McDougall Road, Kuching, Sarawak, tel. 20281-6, 23360, 20 min from airport and seaport, downtown; 82 air-conditioned rooms, dining room, coffee house, bar, nightclub.

Borneo Hotel, Tabuan Road, Kuching, Sarawak tel. 24121 11 km from airport, center of town; 37 rooms, completely renovated, air-conditioned bedrooms, dining room, cocktail lounge, nightclub, beauty and barber shops, conference room.

Fata Hotel, McDougall Road, Kuching, Sarawak; 30 air-conditioned rooms, dining room, bar, money exchange, tours operator.

Holiday Inn Kuching, Jalan Tunku Abdul Rahman, Kuching, Sarawak, tel. 23111, 20 min from airport, on Sarawak River, near Sarawak Museum; 200 rooms, air conditioned, dining room, banquet room, bar, cocktail lounge, weekly entertainment at bar and poolside, swimming pool, beauty and barber shop, laundry, shops.

Hotel Longhouse, Abell Road, Kuching, Sarawak, tel. 55333, 15 min from airport, 5 min from seaport; 50 air-conditioned rooms, dining room, cocktail lounge.

Odeon Hotel, 74 Padungan Road, Kuching, Sarawak, tel. 24211 15 min from airport; 30 rooms, air conditioned, dining room, tour desk, arcade shops, cinema, Chinese restaurant, roof-garden.

Miri

Fatimah Hotel, 49 Brooke Road, Miri, Sarawak; 43 air-conditioned rooms, dining room, Chinese, Malay, European dishes available on order.

Park Hotel, P.O. Box 241, Kingsway, Miri Sarawak, tel. 3761, 15 min from airport, 500 meters from beach; 95 air-conditioned rooms, dining room serving Chinese and European cuisine, coffee house, bar, nightclub, shopping arcade.

Sibu

Capitol Hotel, 19 Wong Wai Siong Road, Sibu, tel. 21044, 31 rooms, bar, restaurant.

Malaysia Hotel, 28 Kpg. Nyabor Road, Sibu, tel. 22299 27 rooms.

Premier Hotel, Sarawak House Komplex, Sibu, tel. 23222. Located downtown; 96 rooms, air conditioned, coffee house, bar restaurant, nightclub, shopping arcade, conference rooms.

Sarawak Hotel, 34 Cross Road, Sibu, Sarawak, tel. 23455, 15 min from airport, 3 min from seaport; air conditioned, dining room serving Chinese and European cuisine, bar, excursion boats, rental bicycles, shopping arcade.

Brunei

Brunei Hotel, 95 Jalan Chevalier, Bandar Seri Begawan, tel. 22373. 100 rooms, airconditioned, restaurant, central position.

Ang's Hotel, Jalan Pasek Lama, Bandar Seri Begawan, tel. 23553. Central position, 100 rooms, air-conditioned, restaurant.

Sheraton Hotel (due to open in 1981) in Bandar Seri Begawan.

---

celebrations

It is difficult to say which is the most exciting spectacle—a blowpipe's bull's-eye in the Borneo interior; a top that spins for fifty minutes under a makeshift canopy on Peninsular Malaysia's east coast; an imperial howl at Penang's Chinese opera; or an Indian dancer with bells on her toes. In Malaysia not only do all these happenings occur, but several may be going on at the same time. The country has a public holiday nearly every month, not counting the market feasts, regal birthdays and religious processions that sprinkle calendar pages like confetti. The only problem is distance. Malaysia spreads out over 5,000 green km and so do its festivals. If you wish to see them you usually have to travel.

The Muslim, Chinese and Hindu calendars, unlike the Gregorian calendar, use the lunar month as their basic unit of calculation. Hence dates vary from year to year.

For this reason, the calendar of festivals and celebrations has been split into two parts: one for festivals with fixed dates and the other for festivals with variable dates. For immediate events, read the daily newspapers and *Kuala Lumpur This Month*, distributed free at leading hotels.

Festivals And Celebrations With Constant Dates

January

New Year's Day: On the 1st January, apart from the familiar tradition of waking up late after the long and lively night before, the public holiday is enjoyed in leisure except by those in the states of Johore, Kedah, Kelantan, Perlis, and Trengganu.

Thai Pongal: On 14th January, essentially a Hindu harvest festival celebrated in an atmosphere of prayer and thanksgiving. Householders rise early, bathe and don new clothes, marking the beginning of the Hindu month of Thai, the luckiest of all months.

Birthday of His Highness the Sultan of Kedah: On the 21st January, celebrated by a guard of honor and the presentation of medals at Balai Besar, followed by a garden party at Istana Anak Bukit near Alor Star.

February

Kuala Lumpur City Day: On 1st February; what began as a small, tin-mining settlement at the confluence of two rivers—hence the name Kuala Lumpur ("Muddy Estuary")—has become in little more than 120 years one of the world's fastest growing cities. The day honors the capital as a "living symbol" of Malaysia's political identity as a nation.

Birthday of His Highness the Raja of Perlis: On 3rd February, the small northern state of Perlis is swept into a festive mood with the highlights of ceremonial pageantry occurring in Kangar, the state capital.

March

Birthday of His Highness the Sultan of Selangor: On 8th March, a public holiday for the state, featuring a ceremonial parade, an investiture and a garden party at the Sultan's palace in Klang, a harbor town about 24 km west of Kuala Lumpur.

May

Giant Turtle Season: Starting May through September, the long, lonely beach at Rantau Abang on the East Coast of the Malay peninsula has, oddly, been chosen as the only spot in the world where the gigantic, leathery turtles lay their eggs. Late at night, the enormous sea beasts creep slowly along the sands, dig a hole, deposit their eggs, waddle back to the seas and vanish.

Kadazan Harvest Festival: On May 10th and 11th celebrated by Kadazan farmers in Sabah with traditional thanksgiving ceremony for a successful harvest as well as feasts for all those who have helped in harvesting the crop. The traditional Kadazan dance, *sumazau,* highlights this festivity.

Kota Belud Tamu Besar: On the 30th and 31st May, colorful congregation of Bajau horsemen, cockfights, native dances and beauty contests mark the gay annual market festival at Kota Belud, a scenic town 77 km from Kota Kinabalu in Sabah. The *tamu*, or weekly market, has been an institutional get-together among Sabah's tribesmen for decades. A good opportunity to view the enduring traditions of Borneo.

Sipitang Tamu Besar: early May, Sipitang, a small coastal town 31 miles from Beaufort in Sabah, holds its annual market celebration. It is one of the few places where blowpipe competitions and ladies' football matches are organized. Other highlights include a beauty contest, agricultural show, handicraft exhibition and traditional dances.

June

Gawai Dayak: On 1st and 2nd June, annual Dayak festival long celebrated throughout Sarawak to mark the closing of the rice season and to pray for another auspicious crop. Key ritual is the *miring* ceremony, conducted by the bard of the tribe. Dayaks gather to make offerings of various foods, fruits and their famed *tuak* rice wine, as the bard recites poems asking for guidance, blessings and long life. A white cockerel, believed to drive away evil spirits, is sacrificed while throughout the day Dayaks entertain themselves with performances of the *ngajat* war dance, demonstrations of blowpipe skills and cockfights.

Birthday of His Majesty the Yang di Pertuan Agung: On 4th June, celebrated throughout Malaysia to honor the Supreme Head of State with regal pageants centering in the capital city of Kuala Lumpur at Stadium Merdeka, Parliament House and Lake Gardens.

Birthday of His Excellency the Governor of Malacca: on 11th June, a state holiday, there are celebrations throughout Malacca.

Birthday of His Highness the Sultan of Trengganu: On the 26th June, grandly celebrated throughout the state, particularly by the Police Special Constables, Territorial Army, Boy Scouts, Girl Guides, Red Cross and schoolchildren participating in the birthday parade on the Sultan Ismail Stadium field in Trengganu.

Festa de San Pedro: On 29th June, Christian holiday especially cherished by the Portuguese-Eurasian community of Malacca in honor of the patron saint of fishermen. Merrymakers hold a feast in the evening when gaily decorated boats lit by candles are blessed by the priest. Folk dances and prizes for the most beautiful boat accompany the services at the Church of Assumption in Banda Praya, Malacca.

July

Keningau Tamu Besar: On 1st July, market feast at Keningau in Sabah, 48 km from Tenom, is held, at which villagers amuse themselves with pony and buffalo races, blowpipe competitions, talent shows, beauty contests, sports, dances and handicrafts shows.

Birthday of the Governor of Sarawak: On 7th July, birthday parade on the central *padang* in Kuching culminates state-wide ceremonies.

Puja Umur: Birthday of His Highness the Sultan of Kelantan, on 10th and 11th July, begins with a big parade and guard of honor at the Padang Merdeka in Kota Bharu, followed by colorful ceremonies at Istana Balai Besar where His Highness bestows honors on his subjects for their distinguished service to the state. Sideshows and competitions keep Kelantan in a festive mood.

Birthday of His Excellency the Governor of Penang: On 16th July, the island celebrates with big parades, free cinema shows, brightly lit streets and public buildings and with the donation of cash gifts to nursing homes and orphanages.

Birthday of His Highness the Yang di Pertuan Besar of Negri Sembilan: On 19th July, public celebrations for the state include the investiture ceremony held in the Istana at Sri Menanti, a garden party in the evening and an all-community dinner and dance. Prayers are offered in mosques, churches and temples.

Tuaran Tamu Besar: On 29th July, the road to Tuaran, a scenic town in Sabah, 35 km from Kota Kinabalu, passes modern residential districts, rubber plantations, rice fields and small villages. During *tamu besar*, the annual market festival held at the end of July, the little town makes merry with water sports, boat races, mounted Bajau horsemen, night markets and dances.

August

Wild Game Hunting: On 15th August the season opens for Green Pigeons in Negri Sembilan, Selangor, Malacca and Penang. Game birds may also be shot in other Malaysian states on license from the state game warden. Season runs until the end of November.

National Day: On 31st August, anniversary of *Merdeka*—Independence—in 1957, known as *Hari Kebangsaan Malaysia* (National Day), stirs up patriotic celebrations from the smallest village to the largest town. The most outstanding are held in Kuala Lumpur where bright city lights illuminate public parks and stately Moorish buildings. All roads leading to the city are crowded with pedestrians on holiday, and schoolchildren fill Merdeka Stadium to view the lavish national parade. Festivities begin at eight in the morning amidst the roll of drums and fanfare of trumpets when His Majesty the Yang di Pertuan Agung and his consort arrive to preside over the affair. Parades there continue through the night when police bands and military personnel display their marching skills. The city's Lake Gardens are transformed into open stages entertaining huge crowds with traditional Malay and Indian classical dances, Chinese operas and all-community variety shows.

Beaufort Tamu Besar: On 31st August, annual market day at Beaufort in Sabah, 90 km by train from Kota Kinabalu, is filled with a colorful program of float parades, *kampung* handicraft exhibits, fun fairs, native dances and a shop-house decoration competition.

September

Feast of Santa Cruz: From 1st to 31st September Catholics honor the Exaltation of the Holy Cross by making a pilgrimage to the Church of Santa Cruz at Malim, Malacca. Tradition says that some ninety years ago, an ailing Malaccan lady living on Jalan Portuguese had a vision telling her she would be cured if she touched the cross in her dream. When the jungle was cleared a cross was found buried there. It cured the woman as the vision had promised. To this day, Malacca's Catholics visit the church enshrining the cross.

Birthday of His Highness the Sultan of Perak: On 15th September, holiday mood pervades the State of Perak honoring its ruler through royal celebrations and sports contests.

Papar Tamu Besar: From 15th to 20th September, market day in Papar, among the largest rice-growing districts in Sabah known particularly for its lovely Kadazan girls, includes native dances, costume contests, cultural shows and sports events. The town is 38 km from Kota Kinabalu.

Birthday of His Excellency the Yang di-Pertuan Negara of Sabah: On 10th September, ceremoniously honored throughout the state.

October

Puja Ketek: From 1st to 31st October, Siamese temples in Kelantan on Peninsular Malaysia's East Coast celebrate this day with pilgrimages to the *ketek*—holy shrine. The largest *ketek* in the state is at Batu Tiga in Repek. During the ceremony, thousands of Buddhists bearing offerings to the shrine attend local sideshows featuring traditional dances, such as *menora* and *wayang gedek*. The forefathers of many worshipers were Siamese who settled in the state.

Menggatal Tamu Besar: From 1st to 31st October, market festival in the pleasant town of Menggatal in Sabah, 13 km from Kota Kinabalu. It features a gay gathering of the local population who join in beauty contests, cultural shows, agricultural and handicraft exhibits and native dances.

Universal Children's Day: On 7th October, in Kuala Lumpur, a giant rally for children from schools, homes and orphanages opens with the release of balloons, followed by band music, fancy dress football, motorcycle acrobatics and the presentation of an award to the most gallant child of the year. The winner has his big moment when his award is presented by His Majesty the Yang di Pertuan Agung.

Kudat Tamu Besar: Around mid-October, Festival of Kudat, a town on the northern coast of Sabah, is celebrated by the Rungus tribe, longhouse dwellers who wear gold-colored rings around their arms, necks, ankles and waists. Apart from baby shows, livestock competitions and beauty contests, there is a grand display of folk dances rare to the region such as *sumazau, magangon, dindang* and the ever popular *joget*.

Birthday of His Highness the Sultan of Pahang: On 24th October, big celebration throughout the state of Pahang, featuring a parade, investiture and garden party at the town of Pekan. There are polo matches at the Sultan's polo ground, a state ball at the Abu Bakar Palace, and evening performances of traditional shows in the compound of Kota Beram Palace.

Birthday of His Highness the Sultan of Johore: On 28th October, crowds line the waterfront facing the palace for a good view of the sea-sports staged for the day, followed by games and athletic meets among schoolchildren and sportsmen. Musical troupes take over at night to entertain the crowds at Johore Bahru.

November

Guru Nanak's Birthday: On 22nd November, the great guru of Sikhism, Nanak, was born in 1496, and stated that there should be no sects and ceremonies, only pure love and devotion to God. Sikhs in Kuala Lumpur honor his birthday by reading the Guru Granth Sahib, singing devotional hymns and attending religious lectures and feasts at the Sikh temples.

December

Pesta Pulau Penang: a month-long carnival on Malaysia's holiday island. The water carnival features speed boat races, marathon swimming and others events. Dragon boat races are held towards the end of the festival. The Pesta Queen contest and the Chingay flag procession in George Town are other highlights.

Christmas: Christians of all races spend Christmas eve at midnight mass and carol parties, preceding a public holiday enjoyed by all.

* * *

Below follow the festivals and celebrations with variable dates—these probably include some of Malaysia's more exciting events, which still follow ancient calendars and seasons.

Festivals And Celebrations With Variable Dates

The dates given are applicable to 1980 and may vary by as much as a month from year to year.

January–February

Chinese New Year's Day: First day of the first moon (between January and February). Traditionally, the holiday season explodes with a big bang of firecrackers and jubilant merrymaking. People, especially children, wear their best clothes and receive lots of *ang-pows* (money wrapped in red packets) from parents, relatives and family friends. Every home and business holds "open house" for everyone. Bright red lucky scrolls, inscribed with ancient proverbs in gold Chinese characters, decorate many homes, signifying the birth of a new span of life and the arrival of a new year. The season's greeting is "Kong Hee Fatt Choy," meaning "A Happy and Prosperous New Year." Chinese shop houses in most Malaysian towns are splashed with day-glow colors to set the mood for dragon dances and pedestrian parades.

* * *

Birthday of Chor Soo Kong: Between January and February, on the sixth day of the first moon the number of pit vipers slithering among the altars of Penang's famous Snake Temple is believed to be greatest. A Chinese priest built the temple in 1850 as a sanctuary for the snakes, venerated as disciples of the god Chor Soo Kong. Hundreds of Chinese visit the temple on this day to offer prayers to the god, while outside courtyards flourish with Chinese opera.

* * *

Birthday of the Jade Emperor: Ninth day of the first moon (between January and February). Chinese festival honoring Yu Huang, Supreme Ruler of Heaven, who is depicted wearing a robe adorned with peonies and holding a scroll bearing the inscription "May ten thousand treasures seek audience with you." His attendants carry banners proclaiming "May your future be as vast as the Eastern Sea" and "May you live as long as the Southern Mountains." Chinese throughout Malaysia pay homage at temples by offering food, fruits and flowers to the deity.

* * *

Ban Hood Huat Hoay: Day of Ten Thousand Buddhas (between January and February). Celebrated with a twelve-day observance held among the lofty shrines of Kek Lok Si Buddhist Temple in Penang. Devotees gather to pray for world peace, happiness, prosperity and goodwill among mankind. Captive tortoises, fish and birds are liberated as a good deed.

* * *

Kwong Teck Sun Ong's Birthday: (end of February) when celebrations are held at the Chinese temple in Kuching, Sarawak, to commemorate the birth of the child deity. Hundreds of devotees come to pray at the temple and make offerings of buns shaped like tortoises (a symbol of longevity) to the child god. A procession is held in the evening and performances by musicians playing traditional instruments and comic sketches.

* * *

Chap Goh Meh: Fifteenth night of the Chinese New Year and the official ending of celebrations in ancient China (between January and February). In Chinese lore, it is a bright night for young ladies seeking good husbands. At Penang's Esplanade and New Coast Road, single girls in full finery stroll along the promenade—the more fortunate among them making the scene in gaily decorated cars followed by musicians playing old songs. Tradition tells of these young ladies throwing oranges, pebbles or groundnuts into the sea with a wish for a handsome husband. Nowadays, many young Malaysian Chinese celebrate Chap Goh Meh with a swinging party.

* * *

Chingay: Twenty-second day of the first moon (between January and February). An annual procession staged on the waterfront in Johore Bahru. Long bamboo poles, 6–12 meters high, serve as tapering masts for huge triangular flags carried by brawny Malaysian Chinese amid a cacophony of drums and gongs. Flag-bearing teams compete in a skillful display of acrobatics and balancing acts while marching past the crowds.

* * *

March—April

Tua Peck Kong: Twenty-sixth day of the eight moon (beginning of March 1980). Spirit money and spirit property fashioned from paper, augmenting the riches of the deceased, are burnt at the temple of Sia San Ten in Kuching, Sarawak, as devotees pray for the well-being of their ancestors.

* * *

Palm Sunday: The Sunday before Easter (late March or early April). The congregation of St. Peter's Church of Malacca, the oldest ecclesiastical edifice in all Malaysia, celebrates Palm Sunday with a vivid candlelight procession headed by the figure of Christ bearing the Cross. Hundreds of Malaysians of all races attend the Church of the Portuguese Mission, built in 1710.

* * *

Panguni Uttiram: Occurs on the day of the full moon in the Tamil month of Panguni (between March and April). Very popular day among Hindus as it marks the occasion of two celestial marriages, that of Siva to Shakti and Lord Subramaniam to Theivani. Thandayuthapani Temple at Sentul, Kuala Lumpur, celebrates the holiday with a grand procession bearing the image of Lord Subramaniam on an illuminated silver chariot.

* * *

Good Friday: The Friday before Easter (late March or early April). Among the many services held in Christian churches and cathedrals throughout Malaysia is a dramatic candlelight procession round the centuries-old St. Peter's Church in Malacca. Thousands of worshipers gather to witness the solemn figure of Christ lying in a canopied coffin and the life-size statue of the Blessed Virgin Mary borne above a sea of candlelight.

* * *

Easter Sunday: The first Sunday following the full moon that occurs on or after 21 March (late March or early April). Traditional services held in all Malaysia's churches. The old Catholic churches in Malacca, built by Dutch and Portuguese settlers centuries ago, are particularly festive during Easter.

* * *

Birthday of the Goddess of Mercy: Nineteenth day of the second moon (between March and April). Women especially remember the birthday of Kuan Yin, a deity well beloved by Malaysia's Chinese. Her full title translates as "The most merciful and compassionate Bodhisattva, protector of the afflicted, who looks down on the world and hears its prayers." Hundreds of devotees, bearing joss sticks, fresh fruit, flowers and sweet cakes, gather at the popular temples dedicated to Kuan Yin in Kuala Lumpur and Penang.

* * *

Cheng Beng: It falls 106 days after the winter solstice, usually about the end of the second or the beginning of the third moon (between March and April). "All Souls' Day," when Chinese visit the ornate tombs of their ancestors. Families burn incense sticks, candles and joss papers and make sacrificial offerings of food. Cleaning and repainting of the graves are also carried out during their annual visit to the cemeteries. In Cantonese, the ceremony is called "Cheng Ming."

* * *

Sri Rama Navami: The ninth day of the month Caitra (between March and April). A popular nine-day festival among the Brahman caste, held to honor Sri Rama, hero of the Hindu *Ramayana* epic. Several Hindu temples feature devotional songs, music recitals and the reading of the *Ramayana*. Mariamman Temple in Kuala Lumpur holds special prayers in the evenings.

* * *

April—May

Songran Festival: Traditional New Year honored by Thai Buddhists throughout Asia (between April and May). Celebrated in the Thai temples of Penang by removing the image of Lord Buddha and bathing it with holy lotion or fragrant waters. Devotees join in a water sprinkling ceremony and request monks to chant prayers to Buddha and their ancestors, seeking blessings and forgiveness for their ill-doings during the year.

* * *

Chithirai Vishu: The Hindu New Year begins on the day the sun enters the zodiacal house Medam (Aries) in the month Chithirai (between April and May). The Hindu Almanac begins its calculations for the year from this day, a day of rejoicing for Hindu devotees. The house has been cleaned and washed, the ceremonial vessels and lamps polished. Housewives rise early and light prayer lamps before the household deity. Traditionally, when other members of the family have woken, they are not allowed to open their eyes until they have been led to the family altar, where their first sight in the new year is the family deity.

* * *

Puja Pantai: Big beach festival 5 km south of Kuala Trengganu on Peninsular Malaysia's East Coast when 25 000 people have a three-day beach party in early May. The festival, coinciding with the full moon and the end of the rice harvest, has been going on longer than any person can remember. Vacationers camp on the beach in rows of makeshift huts, where there are hundreds of shops and bicycle peddlers. Food and drink stalls give women an opportunity to leave the kitchen for a change. Until a dozen years ago, the days were filled with *Wayang Kulit* shadow plays, dramas and ancient dances. Now, these have given way to blaring portable radios and outdoor theaters with noisy electric generators showing Malay, Indian and cowboy films, and singers touring the scene in souped-up Volkswagen vans equipped with flashy lights and megaphones.

* * *

Birthday of the Queen of Heaven: Twenty-second day of the third moon (between April and May). Seamen, fishermen, and many others flock to Chinese temples dedicated to Ma-Chu-Po, Queen of Heaven and goddess of the seas. To her they make supplications for fair weather and good fishing, and to her they pay tribute for successes in the past twelve months.

* * *

Vesak Day: The day of the full sixth moon (between April and May). Celebration of Lord Buddha's birth, death and enlightenment. Throughout the day Buddhist monks in saffron robes chant *sutras* while worshipers by the thousands offer prayers and perform good deeds. Caged birds are set free by devotees as a symbol of releasing a captive soul. Many Buddhist temples stage picturesque lantern processions.

June—August

Isra Dan Mi'raj: (June 11th in 1980) Muslim holiday observed in mosques and private homes by offering prayers to commemorate the ascension of Prophet Muhammad. After the last evening prayers (*Isha*), devotees gather to listen to the account of the night journey from Mecca to the great mosque of Jerusalem, and of all the wonderful things the Prophet saw along the way.

* * *

Dragon Boat Festival: Fifth day of the fifth moon (mid-June). A holiday commemorating an ancient Chinese legend that tells of an unsuccessful attempt to save the life of the celebrated poet Ch'u Yuan. Previously, crowds gathered at the waterfront in Penang to watch the dragon boat races. Now the Chinese festival is simply celebrated by eating "Chung"—steamed dumplings prepared especially for the occasion.

* * *

Birthday of the God of War: (June) Kuan Ti, one of three sworn brothers of the famous trio in the "Romance of the Three Kingdoms," rose in prominence within the Chinese pantheon to become God of War—he who has the ability to avert war and protect people from its horrors. Devotees offer special prayers to the popular deity in many Chinese temples.

* * *

Lumut Sea Carnival: held at the Lumut Esplanade annually towards the end of July. Sea sports, hydroplane racing, cross channel swimming, go-karting, cycle racing and a big walk are held during the day. At night there are amateur boxing, Chinese operas, performances of traditional dances and the Pesta Ball and Pesta Queen contest.

* * *

Birthday of the Goddess of Mercy: Nineteenth day of the sixth moon (July). Kuan Yin's "birthday" is once again celebrated when devotees visit her temples in Kuala Lumpur and Penang to pray for her benevolence. The old temple at Jalan Pitt, Penang, stages puppet shows.

* * *

Nisfu Night: Fifteenth day before Ramadan (between July and August in 1980). Muslim holiday when it is popularly supposed the souls of the dead visit the house. Celebrated by gathering at the mosque or in the home between sunset and late evening prayers for Koran readings and reciting special prayers asking for the welfare of the dead and the living at all times and places.

* * *

Ramadan: Is the month of fasting in the Muslim calendar in accordance with the third tenet of the Islamic faith. For thirty days, Muslims take no food or drink from the break of dawn to sundown.

* * *

Lailatul Qadar: (During Ramadan) "Night of Grandeur," among the most blessed and auspicious nights in the Muslim calendar. It was on this evening that the complete Koran in spiritual form was brought down to earth from heaven before being revealed over the months to Prophet Muhammad. Many Muslims believe there is a blessed moment during the night when any prayer from the faithful is heard and any request to God is granted. No special services mark the occasion but in the *kampungs* families keep rows of lights around the house burning all night.

* * *

Koran Reading Competition: this is an international competition and major event in Malaysia. It is held annually at the Merdeka Stadium in Kuala Lumpur during the middle of Ramadzan. The competition lasts for six days and a prize-giving ceremony is held on the final night.

* * *

Sri Krishna Jayanti: Eighth day of the Sanskrit month Sravana (between July and August). Hindu festival celebrated in honor of Lord Krishna, especially popular among North Indians. Songs, dances and dramas depicting the life of Krishna— famous as a cheeky lover, a warrior and God incarnate—continue for ten days, focusing on the eighth day, Krishna's birthday when the Lakshmi Narain Temple in Kuala Lumpur holds special prayers at midnight.

* * *

Festival of the Seven Sisters: (August) On this night, Chinese maidens pray to the Weaving Maid for good husbands by burning joss sticks and joss papers. Sacrificial tables are laden with paper combs, mirrors, hairpins, rouge and other beauty aids. The night remembers the legend of the seventh and most beautiful daughter of the sun god, whose true love was a cowherd whom she married. The union so disappointed her awesome father that he banished his daughter and her husband to separate star palaces in the sky, allowing the young lovers to meet only once a year—on the seventh night of the seventh moon.

* * *

Festival of the Hungry Ghosts: Fifteenth day of the seventh moon (August). Chinese traditionalists believe that on the seventh moon the souls of the dead are released from purgatory to return to earth for feasting and entertainment. In large Malaysian towns, marketplaces are filled with offerings to the wandering spirits, while traditional Chinese operas and puppet shows enjoy a grand revival.

* * *

Vinayagar Chathuri: Fourteenth day of the Tamil month Avani (between August and September). Hindu worshipers pray to Vinayagar (Ganesh) for great wisdom, spiritual powers and peace of mind. Special *pooja*, prayers said with twenty-one types of flowers and twenty-one types of grass, are offered to the sagacious, elephant-headed deity at Koddu Malai Vinayagar Temple at Jalan Pudu in Kuala Lumpur.

* * *

Hari Raya Puasa: (in August for 1980) Hari Raya marks the end of the fasting month and the beginning of three days of rejoicing and merrymaking. The day is ushered in with prayers of thanksgiving in all mosques. Muslims are grateful to Allah for enabling them to successfully observe the fast and they show their gratitude by rejoicing, donning new clothes and visiting one another to strengthen the bonds of friendship and to renew love and goodwill among mankind.

September–October

Fire-Walking Ceremony: (September) Sometime during the month of September the Hindu temple at Gajah Berang, Malacca, revives this ancient ritual whereby devotees prove their spiritual probity by treading barefoot on hot coals.

Isra Dan Mi'raj: (September) Muslim holiday observed in mosques and private homes by offering prayers to commemorate the ascension of Prophet Muhammad. After the last evening prayers (*Isha*), devotees gather to listen to the account of the night journey from Mecca to the great mosque of Jerusalem, and of all the wonderful things the Prophet saw along the way.

* * *

Moon Cake Festival: Fifteenth day of the eighth moon (September). Sometimes called the Mid-Autumn Festival, this day marks the overthrow of the tyrannical Mongol warlords in ancient China. It now lends special respect to poets, children and women, and is celebrated with the exchange and eating of moon cakes. In the evening, children light festive paper lanterns in the shape of anything from a magic fish to a moon rocket and parade around their homes. Women pray to the Goddess of the Moon for it is believed the moon shines brightest on this night.

* * *

Navarathri: Begins on the first day of the bright fortnight of the Tamil month Purattasi (between

September and October). Hindu festival, literally meaning "Nine Nights," is dedicated to the wives of Siva, Vishnu and Brahma. Young girls enjoy special prominence by being dressed up as the goddess Kali and honored with offerings of flowers, sandalwood, fruits, new clothes and sweet meats. This is in reverence of their innocence and in hope that they grow up with good qualities. In Kuala Lumpur, the Sangitha Apriviruthi Sabha, an organization devoted to fostering classical Indian music, stages a music festival.

* * *

Hari Raya Haji: Tenth day of the month Dzulhijjah, last month of the Muslim calendar (mid-October in 1980). Celebrated throughout Malaysia as a national holiday honoring particularly those Muslims who have made a pilgrimage to Mecca. The day literally means "Festival of the Pilgrimage" and symbolizes the reunion of all mankind. Muslims throughout the world assemble in the Holy City to visit the Baitulla, place of congregation for all devotees fulfilling the fifth tenet of Islam. Henceforth, a male pilgrim is entitled *Haji* and a woman *Hajjah*. In the morning, prayers are offered at all mosques. Later, Muslims play host to friends in their homes and visit relations.

* * *

Festival of the Nine Emperor Gods: Ninth day of the ninth moon (between September and October). Nine days of Chinese operas, prayers, processions and devotions honoring the Nine Emperor Gods in Chinese mythology. Many devotees turn vegetarian during this time and make a pilgrimage by climbing the famous 1 002 steps to the Kew Ong Yeah temple on top of Paya Terubong Hill in Penang. On the ninth day, a grand procession is held to commemorate the return of the gods to heaven. Kau Ong Yah temple in Ampang Village, Kuala Lumpur, holds a spectacular fire-walking ceremony on that evening.

* * *

October–December

Kantha Shashithi: Sixth day of the bright fortnight of the month Aipasi (between October and November). Hindu celebration commemorating the defeat of an evil spirit by Lord Subramaniam. Orthodox observers fast for six days, praying frequently. In Kuala Lumpur, the Selangor Ceylon Saivite Association celebrates the festival at Kandaswamy Temple at Jalan Scotts. Subramaniam is worshipped as the great fighter against the forces of evil, one who liberates an individual from sin.

* * *

Deepavali: Fourteenth day of the dark fortnight of Aipasi (between October and November). Hindus celebrate the "Way of the light" by burning tiny oil lamps outside their homes, signifying the triumph of good over evil. On this day in the scriptures Lord Rama killed the demon King Rawana. It is one of the few Hindu festivals during which merrymakers invite all Malaysians.

Hindu families take full advantage of the holiday by holding "open house" for friends and relatives. Around the rubber estates, Tamil cinemas are packed.

* * *

Muslim New Year: First day of the Muslim month of Muharram (November 9th in 1980). It marks the beginning of the Muslim year, and is a public holiday for Malaysians.

* * *

Ashura Day: Tenth day of Muharram (November 19th in 1980). Historically, a day of mourning in memory of the tragic death of Hussain, favorite grandson of the Prophet, who was killed in battle at Kerbala. Devout Muslims commemorate the day by fasting, sometimes joining with a small group of close friends to break the fast. In Penang, local amateurs stage a drama called "Boria," reenacting the Kerbala tragedy.

* * *

Birthday of the Goddess of Mercy: Nineteenth day of the ninth moon (between October and November). Kuan Yin's "birthday" is once again celebrated when devotees visit her temples in Kuala Lumpur and Penang to pray for her benevolence. The old temple at Jalan Pitt, Penang stages puppet shows.

* * *

Kartikai Deepam: On the day of the full moon of the Tamil month Kartikai (between October and November). Hindu festival marking the day on which Siva is said to have changed himself into a pillar of fire to settle an argument between Brahma and Vishnu as to who was the greater. High bonfires are lit in temples to recall the eminence of Siva. Local festivities are grandest at Thandayuthapani Temple in Muar, 190 km south of Kuala Lumpur, where hallways are decorated with thousands of tiny wick-lamps and night processions are held.

* * *

Winter Solstice Festival: No fixed day; sometime in December. Chinese holiday, sometimes known as the farmers' festival when thanks are offered for good harvests. Early in the morning, dumplings made from glutinous rice are cooked and served in a mixture of sugar and bean powder, but before they are eaten they are placed at the ancestral altars, and the family recites prayers.

* * *

Mandi Safar: Occurs in the second Muslim month, Safar (December in 1980). A once colorful bathing festival unique to Malaysia when Muslims from all walks of life dressed in rainbow colors and visited the sea beaches as a time of "religious cleansing of the body and soul with water." Though to orthodox Muslims Mandi Safar is more a picnic than a religious rite (there is no mention of it in the Koran), the holiday remains merry on a small scale. The most famous gathering grounds are the beaches at Tanjong Kling near Malacca and those of Penang.

* * *

speaking malay

Malay, mother tongue of more than 150 million Asians, is as ancient as a Grecian urn, and nearly as practical. A man can travel from the tip top of the Malay peninsula, through the southern Philippines and all along the island-hopping trail that zigzags across the Indonesian archipelago—speaking Malay. New nations have adapted the old language to their own ends, lending it a variety of sophisticated nuances in grammar, spelling and scientific terms. But all countries with official letterheads in Malay trace them back to the trade fairs of antiquity when merchants bargained over gold dust and rhinoceros horn in a tongue similar to today's "Bazaar Malay," the language of the marketplace.

While Europe droned through the Middle Ages, Malay rulers conversed in an increasingly refined and eloquent "Classical Malay," until, by the time the cosmopolitan Malacca Sultanate had set up its throne in the 1400s, the language had reached the heights of epic grandeur. The *Sejarah Melayu*, "Malay Annals," written by a scribe in the Malacca court "for the greater pleasure of his lord the king," achieves a stylistic grandiloquence that would delight the most venerable of storytellers.

The Annals' version of an Indian Raja on the march to conquer China reeks with romance no troubadour would deny: "So vast was his army on the march," the tale relates, "that boundless tracts of forest became treeless plains, the earth rocked as though convulsed by an earthquake, mountains were moved and their summits came toppling down: even the highest hills were brought low, and mighty rivers ran dry and became land . . ."

Classical Malay relapsed to the marketplace during the colonial era when the social elite, though retaining Malay as an official language, spoke only English among themselves. Independence in 1957 unanimously changed the conversation back to Malay, stressing its new importance as the National Language, symbol of unity among all Malaysians. Posters, banners, car stickers and special badges, exhorting people to speak as the ancients spoke, popped up in schoolrooms and government buildings. Certain theme songs played heavily on Radio Malaysia, such as *Bahasa Jiwa Bangsa*—"Language is the Soul of the Nation"—contributed to the superior status Classical Malay now enjoys. With new words from the age of technology enriching its reserves, and patriotic proprieties making it the language of monarchs and citizens alike, Malay can look forward to a future as refined and functional as its past.

Though formal Malay is a complex language demanding some time of serious study, the construction of "Basic Malay" is fairly simple, with many things about the language conducive to learning. Malay is written in the Latin alphabet and, unlike some Asian tongues, is not a tonal language. There are no articles in Malay—*buku* means "the book" or "a book," *anak* means "the child" or "a child." Plurals are made simply by doubling the noun—*buku-buku* means books. Nor are there any complicated verbal tenses. To denote time, a few key adverbs are used, the most useful being *sudah* "already," indicating the past, and *belum*, "not yet," indicating the future.

When speaking Malay, you need a few basic rules. Adjectives always follow the noun. *Rumah* (house) and *besar* (big) together as *rumah besar* mean "a big house" and so on. When constructing a sentence the order is: subject—verb—object. *Dia* (he) *makan* (eats) *nasi* (rice) *goreng* (fried). *Dia makan nasi goreng:* He eats fried rice. The traditional greeting in Malay is not "Hello!" but rather *Kemana?*—"Where are you going?" The question is merely a token of friendliness which does not require a specific answer. One simply returns the smile by replying *Tak ada ke mana*—"Nowhere in particular" and passes on.

Below are some very general guidelines for the pronunciation of Malay, or *Bahasa Malaysia* as it is known here. No written descriptions of the phonetics can replace the guidance of a native speaker, but once you've tried pronouncing a few words, Malaysians are quick to understand and their response is the best way to pick up a feeling for the language.

a	is pronounced short as in *father* or *cart*. *apa*—what; *makan*—to eat
ai	is pronounced like the sound in *aisle*. *kedai*—shop; *sungai*—river
au	sounds like the *ow* of *how*. *pulau*—island; *jauh*—far
e	is very soft, hardly pronounced at all. *membeli*—to buy; *besar*—big
g	is pronounced as in *go*, never as in *gem*. *pergi*—go; *guru*—teacher
h	is pronounced as in *halt*. *mahal*—expensive; *murah*—cheap
i	sounds like *i* in machine or *ee* in *feet*. *minum*—to drink; *lagi*—again
j	sounds like the English *j* in *judge*. *Jalan*—Street; *juta*—million
ny	is similar to *ni* in *onion* or *n* in *news*. *harganya*—price; *banyak*—a lot
o	is most similar to the *o* in *hope*. *orang*—human being; *tolong*—help
u	is pronounced as *oo* in *pool*. *tujuh*—seven; *minum*—to drink
y	sounds like *y* in *young*, never as in *why*. *wayang*—opera; *kaya*—rich

Useful Phrases

Good morning.	*Selamat pagi.*
Good afternoon.	*Selamat tengah hari.*
Good evening.	*Selamat petang.*
Please come in.	*Sila masuk*
Please sit down.	*Sila duduk.*
Thank you.	*Terima kasih.*

English	Malay	English	Malay
You're welcome.	*Sama-sama.*	where? (place)	*di mana?*
Where do you come from?	*Anda datang dari mana?*	where? (direction)	*ke mana?*
		when?	*bila?*
I come from . . .	*Saya datang dari . . .*	how	*bagaimana?*
What is your name?	*Siapa nama anda?*	why?	*mengapa?*
My name is . . .	*Nama saya . . .*	which?	*yang mana?*
Can you speak Malay?	*Boleh anda bercakaɟ dalam Bahasa Malaysia?*	how much?	*berapa?*
		to eat	*makan*
Yes.	*Ya.*	to drink	*minum*
No.	*Tidak.*	to sleep	*tidur*
Only a little.	*Sedikit sahaja.*	to bathe	*mandi*
I want to learn more.	*Saya hendak belajar lebih lagi.*	to come	*datang*
		to go	*pergi*
How do you find Malaysia?	*Apakah pendapat anda mengenai Malaysia?*	to stop	*berhenti*
		to buy	*beli (membeli)*
I like it here.	*Saya suka berada di sini*	to sell	*jual (menjual)*
The weather is hot, isn't it?	*Cuaca di sini panas, bukan?*	street/road	*jalan*
		airport	*lapangan terbang*
Yes, a little.	*Ya, sedikit.*	post office	*pejabat pos*
Where are you going?	*Pergi ke mana?*	shop	*kedai*
I am going to . . .	*Saya pergi ke . . .*	coffee shop	*kedai kopi*
Turn right.	*Belok ke kanan.*	money	*wang; duit*
Turn left.	*Belok ke kiri.*	dollar	*ringgit*
Go straight.	*Jalan terus.*	cent	*sen*
Please stop here.	*Sila berhenti di sini.*	1. one	*1. satu*
How much?	*Berapa?*	2. two	*2. dua*
Wait a minute.	*Tunggu sekejap*	3. three	*3. tiga*
I have to get change.	*Saya hendak tukar duit.*	4. four	*4. empat*
Excuse me.	*Maafkan saya.*	5. five	*5. lima*
Where is the toilet?	*Di mana tandas?*	6. six	*6. enam*
In the back.	*Di belakang.*	7. seven	*7. tujuh*
Where may I get something to drink?	*Di mana boleh saya minum?*	8. eight	*8. lapan*
		9. nine	*9. sembilan*
Over there.	*Di sana.*	10. ten	*10. sepuluh*
One cup of coffee.	*Kopi se cawan.*	11. eleven	*11. sebelas*
One cup of tea.	*Teh se cawan.*	12. twelve	*12. dua belas*
Fried noodles.	*Mee goreng.*	13. thirteen	*13. tiga belas*
Fried rice.	*Nasi goreng.*	20. twenty	*20. dua puluh*
The food was tasty.	*Makanan tadi sedap.*	21. twenty-one	*21. dua puluh satu*
How much does this cost?	*Berapakah harganya?*	22. twenty-two	*22. dua puluh dua*
		23. twenty-three	*23. dua-puluh tiga*
Ten dollars.	*Sepuluh ringgit.*	30. thirty	*30. tiga puluh*
That's quite expensive.	*Mahal sangat.*	40. forty	*40. empat puluh*
Can you make it less?	*Boleh kurangkan?*	58. fifty-eight	*58. lima puluh lapan*
Seven dollars.	*Tujuh ringgit.*	100. one hundred	*100. seratus*
Fine.	*Baiklah.*	263. two hundred and sixty three	*263. dua ratus enam-puluh tiga*
I'll buy it.	*Saya nak membelinya.*		
Good-bye.	*Selamat tinggal.*	1 000. one thousand	*1 000. seribu*

Useful Words

Mr.	*Encik*
Mrs.	*Puan*
Miss	*Puan, Cik*
I	*Saya*
you (friendly)	*awak*
you (formal)	*tuan-tuan*
he, she	*dia*
we	*kami*
they	*mereka*
what?	*apa?*
who?	*siapa?*

reading on

Books on Malaysia probe the far reaches of the Borneo wilds, flashback to old Penang when secret societies were on the rampage, linger among the genteel life in Malay *kampungs*, or chase surrealistic tracks of elusive, 3-meter jungle "giant men." The arcades of large hotels and drugstores sell popular and peculiar paperbacks on Malaysia. MPH Bookstore, on Tuanku Abdul Rahman Road in Kuala Lumpur, is a good place for browsing. So are the haphazard bookshelves at Caxton Stationers. The library at the University of Malaya, open to the public every day but Sunday, has the finest collection of all.

Alliston, Cyril, *Threatened Paradise: North Borneo and Its Peoples*. London: Robert Hale, 1966. Quick, stimulating reading on native tribesmen, Malays, Chinese and English colonialists in Sabah who have created the peculiar way of life there.

Chapman, F. Spencer, *The Jungle is Neutral*. London: Corgi Books, 1949. Malaysia's classic on the terrible reality of jungle warfare in World War II as told by a British officer who wandered the wilderness for three long years, and survived.

Fauconnier, Henri, *The Soul of Malaya*. Kuala Lumpur: Oxford University Press, 1965. The book is sheer mood. No other man has written so powerfully on the seductions of Malaya. We remember Conrad's *Heart of Darkness*—"Mr. Kurtz, he dead."

Glaskin, G. M., *The Beach of Passionate Love*. London: Barrie and Rockliff, 1961. An average novel but the setting certainly is not. Behind the turbulent drama of love emerges a portrait of the cultured Malays of Kelantan and the society they honor.

Harrison, Tom, *World Within: A Borneo Story*. London: The Cresset Press, 1959. Harrison has a style of descriptive writing that makes the inland peoples of Sarawak—peoples he knows—spring from the pages in third dimension, cracking jokes or chanting glorious songs as they go.

Lat, *kampong Boy:* Kuala Lumpur, Straits Times Publishing, 1979. Popular Malaysian cartoonist, Lat, gives an hilarious account of life in a typical Malay kampung (village) seen through the eyes of a child. The affectionate drawings and autobiographical text are both by Lat.

MacDonald, Malcolm, *Borneo People*. London: Jonathan Cape, 1956. A revealing account of his travels throughout Sarawak as an officer in the British colonial service during the forties and fifties.

Morrel, R., *Common Malayan Butterflies*. Kuala Lumpur: Longmans, 1960. Malaysia harbors 900 species of butterflies compared with Great Britain's 68. Visitors can encounter "The Painted Jezebel," "The Orange Albatross" or "The Black-Veined Tiger." This well-illustrated book shows them all and gives good tips to aspiring lepidopterists.

Runciman, Steven, *The White Rajahs: A History of Sarawak from 1841 to 1946*. Cambridge: University Press, 1960. A historian's tale of the extraordinary Brooke dynasty and the personalities of three men who fashioned a state from medieval Borneo.

Ryan, N. J., *The Cultural Heritage of Malaya*. Kuala Lumpur: Longman, 1962. A slightly pedantic but brief and very inclusive summary of the fusion of Malay, Chinese, Indian and Western societies to form Malaysia's multi-racial identity.

Sheppard, Mubin, *Taman Indera: Malay Decorative Arts and Pastimes*. Kuala Lumpur: Oxford University Press, 1972. A colorful survey of what many see but few write down with such precision—the culture of the Malays and the beauty of their arts.

Shuttleworth, Charles, *Malayan Safari*. London: Dent, 1965. The author, a British guide, tells cynically and amusingly of visits to the National Park and the East Coast islands; of the animals he encountered and the people he guided.

Tweedie, M. W. F. and Harrison, J. L. *Malayan Animal Life*. Kuala Lumpur: Longman, 1954. Malaysia's animal kingdom is so exotically profuse it would astonish a sophisticated zookeeper. The authors present an intriguing cast for a jungle play: from Moon Rats to Clouded Leopards to Spider-Hunting Sunbirds.

Wang Gung Wu (Ed.), *Malaysia, A Survey*. London: Pall Mall Press, 1964. A collection of essays by local and foreign scholars on Malaysia's history, geography, economics and society, which Malaysian intellectuals are likely to recommend to visitors as a good introduction to the country.

Wavell, Stewart, *The Lost World of the East: An Adventurous Quest in the Malayan Hinterland*. London: Sovenir Press, 1958. Follow the offbeat trail of a chess-playing BBC journalist who penetrates deep into the "blue jungle" in search of the fabulous lost city of Chini. With microphone in hand, he barely escapes terrorist guns by disguising himself as an aborigine, only to drop in later on a Malay magician's seance. Easily-read strange tales of mysterious Malaysia.

* * *

Malaysia is a veritable Garden of Eden of fruits all the year round, but besides the all-time tropical favorites such as golden pineapple, rosy papaya, juicy water-melon and all sorts and sizes of bananas, there's a host of others you may not have seen before. Many are seasonal — all are delicious.

Durian is king of fruits to the Malaysian. Once you get past the powerful smell, the taste is indescribably delicious. No two durians taste alike but some claim it is best likened to fruity-creamy-caramel.

Jambu Batu is also known as guava. Some people eat only the green outer layer, some only the pulp, but the wise eat the whole fruit.

Rambutans have marvelous hairy red-tinged-with-gold skins. The flesh is rather like lychees, juicy and sugar-sweet.

Mango comes long or rounded, green or yellow, and the golden flesh inside is soft, sweet and luscious.

Mangosteen is purple on the outside, white, sweet and juicy on the inside. The mangosteen ripens at the same time as the durian and they go well together. The Chinese believe that the "heatiness" of the durian is balanced by the "coolness" of the mangosteen.

Nangka or **Jackfruit** is the huge green fruit which you can often see on trees in the villages covered with sacks or paper bags to protect them from the avid birds. The pulp is juicy and chewy at the same time. It can be eaten both raw and cooked and even the seeds are edible.

Starfruit, yellow and shiny, is a good thirst quencher. Cut it horizontally into star-shaped wedges and dip it in salt.

Pomelo looks and tastes like a sweet, over-grown, slightly dry grapefruit.

Buah Duku. To open a duku, just squeeze gently. The flesh is sweet with a sour tinge. You'll probably eat dozens of dukus at one time, but watch out for the hard greenish center which can be bitter.

Buah Susu, literally translated 'milk fruit', is better known as passion-fruit. There are many different varieties, all equally delicious. Crisp-skinned and orange from Indonesia, purple from Australia and California, but the local ones have soft, velvety yellow skins. The grey seeds inside are sweet and juicy.

Buah Durian Blanda, or **Soursop**, resembles a chunky durian without the smell or the prickles. The soft, creamy flesh inside has just the hint of a sour tang.

Index
Glossary

A

Abdul Rahman, Tunku, 23
Abdul Razak, Tun, 23
aborigines see indigenous tribes
Abu Bakar Mosque, Johore, 200
accommodation, 100, 218-288
agriculture, 52-58
air travel, 98, 247, 274 see travel
airlines, 279
airport, 274
Akwhi, Captain, 140
Allied War Cemetery, 140
Alor Star, Kedah, 163-164
ang pows (red packets), 93
antiques, 115, 148, 163, 178
aquarium, 259, 269
    Brunei, 269
    Penang, 159
    Sarawak, 259
    Selangor, 121
archaeological sites, 164, 202, 262
architecture
    Chinese, 176
    Dutch, 179
    Malaysian, 140, 161, 170
    Moorish, 105
area, 13, 97
art, 93, 278
art galleries, 278
    National Art Gallery, K.L., 113
    Penang Art Gallery, 148
    Yahong Art Gallery, Penang, 163
Aw Potteries, 199
Ayer Hitam, Johore, 199
Ayer Itam Dam, Penang, 156

B

Bajau, 231, 242, 244, 245
baju kurong (a form of Malay dress for women), 198
Bandar Seri Begawan, 268
banks, 280
Bako National Park, Sarawak, 260
batek, 115, 209, 212, 224, 225
Batek Center, Kuantan, 212
batek painting, 163, 278
Batu Caves, 69, 87, 122, 122
Batu Ferringhi, Penang, 163
Batu Maung, Penang, 160-161
Bayan Lepas Airport, Langkawi Island, 160
Beach of the Beautiful Princess, Pangkor Island, 136
Beach of Passionate Love, Kota Bharu, 227
beaches, 48, 119, 165
    Batu Ferringhi, Penang, 163
    Bisikan Bayu Beach, East Coast, 225
    Chendor Beach, 216
    Dungun, 215
    Jason's Bay, Johore, 203
    Kelantan, 47
    Mersing, Johore, 203
    Muka Head, Penang, 162
    Pantai Dasar Saba, 226
    Pantai Irama, 226
    Port Dickson, 171-173
    Rantau Abang, 216-217
    Tanjong Aru, Sabah, 235
    Tanjong Penawar, Johore, 202
    Telok Chempedak, Kuantan, 212

Beaufort, Sabah, 245
Berdikir Barat (a verbal art form), 221
bibliography, 297
bird-singing, 225
bird's nest, 247, 264
birth rate, 97
Bisikan Bayu Beach, East Coast, 225
blowpipes, 132
boating, 172, 202
bomoh (Malay village medicine man), 76
Botanical Gardens, Penang, 155, 156, (Waterfall Gardens)
British, 23, 46, 48, 56, 198, 231, 243
British North Borneo Chartered Company, 234, 243, 247
brocade, 212
Brocade Weaving Center, Kuantan, 212
Brooke, Charles, 251, 253, 254, 255
Brooke, Charles Vyner, 255
Brooke, James, 22, 46, 251, 252, 253, 261, 269
Brunei Museum, 265, 269
Brunei River, 268
Buddha, 134, 153, 154, 155, 214
Buddhism, 153, 154, 213
buffaloes, 244
Bugis, 174
bunga raya (hibiscus flower), 224
Bukit China, Malacca, 185
Bumiputras ("Sons of the Soil"), 74
burong baskets (woven native baskets), 238
burong ketitir (merbok, jungle bird), 225
bus, 274 see travel
business hours, 108, 275
butterflies, 132, 165, 212

C

Cameron Highlands, 129, 131
camping
    East Coast, 213
    Endau River, 205
    Lake Chini, 212
    National Park, 193
    Penang Island, 162
carvings, 115
casino, 123
caves, 129, 133-134, 166, 213, 214
    Batu caves, Kuala Lumpur, 69, 87-89, 121-123, 122
    Charah Cave, Pahang, 213
    Gomantang Caves, Sabah, 247
    Gua Cerita or Story Cave, Langkawi, 166
    Niah caves, 35, 262, 265, 265
celebrations, 288-294
Charah Cave, 213
Chartered Company see British North Borneo Chartered Company
Cheng Ho, Admiral, 22, 45, 160, 167, 176-177, 180, 185
Cheng Hoon Teng Temple, Malacca, 176, 177
Cherating, 215
Cherating River, 215
Chinatown, Penang, 144
Chinese, 13
    angpows 93
    architecture, 176
    clan house, 72-73
    clan piers, 159
    clan wars, 130, 140
    early traders, 40

    festivals see festivals
    lion dance, 90
    medicines, 29
    New Year, 90, 93, 152, 154
    opera, 18, 75
    population, 15, 18, 75
    secret societies, 26, 64
    temples see temples
    tin miners, 54, 56
Chinese Assembly Hall, 114
Christ Church, Malacca, 183
churches, 276
    Christ Church, Malacca, 183
    St Paul's Church, Malacca, 182
    St Peter's Church, Malacca, 182
Christian Cemetery, Penang, 148
Churchill, Winston, 23, 269
Churchill Museum, 268, 269
cinemas, 278
Clarke, Andrew, Sir, 130
climate, 97, 275
Clock Tower, Penang, 147
Club Mediterranée, 215
clothing, 275
cockfighting, 244
Columbus, 42
communist, 23, 251
corals, 166, 210, 232
"Crab Island", 129
credit cards, 275
Cristao (a medieval Portuguese dialect), 184
cultural dances
    changggong, 220
    Dindang, 290
    Hadrah, 220
    Joget, 119
    Kudang Kepang, 203
    Mak Yong, 212, 220
    Menora, 220, 290
    Rodat, 212
    Ronggeng, 220
    Sumazau, 290
    Tari Piring, 220
    Zapin, 220
cultural expressions, 74-93
cultural pastimes
    berdikir barat, 221
    bird singing, 225
    cock fighting, 244
    dance, see cultural dances
    kite flying, 209
    sepak raga, 74, 80, 232
    silat, 78, 212
    top spinning, 13, 74, 80, 81, 209, 221
    wayang kulit, 54, 83, 209, 212
cultural show, 119
currency, 97, 275
custom formalities, 274

D

d' Albuquerque, 48, 180, 181
dance see cultural dances
Dayang Bunting Island, 167
death rate, 97
Desaru, 202
Dindings River, 137
discotheques, 119
Dunlop, John, 23, 58, 138
Dutch, 22, 46, 136, 147, 179, 182
    architecture, 137, 179
Dyaks, 35, 253, 254, 259, 261

E

East Coast, 209-227
East India Company, The, 22, 45, 146, 147, 167

economy, 18, 232
electricity, 97, 276
embassies, 281
Endau River, 36, 205
Eurasians, 13, 182
    Portuguese Eurasians, 182, 183, 184
exports, 97

F

Fa-Hsien, 42
facts at a glance, 97
fauna, 29-30, 165, 190, 192, 213, 215, 260 see also wildlife
Festa de San Pedro, Malacca, 184
festivals, 219, 220, 221, 288-294
    Chinese New Year, 90-93, *90*
    Festa de San Pedro, 184
    "Intrudu", 184
    Kayu Papan, 203
    Pesta Lumut (sea carnival), 138
    Thaipusam, 87-89,*89*
fishing
    occupation, 40, 48, 160, 209
    sport, 192, 193, 204, 205, 213, 219
flora, 125, 190, 238, 239, 260
flying club, 116
food, 116, 118-119
    malay food, 163, 170
    seafood, 163, 199
foreign exchange, 275
Fort Cornwallis, 147
Fort Margherita, 254
Fraser's Hill, 125, 129
fruits, 298
funicular railway, 157

G

gambling, 75, 105, 117, 123, 125
gardens and parks
    Botanical Gardens, Penang, 155-156
    Istana Gardens, Johore Bahru, 200
    Lake Gardens, Taiping, 140
    Taman D.R. Seenivasagam Park, 133
    Templer Park, K.L., 121
Gaya Island, 232
Genting Highlands, 123
George Town, 144, 150
Gomantang Caves, Sabah, 247
golf courses
    Cameron Highlands, 132, *132*
    Desaru, 203
    Fraser's Hill, 125
    Genting Highlands, 124
    Kuala Trengganu, 218
    Kuantan, 212
    Langkawi, 165
    Mersing, 203
    Pekan, Pahang, 211
    Penang, 157
    Port Dickson, 172
    Taiping Lake Gardens, 141
Gombak River, 105
Good Friday, 183
Government Rest House see Rest House
Grik, Perak. 139
gua (cave), 166
Gua Cerita Cave, 166
Guillemard Reservoir, 156
gunong (peak)
    Gunong Brinchang, 132
    Gunong Jerai (Kedah Peak), 163
    Gunong Kinabalu, 33, 235

Gunung Ledang, 198
Gunong Raya, 165
Gunong Tahan, 189. 193

H

Half Way House, 141
handicrafts, 115, 212, 222-223, 259
Hang Tuah (a heroic Malay warrior), 87
"Hash House Harriers", 237
headhunting, 16,33
Head of State (Yang di-Pertuan Agong), 97
health, 276
highest point, 97
hill stations, 129, 141
    Cameron Highlands, 131-133, *131, 132, 133*
    Fraser.s Hill, 125, *125*
    Genting Highlands, 123-124, *124*
    Maxwell Hill, 141
    Penang Hill, 156, 157, *157*
Hinduism, *17,* 22, 35, 59, 77-79, *78,* 89, 122
history, 13, 22, 74, 173
hot springs,
    Poring, Sabah, 240, 242
    Sungei Kesang, Johore, 199
    Telaga Air Panas, Langkawi, 166
hotels, 281-288
Hong San Temple, Sarawak, 259
Hornaby, William, 122
horse-racing, 116 see Turf Clubs
horseback riding, 163, 165, 202
hostesses, 120
Hussein Onn, Datuk, 23

I

Iban, 16, 33, 261, 262
ikan bilis (anchovies), 159
Illanuns, 231, 232
Imam, 108
immigration formalities, 274
imports, 97
income, 97
independence, 97
Indians, 13, 16, 22, 58, 75, 144
    Bengalis, 16
    Sikhs, 16
    Tamils, 16
indigenous tribes
    Dyaks, 253, 254, 259,
        Land Dyaks, 35
        Sea Dyaks, 261
        Sru Dyaks, 258
    Negritos, 27, 30, *31,* 35, 189, 190-192
    Orang Asli, 33-34, 132, 139, 205, 213
    Sabah tribes
        Bajau, 231, 242, 244, *245*
        Kadazan, *229,* 231, 233, 235, *235,* 244
        Murut, 231, 232, 245
        Illanun, 231
        Rungus, 232
    Sarawak tribes
        Kayan, 251
        Kenyah, 251
        Murut, 251
        Kelabit, 251, 258
        Punan, 251
    Semang, 80
"Intrudu", 184
Ipoh, 133, 135
Islam, 15, 22, 45, 74, 76, 108, 185, 211, 219

islands
    Besar Island, 176
    Crab Island, 129
    Dayang Bunting Island, 167
    Duyung Island, 219
    Gaya Island, 232
    Pangkor Island, 129. 136
    Perhentian Island, 210
    Rawa Island, 204
    Redang Island, 219
    Sibu Island, 205
    Song Song Island, 129
    Tenggol Island, 210
    Tioman Island, 203
    Ular or Snake Island, 215
istana (palace)
    Istana Kuala Kangsar, 139
    Istana Besar, Johore, 200
    Istana Balai Besar, 225
    Istana Mazia, K. Trengganu, 219

J

Jame Mosque, 106
Japanese 23, 135, 141, 226, 242
Jason's Bay, 203
Jesselton, 234
Johore Bahru, 200
Johore Lama, 198, 202
Johore River, 197
Johore Zoo, 200
jungle, 18, 27, 141, 189

K

Kadazan, 35, 231, 234, 235, 244
kain songket (silk woven with gold and silver thread), 222
kampungs (villages), 52, 74, 83
Kampung Ayer, Brunei, 269
Kampung Ayer, Sabah, 233, 234
Kampung Baharu, K.L., 115
Kapit, 260
kavadis (cage used at Thaipusam and Hindu mortification ceremonies), 89, 122
Kayan, 251
Kayu Papan Festival, 203
Kedak Museum, 278
Kedah Point, 145
Kek Lok Si, Penang, 155
Kelabit, 251, 258
Kelantan, 46, 224, 225
Kelantan State Mosque, 225
Kellie's Castle, 136
Kenyah, 16, 251, 258, *263*
Khoo Kongsi, Penang, 150
Kinabalu National Park, 236, 237
kites, 74, 221
kite-flying, 209
Klang River, 105
Kota Bharu, 225
Kota Belud, 244
Kota Kinabalu, 48, 231, 232
Kota Tinggi Waterfalls, 201
Koran, 74, 78, 162, 166
kris (a wavy-bladed double-edged dagger), 23, 78, 84, *86,* 87, 115, 148, 176, 231, 254, 278
Kroh, 130, 139
Kuala Besut, 225
Kuala Dungun, 215
Kuala Kangsar, 138
Kuala Lumpur, 13, 23, 62, 69, 105
Kuala Perlis, 164
Kuala Trengganu, 218
Kuan Yin, 134, 152, 153
Kuan Yin Temple, Penang, 151,
Kuantan, 211
Kuantan River, 211

Kuching, 252
Kudang Kepang dance, 203

L

Labuan, 232
Lake Gardens, 66, 110, 111
lakes,
    Dayang Bunting Lake, 167
    Lake Chini, 36, 212
    Sultan Abu Bakar Lake, 131
    Tasek Chenderoh, 139
Land Dyak, 35
Langkawi Islands, 129, 130, 160, 164-167
language, 15, 75, 97, 184, 276, 295
Lebir River, 189, 191
Leboh Ampang, K.L., 115
Light, Francis, Captain, 22, 145, 161, 167
Limbang River, Brunei, 268
lion dance, 90
Loke Yew, 114, 117
longhouse, 93, 260, 262, 264
Lord Siva, 110
Lord Subramaniam, 89
Low Hugh, 235
Lumut, 136

M

Magellan, 42
Magic Arrow rail service, 274
Mahsuri, 167
Malacca, 22, 42, 174
Malacca Museum, 175, 179, 278
Malacca River, 174, 180
Malacca Straits (Straits of Malacca), 22, 40, 46, 48
Malay, 13, 15, 76, 161
Malay food, 163, 170
Malay kings, 22
Malay language, 45, 295
Malaya, 23
Malayan Railway, 274
Malaysia, 13
Malaysian Air Charter, 164
Malaysian Grand Prix, 117, 157
marine life, 166, 173, 204, 210, 216, 216-218
markets, 66
    Central, Kuala Lumpur, 109, 115
    Central, Trengganu, 42, 218
    Kota Bharu, 225
    Kota Kinabalu, 233
    Kota Belud, 243
    Kuching, 256
    Penang (night market), 139
    Taiping (night market), 131
martial art, 78
Masjid Jame, K.L., 106
Masjid Negara, K.L., 107
Mat Aris, 80
Mat Salleh, 246
Maxwell Hill, 141
Mecca, 74
Mersing, 203
Mersing River, 203
Mimaland, K.L., 123
Minangkabau, 170
Ming Dynasty, 177, 185
Ming pottery, 204
Moluccas Islands, 42, 83
monsoon, 40, 51, 174, 191, 193, 202, 209, 215, 226
mosques
    Abu Bakar Mosque, Johore, 200
    Jame Mosque (Masjid Jame) K.L., 106

Kampong Nilam Puri Mosque, Kota Bharu, 225
    National Mosque (Masjid Negara), KL, 69, 101, 107
    Omar Ali Saifuddin Mosque, Brunei, 268, 269
    State Mosque, Kota Bharu, 225
    State Mosque, Seremban, 160
    Tranquerah Mosque, Malacca, 185
    Ubudiah Mosque, Perak, 139
    Zahir Mosque, Kedah, 163
motor racing, 117, 157
Mount Kinabalu, 33, 235
mountains see gunong
muezzin, 76
Muka Head, Penang, 162
Murut, 35, 231, 245, 251
museums,
    Brunei Museum, 169
    Churchill Museum, 169
    Kedah Museum, 278
    Malacca Museum, 175, 179, 279
    National Museum, K.L., 112, 278
    Penang Museum, 148, 278
    Perak Museum, 278
    Sabah Museum, 235
    Sarawak Museum, 257-259, 278
    Seremban Museum, 278
    Taiping Museum, 130
Muslim, 13
Muzium Negara (National Museum), 112, 278

N

National Art Gallery, 113, 278
national language, 15
National Monument, K.L., 111
National Mosque, K.L., 69, 106
National Museum (Muzium Negara), 112, 278
National Parks,
    Bako National Park, 360
    Kota Kinabalu National Park, 236, 237
    National Park (Taman Negara), 30, 189-193
National Stadium, 69, 108, 278
National University, 69
National Zoo, 120
Nattukotai Chettiar Shrine, Penang, 156
Negritos, 27, 189, 190, 191, 192
Negri Sembilan, 170
Niah Caves, Sarawak, 35, 262, 265, 265
nien koay ("cakes of the year"), 90
night life, 279
    George Town, Penang, 150
    Kota Kinabalu, Sabah, 233
    Kuala Lumpur, Selangor, 119-120

O

oil industry, 48, 209, 251, 268, 269
oil palm (see palm oil)
Omar Ali Saifuddin Mosque, Brunei, 268
opium, 75, 105, 125
Orang Asli, 30, 33, 36, 74, 131, 132, 139, 189, 192, 205, 212
orang utans, 30, 35, 242, 247

P

packing, 276
padang, (wide field), 66, 105, 106, 110, 111

Padus River, 245
Pahang River, 209, 211
Paka River, 215
palm oil, 18, 58, 201
pandanus, 223
Pangkor Island, 129, 136
pantai (beach) see beaches
Parameswara, 22, 45, 175, 177, 185
parang (working knife), 245
Parliament House, 69, 112
pasar malam (night market) 141, 149
    see also markets
Pasi Bogak, 137
Pasir Puteh, 226
pawang (tribal medicine man), 33
Pekan, Pahang, 209, 211
Pekan Kuah, Langkawi Island, 165
Penang, 44, 45, 129, 158, 274
Penang Buddhist Association, 153
Penang Hill, 156
Penang Museum, 148
Penghulu Koh, 262
Perak Tong, 133
Pesta Lumut (sea carnival), 138
Petaling Jaya, 70
petroleum, 18 see also oil industry
pewter, 115, 115
photography, 277
pictographs, 129
piracy, 22, 48, 130, 137, 165, 174, 199, 231, 269
Poring Sabah, 242
Port Klang, 274
Polo, Marco, 22, 45-46
population, 13, 15, 16, 75, 97
Port Dickson, 66, 171-173, 172, 173
Portuguese, 22, 46, 173, 175, 180, 181, 197
prahus (sailing boats), 40
press, 97, 277
Prime Minister, Datuk Hussein Onn, 23, 97
Prophet Muhammad, 69, 108, 293
Ptolemy, Claudius, 22
pulau (island) see islands
Punan, 35, 251

R

raayat-raayat (common people), 52
Rachado Lighthouse, 173
radio, 277
Raffles, Sir Stamford, 181, 185
railway, 98, 108, 244, 274
Ramayana, 83, 84
Ranau, 240
Rantau Abang, 216
religions, 97
Rentap, 261
Rest House, 132, 137, 139, 140, 199, 232
    Ayer Tawar, 225
    Keningau, Sabah, 246
    Kota Kinabalu, 242
    Langkawi Island, 165
    Lumut, 138
    Mersing, 203
    Pulau Perhentian, 210
    Pulau Tioman, 204
    Telok Assam, Sarawak, 260
    Telok Chempedak, 212
    Temerloh, 209
restaurants, Kuala Lumpur, 118
rice, 52, 54
Ridley, Henry, 58
river expeditions
    Endau River, 205
    Rajang River, 260
    Taman Negara, 191

rivers,
    Brunei, 268
    Cherating, 215
    Endau, 36, 205, *205*
    Gombak, 105
    Johore, 197, 202
    Kelantan, 225, 226
    Klang, 105
    Kuantan, 211
    Lebir, 189, 190, 191
    Limbang, 268
    Malacca, 174, 180
    Mersing, 203
    Paka, 215
    Padus, 245
    Pahang, 209, 211
    Perak, 138, 139
    Rajang, 260
    Sarawak, 252, *252*
    Sok, 189
    Tembeling, 189
    Tempasuk, 242
    Trengganu, 219
rubber, 18, 23, *54*, 58, 138, 201
Rungus, 232

S

Sabah, 13, 16, 23, 35, 66, 228-247
Sabah Museum, 235
safari
    Endau River, 36, 205
    National Park, 30, 189-193
    Pahang River, 209, 211
Sahil Waterfalls, Johore, 199
sailing, 163, 172
St. Francis Xavier, 182, 183
St. John's Fort, Malacca, 184
St. Paul's Church, Malacca, 182
St. Peter's Church, Malacca, 182
salt licks, 192, 260
Sam Poh Tong Temple, Ipoh,
    Perak, 134
Sandakan, 247
Santiago gate, 179, 181
Santubong, 259
Sarawak, 13, 16, 23, 35, 46, 251,
Sarawak art, 93
Sarawak River, 252
Sarawak Museum, 257, 258, 259,
    278
satay (tasty tidbits of meat served
    on skewers), 116, 170
scuba-diving, 204
Sea Dyaks, 261
seafood, 163, 199
secret societies, 23
Secretariat, 106
See Yeoh Temple, K.L., 109, *109*
Sekayu Waterfalls, 219
Selangor Club, 106
Selangor Flying Club, 116
Selangor Pewter, 115
Selangor Turf Club, 116
Semporna, 231
Sen Ta, 109
sepak raga (Malay ballgame), 74,
    80, 232
Sepilok Sanctuary, Sabah, 247
Seremban, 170
Seri Rambai, 147
Seria, 269
shipbuilding, 219
shopping,
    Kuala Lumpur, 113, 114
    Malacca, 178
    Penang, 148
Sibu, 260
Sibu Island, 205
silat (Malay art of self-defence), 78,
    212

silver, 209, 222, 224
Singapore, 23, 175, 185, 200
skin-diving, 232
Snake Temple, Penang, 159, 160
Sok River, 189
Song Song Island, 129
songkok (cap), 76
South China Sea, 40
Southeast Asian Games, (SEA
    Games), 83
Southern Cross Express, 274
speed-boating, 165
Speedy Bungalow, 141
Spice Isles, 42, 46
spice trade, 40, 42, 162, 174, 175,
    181
sports
    boating, 165, 202
    fishing, 192, 193, 204, 205, 213,
      219
    golf see golf course
    horse racing, 116, 135 see Turf
      Clubs
    horse riding, 125, 163, 202
    motor racing, 117, 151
    sailing, 163, 172
    scuba-diving, 204
    skin diving, 219 see also corals
    tennis, 125, 132, 165, 202
    water-skiing, 163
    wild-game hunting. 289
Sri Kandaswamy Hindu Temple,
    K.L., 110
Sru Dyaks, 258
Stadhuys, 179
stalactites, 123, 166
State Museum, Taiping, 140
Straits Settlement, 23, 54
strippers, 120
Subang Airport, 274
Sultan, 15, 45, 46, 52, 72, 202, 211
Sultan Abu Bakar, 198
Sultan Abu Bakar Lake, 131
Sultan Mansur Shah, 185
Sultan of Johore, 185
Sultan of Kedah, 145, 146
Sultan of Pahang, 211
Sultan's Well, 185
Sungei Kesang hot springs, 199
Sunghai, 136
Swettenham, Frank, 105

T

Taiping, 130, 140
Taiping Lake Gardens, 140
Taiping Zoo, 140
Taman D.R. Seenivasagam Park,
    133
Taman Negara, 30, 189
tamu (open-air weekly market),
    243, 244 see markets
Tambunan, 246
Tanjong Jara, 215
Tanjong Aru, Sabah, 235
Tanah Rata, Cameron Highlands,
    131
tasek(lake) see lakes
Tasek Chenderoh, Perak, 139
tattoos, 93, 262
taxis, 274
tea, 132, 141
Telaga Air Panas, 166
Telaga Tujoh, 166
television, 277
Telok Anson, 129
Telok Belanga, 137
Telok Chempedak, 212
Tembeling River, 189
Temerloh, 209

Tempasuk River, 242
Temple of Azure Cloud (Snake
    Temple), 159, 160
Temple of Tien Hou, Sarawak, 259
temples,
    Buddhist,
      Penang Buddhist Assn., 153
      Sleeping Buddha Statue,
        Charah Cave, Pahang,
        214
      Wat Chayamangkalaram,
        Penang, 153
    Chinese
      Batu Maung Shrine,
        Penang, 160
      Cheng Hoon Teng,
        Malacca, 176-178
      Hong San Temple,
        Sarawak, 259
      Kek Lok Si, Penang, 155
      Kuan Yin Temple, Penang,
        151
      Perak Tong, 133-134
      Sam Poh Tong Temple,
        Perak, 135
      See Yeoh Temple, K.L.,
        109, *109*
      Temple of Azure
        Cloud (Snake Temple),
        Penang, 160
      Temple of Tien Hou,
        Sarawak, 259
      Tua Pek Kong Temple,
        Sarawak, 259
    Hindu
      Hindu Temple, Penang
        Hill, 157
      Nattukotai Chettiar Shrine,
        Penang, 156
      Sri Kandaswamy Hindu
        Temple, K.L., 110
Templer Park, 121
tennis, 125, 132, 165, 202
Thaipusam, 69, 87-89, 122, 156
'The Gap", 124
Thompson, Jim, 132
timber, 18, 30
time zone, 97
tin, 18, 54, 106, 214
Titi Kerawang, Penang, 162
To' Dalang ("Master of Mysteries",
    puppeteer). 84
top spinning, *13*, 74, 80, *81*, 209,
    221
Tourist Development Corporation,
    100, 212, 279
trading, 97
train, 98, 274
Tranquerah Mosque, Malacca, 185
travel
    air, 98, 274
    rail, 98, 274
    road, 99, 274
Traveler's Checks, 275
Trengganu, 42, 218-222
Trengganu River, 219
trishaw, 149, 150, 176
Tua Pek Kong Temple, Sarawak,
    259
tuak (palm wine), 251
Tumasek, 175, 185
Tun Abdul Razak National Park,
    Sabah, 232
Tunku Abdul Rahman Aquarium
    and Laboratories, 160
Tunku Kuddin, 105
Turf Clubs,
    Penang Turf Club, 116, 157
    Selangor Turf Club, 116
    Singapore Turf Club. 116

302

Turf Club, Ipoh, Perak, 116,
135
turtle, 216-218, *216*

U

Ubùdiah Mosque, Perak, *138*, 139
Ulu Tiram, 201
unicorn, 30

V

visas, 274

W

Wat Chayamangkalaram, Penang,
154
Waterfall Gardens, Penang, 155
(Botanical Gardens)
waterfalls, 121, 132
Botanical Gardens, Penang,
155-156
Kota Bharu, 226
Kota Tinggi, Johore, 202
Sahil Waterfalls, Johore, 199
Sekayu, Trengganu, 219
Telaga Tujoh, Langkawai, 166
Titi Kerawang, Penang, 162
waterskiing, 163
Watson, Malcolm, Sir, 23
wayang kulit (shadow play), 54, 83,
209, 212,
weaving, 212, 222-223, 227
"white Rajahs", 16, 22, 46, 66, 251-
253, 255, 258
wildlife, 189, 193, 205, 260
Wisma Loke, 117
wood carving, 212

Y

youth, 74, 75, 78
Yap Ah Loy, 64, 105, 106, 109, 117
Yang di-Pertuan Agong, 23, 52,
163, 211, 278

Z

Zahir Mosque, Kedah, 163
zoos, 140
Johore Zoo, 200
National Zoo, K.L., 120-121
Taiping Zoo, 140

DISTRIBUTORS

AUSTRALIA: Lonely Planet Publications, P.O. Box 88 South Yarra, Victoria 3141.

BENELUX: Elsevier Focus, Gebouw Rivierstaete, Amsteldijk 166, Amsterdam, Netherlands.

CANADA: See USA

DENMARK: Medicinsk Forlag ApS, Tranevej 2, 3650 Olstykke.

HAWAII: APA Productions Hawaii Inc., 339 Saratoga Road, Suite 21, Honolulu 96815.

HONGKONG: Harris Book Co. Ltd., 115 Prince's Bldg.

INDONESIA: N.V. Indoprom Co. (Indonesia) Ltd, SGV Building, 2nd Floor, J1 Letjend S.Parman Kav. 56, Slipi, Jakarta Barat.

ISLAND OF BALI: Bali Hyatt Hotel, Sanur, Bali, Indonesia.

JAPAN: Charles E. Tuttle Co. Inc., 2-6, Suido 1-chome, Bunkyo-ku, Tokyo 112.

KOREA: Universal Publications Agency Ltd., UPA Building, 54 Kyonji-Dong, Chongnoku, C.P.O. Box 1380, Seoul.

NEPAL: Tiger Tops Jungle Lodge, P.O. Box 242, Kathmandu.

NEW ZEALAND: Publishers Services, 115 Khyber Pass, P.O. Box 9659, Newmarket, Auckland.

PHILIPPINES: Erehwon Bookshop Inc., P.O. Box 86, Makati, Metro Manila 3117.

SINGAPORE & MALAYSIA: APA Productions Pte Ltd., 349, Pasir Panjang Road, Singapore 0511.

SRI LANKA: K.V.G. De Silva, 415 Galle Road, Colombo 4.

SWITZERLAND: EMA-Handel AG, 4410 Liestal, Burghade 34,Basel 40-13 308.

THAILAND: Chalermnit Bookshop, 1-2 Erawan Arcade, Bangkok.

UNITED KINGDOM: Roger Lascelles, 3 Holland Park Mansions, 16 Holland Park Gardens, London W14 8DY.

USA (Mainland): Sino Publishing Co., 745 Fifth Ave., New York, NY 10151.

WEST GERMANY & AUSTRIA: Geo Center, Honigwiesenstrasse 25, D7 Stuttgart 80, Postfach 800830, West Germany.